Building a Sustainable Political Economy: SPERI Research & Policy

The Sheffield Political Economy Research Institute (SPERI) is an innovation in higher education research and outreach. It brings together leading international researchers in the social sciences, policy makers, journalists and opinion formers to reassess and develop proposals in response to the political and economic issues posed by the current combination of financial crisis, shifting economic power and environmental threat. Building a Sustainable Political Economy: SPERI Research & Policy will serve as a key outlet for SPERI's published work. Each title will summarise and disseminate to an academic and postgraduate student audience, as well as directly to policy-makers and journalists, key policy-oriented research findings designed to further the development of a more sustainable future for the national, regional and world economy following the global financial crisis. It takes a holistic and interdisciplinary view of political economy in which the local, national, regional and global interact at all times and in complex ways. The SPERI research agenda, and hence the focus of the series, seeks to explore the core economic and political questions that require us to develop a new sustainable model of political economy at all times and in complex ways.

speri.

More information about this series at
http://www.palgrave.com/gp/series/14879

Owen Parker • Dimitris Tsarouhas
Editors

Crisis in the Eurozone Periphery

The Political Economies of Greece, Spain, Ireland and Portugal

palgrave
macmillan

Editors
Owen Parker
Department of Politics and SPERI
University of Sheffield
Sheffield, UK

Dimitris Tsarouhas
Department of International Relations
Bilkent University
Ankara, Turkey

Building a Sustainable Political Economy: SPERI Research & Policy
ISBN 978-3-319-69720-8 ISBN 978-3-319-69721-5 (eBook)
https://doi.org/10.1007/978-3-319-69721-5

Library of Congress Control Number: 2017964368

Printed on acid-free paper

This Palgrave Macmillan imprint is published by Springer Nature
The registered company is Springer International Publishing AG
The registered company address is: Gewerbestrasse 11, 6330 Cham, Switzerland

Contents

List of Contributors

Luis Buendía Department of Economics and Statistics, University of León, León, Spain

Mònica Clua-Losada Department of Political Science, University of Texas – Rio Grande Valley, Brownsville, TX, USA

Isabel David Centre for Administration and Public Policies, Institute of Social and Political Sciences, University of Lisbon, Lisbon, Portugal

Neil Dooley Department of Politics and Sussex European Institute, University of Sussex, Brighton, UK

Pavlos Gkasis Department of Business Administration and Economics, The International Faculty of the University of Sheffield-CITY College, Thessaloniki, Greece

Nicholas Kiersey Department of Political Science, Ohio University, Athens, OH, USA

Owen Parker Department of Politics and SPERI, University of Sheffield, Sheffield, UK

Alexandra Prodromidou Department of Business Administration and Economics, The International Faculty of the University of Sheffield-CITY College, Thessaloniki, Greece

Seán Ó Riain Department of Sociology, Maynooth University, Maynooth, County Kildare, Ireland

Dimitris Tsarouhas Department of International Relations, Bilkent University, Ankara, Turkey

List of Figures

List of Tables

CHAPTER 1

Causes and Consequences of Crisis in the Eurozone Periphery

Owen Parker and Dimitris Tsarouhas

Abstract This volume considers the political economy dynamics that both caused and were precipitated by the Eurozone crisis in four of the hardest-hit so-called periphery country cases—Ireland, Spain, Portugal and Greece. This introduction focuses on the broader structures that underpinned the Eurozone crisis, whereas the chapters that follow zoom in on domestic cases. It argues that a single currency designed in accordance with neoliberal 'efficient market' ideas was at the heart of the crisis, exacerbating dangerous economic divergences between a so-called core of creditor states and periphery of debtor states. Responses to the crisis were, it is suggested, premised on the very same neoliberal ideas and made matters worse for a struggling 'periphery'. More effective responses exist in theory, but are politically difficult in practice.

Keywords Eurozone crisis • Core–periphery • Asymmetries • Austerity • Neoliberalism

O. Parker (✉)
Department of Politics and SPERI, University of Sheffield, Sheffield, UK

D. Tsarouhas
Department of International Relations, Bilkent University, Ankara, Turkey

O. Parker, D. Tsarouhas (eds.), *Crisis in the Eurozone Periphery*,
Building a Sustainable Political Economy: SPERI Research & Policy,
https://doi.org/10.1007/978-3-319-69721-5_1

A separation or divergence exists in the Eurozone between those member states—generally 'creditor' or 'surplus' states—that have weathered the financial and economic crisis since the late 2000s relatively well, and those states—generally 'debtor' or 'deficit' states—that have experienced the most upheaval economically, socially and politically in the context of that crisis. The imbalances between debtor and creditor states predate the crisis, as we will show in this chapter. However, the crisis has cast the relationship between the two categories of state in a new light that renders the 'core–periphery' concept increasingly pertinent.

First deployed by various post-Marxist development theorists, the concept denotes not only an imbalance but also a power relationship within global capitalism between an economically and politically dominant wealthy core—often led by a large hegemonic power—and a largely poor, dependent periphery (Wallerstein 1974, 1979). The use of the concept in relation to the European Union (EU) or Eurozone in the aftermath of the crisis can be understood as denoting a similar kind of dynamic, as we will discuss in what follows. A wealthy core led primarily by Germany has, according to such a narrative, guided the response to the crisis in ways that preserve or even exacerbate economic imbalances between a core and periphery, making the latter supplicant to the former. Such a narrative may be partially true, particularly in relation to certain periphery states that have found themselves forced into a harsh austerity politics in the course of the crisis. But it is probably to overstate the power of core states and understate the economic, political and social divisions *within* states on both sides of this divide. As we will suggest later—and as the authors elucidate in greater detail in the following chapters—important elite actors cutting across both the public–private and the core-periphery divide were collectively culpable in precipitating the crisis. And while those in the periphery countries certainly suffered the most, lower social classes in the core also encountered, and continue to encounter, significant hardship.

As the title of this book indicates, we focus here on the impact of the crisis in the 'Eurozone periphery' and, in particular, on those Eurozone states that have been most severely afflicted and received so-called bailouts of one form or another. In the chronological order in which they were first granted loans, the countries that we consider are Greece (2010), Ireland (2010), Portugal (2011) and Spain (2012). Proving that they were capable of producing even more pejorative terms than 'periphery' to denote this group of countries in economic distress, many working in the financial markets came to refer to them collectively by the moniker 'the PIGS' in the early 2010s. Slight modifications of the acronym were used, with Italy sometimes included in this group of 'problem states'; hence, PIIGS. We will, in contrast, purposefully use the abbreviation GIPS in what follows, to denote our four country cases.

The most obvious omission from the book, according to the logic by which these four countries were selected, is not Italy but Cyprus, as it was the fifth country to receive a bailout in 2012. A much smaller member state than those considered (with a population of little over one million), it nevertheless shared certain vulnerabilities with the other four (Trimikliniotis 2013; Michaelides and Orphanides 2016). Italy, as mentioned above, is the other notable omission. Also widely regarded as part of the so-called periphery given its status as a debtor state, it has struggled significantly throughout the crisis, particularly—like GIPS—in terms of refinancing its debt in the years after 2010. Moreover, ongoing weaknesses in its political and banking systems were a pressing concern at the time of writing in 2017. That said, unlike GIPS, Italy had not received a bailout as of that date.

Finally, we should acknowledge that there is another periphery beyond the Eurozone itself (Bohle and Greskovits 2012; Ryner and Cafruny 2017: 137–166). Although not all members of the common currency, a number of Central and Eastern European EU member states were hard-hit by the broader global financial crisis (GFC) and associated 'credit crunch'. In particular, Hungary and the Baltic states had particularly high and rapidly increasing levels of mortgage debt that led to significant economic crises and recessions in the late 2000s and, in the cases of Hungary (2008) and Latvia (2009), to International Monetary Fund (IMF)–EU bailouts.

In offering a close analysis in this book of four important countries at the heart of the so-called periphery, we are particularly keen to explore the domestic dynamics of crisis. The chapters highlight the interconnected economic, political and social dynamics within these states that made them particularly vulnerable to crisis and that guided responses to that crisis. The chapters also document the very real social and political effects of crisis. We should certainly not understate the agency of state-level private and public actors in fostering conditions that made these states particularly vulnerable to the crisis, even if that agency would later become constrained in important ways as a consequence of collective responses to that crisis. At the same time, in considering GIPS together as part of a 'Eurozone periphery' that stands in contradistinction to a 'core', we are also suggesting that there are important structural factors that underpinned similar developmental trajectories. In particular, these states' collective imbrication in the EU and its common currency zone on similar terms were crucial. While the chapters will focus on the domestic particularities of the individual cases in some detail, this introductory chapter will focus largely on the similarities and the broader structural context of European and, in particular, economic and monetary integration.

The chapter proceeds in five steps. In a first, we consider the underlying causes of the crisis in the periphery, highlighting the central importance of growing levels of debt within the Eurozone and the growth in imbalances between (debtor) periphery and (creditor) core. We concur with an emerging political economy literature that the emergence of a 'sovereign debt crisis' from 2010 needs to be understood against a much broader historical backdrop (see, among many others, Matthijs and Blyth 2015; Ryner and Cafruny 2017). In a second step, we consider the particular structural importance of the single currency and the design flaws in the euro that precipitated the asymmetries at the heart of the crisis. We argue that a euro modelled on neoliberal 'efficient market' principles in a broader context of so-called financialization was always destined to be vulnerable. Third, we outline the responses of the EU to the crisis, which consisted largely of the imposition of austerity on increasingly dependent periphery states. We argue that such responses failed to deal with the underlying issues enunciated in the previous sections and, indeed, exacerbated the crisis, particularly for the periphery (such consequences are considered in greater detail in the chapters that follow). Fourth, we consider possible ways forward and the political difficulties inherent in achieving the far more radical reforms that might underpin a functional single currency and overcome the divisions (and social hardship) that growing economic asymmetries have fostered. Having offered this account of the political economy of the Eurozone crisis, in a fifth step, we offer an overview of the chapters that follow. As noted, in contrast to this introduction, the chapters that follow focus on the interconnected political and economic domestic factors have been key and will continue to be key in dictating how the structures described in this chapter are mediated in GIPS.

Growing Asymmetries Between Core and Periphery

While it was widely supported, including in France and Germany, European Monetary Union (EMU) imposed a single currency on what were distinct varieties of capitalism. Crudely, coordinated market economies in the core of Europe with strong traditions of wage coordination (and, crucially, wage restraint), vocational training, research and development and high productivity had long pursued export-led growth strategies (Hall and Soskice 2001). Southern periphery mixed market economies (as well as some liberal market economies—notably, for current purposes, Ireland) with weak wage bargaining structures, and lower skilled workforces had pursued demand-led growth strategies based on, inter alia, macroeconomic stimulus policies and job creation in non-traded sectors such as service and public sectors. These countries had been prone to inflation as a consequence of such strategies and before EMU had used exchange rate policies—devaluations of the currency—to offset the effects of this inflation on trade balances (Hall 2014; Regan 2013). France has oscillated between these models and in general shows elements of both, with wage restraint—based on statist interventionism rather than social partner involvement—and at the same time a large non-traded sector (Johnston and Regan 2016: 324).

EMU worked well for the core countries, allowing them to continue export-led growth rooted in wage repression, in a context where their major trading partners could no longer devalue their currencies. In the periphery, EMU seemed like it would require a shift away from demand-led growth strategies in the absence of currency devaluation as a policy tool and of a *national* central bank able to target inflation (and *real* exchange rates). But the much lower interest rates and greater capital mobility that the euro delivered for these countries offered an apparent way out of this difficulty (Johnston and Regan 2016: 321). Surpluses from the core were borrowed in the periphery, meaning that demand remained strong even in the absence of expansionary fiscal policy. Demand-led growth became underpinned by debt.

Thus, these two models were increasingly intertwined by virtue of monetary union (Regan 2013). Increasingly large capital flows from core countries—particularly Germany but also France, the Netherlands and others—moved to Eurozone periphery countries. While overall the Eurozone current account is more or less in balance—meaning that capital inflows are roughly the size of outflows with the rest of the world—Fig. 1.1

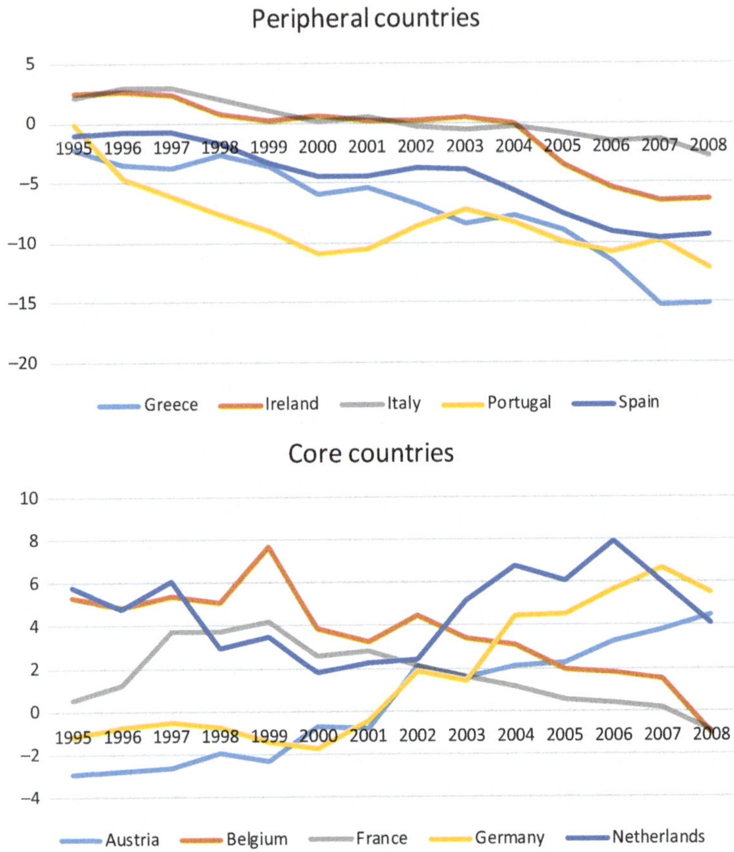

Fig. 1.1 Current accounts as percentage of GDP (Source: IMF-WO, with thanks to Luis Buendia for compiling)

shows that the divergence of flows between countries in the Eurozone is stark. Notably, all of the periphery GIPS ran substantial current account deficits, reflecting their net borrowing from those countries in the core running surpluses. We see that Spain was by far the largest net borrower and Germany the largest net lender. As noted, these capital flows reflected high rates of saving in the core and high rates of borrowing in the periphery.

Many economists did not see the emerging imbalances in the European economy as a significant issue in the early 2000s; they felt that the capital flows were part of a broader pattern of economic convergence, whereby money pouring into the periphery would drive the economic development of poorer economies (Blanchard and Giavazzi 2002; Ryner and Cafruny 2017: 94–99). Crucially, however, against a backdrop of financial deregulation, much of the borrowed money in the periphery did not find its way into the productive economy, but into non-productive consumption and investment that did little to stimulate the export capacities of the periphery. Such intensified deregulation or financialization was a global phenomenon throughout the period, but one that was certainly facilitated by private and public actors including in domestic contexts in GIPS, as the chapters explore in greater detail.

Around the turn of the millennium, domestic demand and export competitiveness started to de-link in both the periphery and the core. In other words, money flooded into the periphery and boosted demand, but it had no impact on exports and the development of a productive economy. In fact, as the authors explore with reference to particular cases in the following chapters, this 'hot' money may even have had a negative impact on export growth to the extent that potentially productive investment was channelled into supposedly quick-win financial assets. Indeed, in many of the country cases under consideration, inflows stimulated domestic demand for both goods exported from the core and for property at home, which created financial bubbles that would eventually burst. Moreover, such hot money meant inflation—including high wages in non-tradable or non-export sectors such as service and public sectors (Johnston and Regan 2016: 324; Hopkin 2015)—in the periphery, which further undermined export competitiveness. This was particularly the case because, despite its export success, Germany kept wages and therefore its own domestic demand low. Indeed, demand and exports diverged in the opposite direction, with the former declining precipitously while the latter gradually rose.

Notably, while in the early 2000s, many were pointing to economic achievements in countries with high debt-led growth—there was, for instance, talk of 'a Spanish miracle' and Ireland was dubbed the 'Celtic tiger' (Ryner and Cafruny 2017: 92)—Germany was described as the 'sick man of Europe'. However, while speculative domestic demand and economic bubbles drove rapid growth in periphery countries such as Spain, apparently anaemic growth in Germany was driven by exports in a context of very weak domestic demand. Thus, even in the early years of the common currency, major structural imbalances were exacerbated by the growing asymmetry between core and periphery. The underlying European growth model was comprised then of both debt-led growth in the periphery economies that permitted excessive spending—though, as the chapters will describe, without in most cases significantly addressing underlying inequalities or substantially developing social models—and low-wage export-led growth in the core, the proceeds of which were saved rather than spent.

In practice, then, capital movements into the periphery did little to address overall balance of payments imbalances as the aforementioned optimistic prognoses of the early 2000s had suggested they would. On the contrary, the asymmetries grew larger in the run up to the crisis. The Eurozone was characterized by a combination of a wage-cutting low-inflation core that actively enhanced its competitiveness and a periphery where demand was boosted by cheap money. As noted, this asymmetry was facilitated by financialization. In other words, by a transnational banking sector—and increasingly liberalized capital market—that fed core surpluses and savings to the periphery via increasingly deregulated and highly leveraged banks in both the core and periphery (Baldwin and Giavazzi 2015). In the crisis context, a broader neoliberal financialization model linked banks in the core to those in the periphery, with important implications for the response to the crisis. In turn, the economic fate of sovereign governments was fatally linked to this highly leveraged and indebted financial sector in both core and periphery as the crisis would reveal and as we discuss below.

Politically, both core and periphery states were content to overlook these imbalances as long as there was growth in the Eurozone. As we have suggested, Germany's dominant manufacturers essentially pursued a neo-mercantilist strategy based on wage repression that enabled the country to support and develop its export sectors. Such a strategy is perhaps unsurprising given the broader context of the costs of German reunification in the 1990s and ongoing efforts in the 2000s to reinvigorate export-led growth. Governments in the periphery states were content before the crisis hit, as long as debt-led economic growth continued to sustain (often weak) social compacts and the various asset prices upon which the tax-take became increasingly reliant. However, the imbalances ultimately proved unsustainable and, when crisis hit, irresolvable.

The underlying causes of such imbalances were, as noted, in large part, the processes of neoliberal financialization (Stokhammer 2016): a deregulation of finance and an associated shifting of capital into financial speculation (at the expense of productive sectors). Such processes had been underway in Europe as in other developed parts of the world (and led by the USA) since at least the 1980s and intensified, first with the preparations for, and later with the realization of, EMU (Ryner and Cafruny 2017: 91–92; Jones 2015). Debt levels that we can associate with financialization ballooned in the period between the start of the single currency and the crisis. In the context of the GFC that started in 2007, such financialization was a direct cause. US mortgage defaults took place in a context of the 'securitization' (a form of financialization) of 'sub-prime' mortgage assets, which led to systemic banking failure in large global banks and prompted a global credit squeeze (the infamous 'credit crunch') and recession. In the context of the Eurozone crisis, the proximate cause appeared to be sovereign debt, but due to the aforementioned interlinked fate of financial institutions (banks) and sovereigns, we would argue that the underlying cause was, as in the USA, this broader financialization and associated indebtedness. Such indebtedness was itself dependent upon wage shares falling from the 1970s as part of a broader neoliberal turn (Bengtsson and Ryner 2015).

Regarding the first trigger for the Eurozone crisis, it was indeed the revelation in 2009 by the incoming Greek government that its predecessors had been concealing the true size of the country's budget deficit. As Chaps. 5 and 9 recount, cronyism and systems of public sector patronage were important factors in the particular Greek case that had seen a long-term increase in public debt and deficits. In light of these revelations, widespread concerns that its public debt might become unsustainable led the financial (specifically, sovereign bond) markets to offload Greek government debt and substantially push up Greece's borrowing costs, ultimately to unsustainable levels. Despite some reluctance and following substantial procrastination, Eurozone states and, crucially, Germany ultimately decided that the potential systemic effects to the euro of allowing a default were too great and stepped in with substantial financial support in 2010. This was not enough, however, to allay the fears of bond markets. Cutting a much longer story short, the spread on Greek government bonds (the cost of refinancing its debts) continued to rise, and the contagion effects meant that other states, particularly the most vulnerable ones in the Eurozone chain, began to feel the effects.

All Eurozone states were, following the effects of the GFC, running government budget deficits. But it was notably the sovereign bonds of peripheral states that had borrowed substantially from abroad (those with the large *current account* deficits described above, namely, GIPS plus Italy) that were rapidly offloaded, pushing their borrowing costs to unsustainable levels. The market fears in all cases related to the sustainability of public financing, either because of high public debt levels or because of the fragility of domestic financial institutions that were likely to require government support. As discussed in greater detail in the individual chapters on GIPS, each of these countries would ultimately receive bailouts from a combination of the IMF, EU and European Central Bank (ECB)—the 'troika'—with significant strings attached and big political implications and effects.

Ultimately, the bailouts were not enough to allay concerns that the possibility of sovereign default was (despite a clause in the Maastricht treaty explicitly proscribing it) becoming ever more real. The second Greek bailout in 2011 included a write-down of debt by private investors that turned a fear of losses into actual losses and caused further market panic. In early 2012 both France and Belgium—notably, countries whose broader current accounts (see Fig. 1.1) saw them moving from surplus to deficit (or from core to periphery by that measure) in the late 2000s—began to experience the contagion effects when a Franco-Belgian bank, Dexia, was nationalized by the Belgian authorities. And in the same period Cyprus—whose banking sector was heavily tied to Greece—requested a bailout. It was interventions by the ECB that ultimately afforded some breathing space and, in particular, President Mario Draghi's now infamous declaration in July 2012 that, 'the ECB is ready to do whatever it takes to preserve the euro. And believe me, it will be enough'. Markets did indeed believe Draghi and sovereign bond yields in the Eurozone saw a significant convergence. The role of the ECB as an active policy entrepreneur, in the face of apparent reluctance by other major EU actors, was thus confirmed.

The Euro

The most obvious common thread connecting the periphery countries under consideration is their participation in EMU. The designers of EMU had chosen not to focus on the aforementioned differences in the varieties of capitalism in the Eurozone that underpinned the asymmetries that predated the single currency. Against the aforementioned backdrop of increasingly unregulated finance and liberalized capital markets, the design arguably exacerbated the imbalances that lay at the heart of the crisis and meant that periphery countries were particularly hard-hit. It was EMU that locked-in German competitive advantages vis-à-vis the periphery, established an environment that made borrowing and growing indebtedness easier in the periphery, and (as noted above) facilitated the intensification of an already liberalized capital mobility from core to periphery.

The design of EMU was based on the prevailing economic ideas of the 1990s. These broadly neoliberal ideas were unsympathetic to active fiscal policy (demand management), promoted a monetary policy focused on controlling inflation (sound money) and pushed supply-side economics—wage cuts, flexibilization of labour markets and promotion of human capital—as the appropriate tool for increasing competitiveness and investment (McNamara 1998, 2006; Ryner and Cafruny 2017: 94–99). In accordance with these ideas, the key plank of EMU was a ECB whose mandate was solely devoted to sound money and a system of economic governance based on maintaining debt and deficit levels within certain limits (the Stability and Growth Pact). It was anticipated that states within the Eurozone would converge economically via the pursuit of broadly supply-side economic policies or so-called structural reforms, an approach that the later Lisbon agenda (2000) would broadly endorse. Indeed, for some, monetary union would 'discipline' states into making such reforms (for a critique of such ambitions, see Gill 1998). Such features of economic governance would, so it was thought, provide the credibility upon which the aforementioned liberalized and heavily diversified financial markets would efficiently allocate capital to the areas where it might accrue the greatest returns (Ryner and Cafruny 2017: 95–96). However, as noted above, capital in fact poured in to highly speculative rather than productive ventures in the periphery; indeed, a broader misallocation of investments by a finance sector with problematically short-term time horizons lay at the heart of the global crisis.

Certainly in hindsight, it seems clear that there should have been some serious doubts about these neoliberal ideas. In the event of growing divergences and asymmetries—and in particular sudden 'asymmetric shocks' (a boom or bust in different parts of a currency area)—it is politically inconceivable that difficult and socially deleterious supply-side policies could underpin economic adjustments. But in the context of a single currency and the absence of control of national exchange rate policy—currency devaluation is no longer an option—there is no alternative to turn to for national governments. EMU was politically popular for GIPS countries (and others) even though participation in the single currency may have been economically deleterious. They would thus commit to meeting the Maastricht criteria and strive for membership regardless of the medium-term effects that participation may have had on their ability to compete with core Eurozone states. The absence of binding mechanisms committing both the core and periphery to sustainable measures assuring *real* economic convergence compounded the problem.

As the economist Paul Krugman (2012) and others (Feldstein 2008, 2012) have convincingly argued, the theory of Optimal Currency Areas (OCA, see Mundell 1961; Kenen 1969) ought to have provided a warning for the designers of EMU.[1] The OCA theory argues that asymmetries in a currency union can be offset by high factor mobility—particularly mobility of labour—or by fiscal integration permitting fiscal transfers. While the EU facilitates some labour mobility—and there has been significant periphery to core movement of labour in the context of the crisis—human mobility is sticky for a variety of rather obvious reasons: people in general do not want to move, and they encounter barriers (linguistic, cultural, no social networks) when they do. As to fiscal transfers, as noted above, this was not an option that was seriously considered; in part because it did not fit with the aforementioned orthodoxy in economic thinking and in part because it did not fit with the preferences of key states, particularly Germany. From this perspective, fiscal integration would have potentially undermined the disciplinary aspect of EMU, discouraging structural reform geared towards austerity and (supposedly) increased competitiveness.

A third important policy tool for dealing with crises in monetary unions is a so-called lender of last resort function. In the context of most currency unions the central bank assumes this role, underpinning the solvency of both banking sectors and sovereigns (de Grauwe 2013). This usually ensures systemic market confidence and militates against market panic of the sort witnessed in the early 2010s. The design of EMU left the lender of last resort function in the hands of national central banks, but, as de Grauwe (2012) has noted, they cannot adequately perform this function given that they are not really 'central' at all in the context of a shared currency; they do not have control of the common currency and so cannot guarantee the solvency of their respective sovereigns (or, by extension, the banks that would be bailed out by them).

It has been convincingly claimed that the absence of political authority attached to the euro renders it distinct from—in Polanyian terms, more socially 'disembedded' than—any previously successful currency union (McNamara 2015). The absence of the political tools required for managing the economic effects of both long-term imbalances and financial crises within EMU was clearly not lost on the financial markets as the broader GFC that hit in 2008 spread to Europe. Indeed, at key moments in the early stages of the Eurozone crisis, both the ECB and Germany explicitly pointed to the absence of such tools in the EU treaties (Matthijs and Blyth 2015: 7). It was to a large extent then the realization that sovereign insolvency may be a possibility within the Eurozone that led to the crisis in the periphery, and it was their significant borrowing (private and public) from abroad—and particularly from banks in the core—that made them particularly vulnerable.

In many ways, the later responses to the crisis enunciated in the previous section can be understood as attempts to address these arguably fundamental shortcomings in the design of EMU. Fiscal transfers were substituted by bailouts (which, unlike transfers, had tough conditionality attached to them as discussed below). And the ECB declaration in 2012 represented a willingness to in fact play the role of a lender of last resort (albeit it denied that this was the case given that to do so would be to controversially expand its legal mandate—see, Schmidt 2016). However, while they averted a disorganized and potentially catastrophic dissolution of the single currency, these responses were both belated and could yet prove insufficient (Cohen 2012; Schmidt 2011; Dyson 2013). The consequences of this mismanagement for the periphery states, both in socio-economic and political terms, have been profound and are proving long-lasting, as the following chapters discuss in some detail.

Austerity

The official EU (and most frequently presented) diagnosis of the crisis tended to seriously simplify, if not refute, the story of imbalance, financialization and the faulty design of the single currency enunciated above. This represented an unwillingness to acknowledge the deeper failures of the neoliberal ideas of efficient markets that underpinned the design of the single currency: '[t]he problem was not the policies pursued, but that they were not pursued far enough' (Ryner and Cafruny 2017: 97). Emphasis was placed on the sovereign debt crisis at the expense of a broader reckoning with both the design of the single currency and finance-driven imbalances. But it is notable that of GIPS, only Greece and Portugal had significant levels of sovereign debt prior to the crisis and the latter was recovering economically before the markets pushed its borrowing costs to unsustainable levels (Fishman 2011).[2] For Spain and Ireland, the root of the problem was private (and especially housing) debt that became public debt only once their banking sectors required rescuing. However, the discourse of sovereign debt effectively permitted the socialization of private sector banking debts, which were paid for through cuts in government spending: in short, austerity (Matthijs and Blyth 2015: 8; Blyth 2013).

Indeed, the bailout packages mentioned above came with significant strings attached. Under various mechanisms[3] 'the troika' agreed memoranda of understanding (MoUs) with GIPS. These agreements differed from state to state. For instance in the case of Spain the agreement focused solely on reform of its banking and financial sector. The terms imposed on the other three varied from country to country, partially taking into account their different problems. Yet what they all included (and, in the case of Greece, still included at the time of writing) was the imposition of austerity measures geared towards the shrinking of the public sector, the imposition of cuts in public services and the flexibilization of labour markets. Periodic monitoring of performance by troika representatives on site made strict conditionality increasingly unpopular in all countries concerned and contributed to the increasing frustration with the EU in general and Eurozone membership in particular.

GIPS have fared very differently in terms of their ability to meet this conditionality, however. Ireland exited its programme at the end of 2013 and Portugal and Spain in 2014. By contrast, Greece almost failed to agree to a new agreement in 2015, and its travails were ongoing in 2017. That said, even those countries that have exited their programmes remain subject to rather intense 'post-programme surveillance' until they have repaid 75 per cent of the financial assistance received. Moreover, under broader reforms to the economic governance of the Eurozone and the EU (Bauer and Becker 2014), such surveillance and monitoring will be continuous within the context of the so-called European Semester. In particular, such monitoring focuses on adherence to EMU rules on budget deficits, public debt and macro-economic imbalances. Its effectiveness, and especially its ability to ensure macro-economic policy coordination and rules' implementation, is far from assured (see Darvas and Leandro 2015).

While the emphasis on macro-economic imbalance is surely welcome in the context of the argument that we present here—which emphasizes the significance of such imbalances—it is important to consider how these can be realistically addressed alongside the imposition of austerity. According to the EU institutions and the prevailing approach to economic governance, such austerity will drive the competitiveness of deficit countries in the periphery, facilitating the development of their productive economies and the expansion of exports to address deficits. But the very notion that austerity could foster such competitiveness and economic growth is incoherent; it serves only to deflate already struggling economies, endangering the very survival of the Eurozone (Blyth 2013; Stockhammer 2016). Such a system of economic governance also fails to address the social plight of workers and citizens in these already struggling countries (Parker and Pye 2017) and exacerbates political instability associated with that plight.

The evidence suggests that such policies have in fact exacerbated imbalances between core and periphery. Rather than increasing, industrial production has in fact collapsed in the periphery, and this has led to the further intensification of industrial activity in Germany (Lavery 2017). Moreover, the asymmetrical emphasis on the problematic nature of deficits (which need to be below 4 per cent to avoid the triggering of the so-called excessive imbalance procedure) and surpluses (which need to be below 6 per cent to avoid triggering the same procedure) serves to ingrain rather than ameliorate imbalances (Bibow 2013). In short, while macro-economic imbalance is now acknowledged as a key concern of the EU, its broader policy agenda works against effectively addressing that very concern.

Continued Deadlock?

In light of this argument, two key reforms present themselves. First, as a range of more critical and (neo)-Keynesian positions have suggested (among others, De Grauwe 2013; Stockhammer 2016), a much stronger focus on Germany's surplus—and its deflationary effect on the Eurozone economy through, in particular, its low-wage policies—will be required in order to begin to genuinely tackle the aforementioned imbalances. This would effectively mean permitting or fostering an increase in long-depressed wages (and inflation) in Germany, and thereby creating the means for increased domestic consumption. Calls for such a change are pretty common (see Watt 2013) but have until now fallen on deaf ears. In a context where demand in the periphery has collapsed following the crisis, it needs to emerge elsewhere if the Eurozone is to avoid a deflationary downward cycle, whereby falling prices lead to a potentially indefinite diminishment of economic activity (Feldstein 2012; Moravcsik 2012;

Schwartz 2012; Lavery 2017). It is precisely those fears that have underpinned ECB activism in recent years; but the consequences of this activism in fuelling asset prices and exacerbating inequalities point to the need for positive action on the part of member states such as Germany.

Second, in accordance with the aforementioned and increasingly acknowledged deficiencies in the design of the single currency, much more serious consideration of some form of intensified economic integration (beyond common rules) will need to be considered. 'Eurobonds'—effectively the collectivization of Eurozone sovereign debt—would be an important step towards such integration inasmuch as they would remove the focus of the sovereign bond markets from any one sovereign state when a crisis hits (Begg 2011). Moreover, a substantive fiscal or transfer union that does not simply further indebt already heavily indebted countries as the current bailout mechanisms do, may be required to genuinely tackle such imbalances. It would do so by, inter alia, directing investment and funds from wealthier to poorer regions in a scaled-up version of regional and cohesion funds (Marsh 2013: 117–119).

The politics of achieving either of these is, and will continue to be, incredibly difficult (on which, see Marsh 2013). In particular, the EU looks destined to continue to have a highly limited fiscal capacity given the extent of change that would be required to achieve a strong transfer union. While the EU has a budget that amounts to around 1 per cent of EU GDP, European state budgets available for fiscal policy can be as much as one third of national GDP (Ryner and Cafruny 2017: 141). The political shifts that would be required to establish a substantive fiscal union are therefore enormous. While such radical solutions may be popular for some in the periphery, at the current juncture this is certainly not the case for a clear-cut majority of key actors. This is true in GIPS and also in Italy and France, where internal political and ideological divergences remain significant. Moreover, it is certainly not the case in the core and, most critically, in Germany, or in the key European institutions (ECB and Commission). Indeed, a broad transnational elite consensus (part of a broader class politics) cuts across the core–periphery divide and remains wedded to the neoliberal efficient markets ideas critiqued in the foregoing.

The economic, social and political consequences of the crisis and the austerity policies that have followed in its wake have been extreme in GIPS (as laid out in the chapters that follow). The appetite for substantial change is therefore certainly significant in these countries. Structurally the status quo is one in which monetary union has meant a significant loss of national (particularly monetary) sovereignty. Eurobonds would appear to be a sellable policy in GIPS and perhaps also Italy and France. However, many in these contexts would baulk at the idea that a loss of monetary sovereignty could or should be offset with deeper political and fiscal integration at European level. For increasing numbers supporting an array of anti-establishment and anti-European or anti-Euro parties, the solution lies, rather, in disintegration of the single currency and/or the euro. That said, survey data show that the majority in these countries continue to show at least tepid support for both the EU and monetary union (Otero-Iglesias 2017) even as they may oppose substantive deeper integration. The upshot for those in a growing periphery (that, as noted, increasingly looks like it includes France) is the status quo of a potentially deflationary 'internal devaluation'—wage cutting—and other 'structural reform' measures. In summary, at the time of writing in 2017 there was something of a political impasse even within the periphery. There was no clear-cut support for measures that would assist in overcoming the problematic pathologies and imbalances within the Eurozone, or for measures that would see its disintegration.

In Germany and other core countries the obstacles to achieving substantive reforms are even greater. To date the German government has been the leader in terms of crisis response despite significant and growing concerns within Germany. Such concerns at a popular level relate to the misguided perception that a virtuous and economically responsible Germany has had to rescue an irresponsible and spendthrift periphery. At a policy level, the German Constitutional Court and an important group of economists and central bankers have expressed concern with respect to aspects of both crisis management and long-term reforms emerging from the Eurozone crisis. The Court has, for instance, suggested that significant increases in German government liabilities in the context of the bailout mechanisms would require parliamentary oversight (Spiegel International 2012). Moreover, the Bundesbank and German representatives in the ECB have consistently opposed unorthodox moves by the ECB of the sort described above (Thompson 2015). According to this line of reasoning, the German government has acquiesced in and led domestically unpopular policy moves in order to preserve the single currency. It has, in short, acted as a 'reluctant' hegemon (Paterson 2011; Bulmer and Paterson 2013).

However, others emphasize that, notwithstanding German discourses framing the crisis as the product of foreign irresponsibility, in fact it was in German (and 'core') interests to ensure the bailouts of periphery countries given substantial exposure of German banks to periphery debt (Thompson 2015; Bibow 2013). This accords with the current account figures highlighted above, which draw attention to the interdependencies and imbalances at the heart of the crisis. More specifically, it is notable that German banks (among others) substantially reduced their exposure in Greece following the first bailout (which, notably, did not include private sector involvement). Moreover, it was the very same unorthodox ECB policies so widely criticized by German central bankers that allowed German private banks to offload periphery assets (Thompson 2015). From this perspective Germany can be conceived as more of a 'self-interested' than 'reluctant' hegemon.

Both narratives contain some element of truth; German actors were variously both reluctant—from a domestic politics perspective—and self-interested—from an economic or materialist perspective—in the course of the crisis. An emphasis on the former position probably suggests a more optimistic prognosis in terms of Germany's ability to support future reform efforts of the sort enunciated above. From this perspective, Merkel's famous declaration—'if the euro fails, Europe fails' (Der Spiegel, 2011)—can be understood as a sincere warning to a reticent but overwhelmingly pro-European domestic audience. However, even from this perspective, there are clear domestic limits on Germany's pro-Europeanism as reflected throughout the course of the crisis in the ways discussed and in the emergence of an explicitly anti-euro political party in the AfD (Alternative for Germany).

From a more materialist perspective, the prospects of substantive reform look even bleaker. Given that Germany's economic exposure to the periphery is far less than it was in 2010, it may be that the material economic incentives to further expand its reform efforts are dwindling. Moreover, in terms of global political-economic structures, it has been convincingly argued that German surpluses permit the accumulation of foreign exchange reserves in ways that have protected Germany to some extent from the vagaries of US-led global finance. From this perspective, Germany is unlikely to do anything that might undermine its current surpluses and the economic model on which they are based (Ryner and Cafruny 2017: 109–111). As Marsh (2013: 115) has put it, for Germany, '[t]he two objectives of domestic and European stabilization, which used to run in parallel, are [now] proceeding along divergent lines'.

Indeed, from whichever perspective we understand Germany's position throughout the crisis, it seems unlikely that it will substantially reform its growth model by stimulating domestic demand and permitting wage inflation. The *raison d'être* of German monetary policy before and since EMU has been price stability, and it seems difficult to envisage substantive moves away from such a deeply ingrained philosophy, which became synonymous with the country's economic miracle in the post-war era and its strong economic performance in more recent years. It is also difficult to foresee German agreement to increased risk sharing in the Eurozone, whether through the establishment of Eurobonds or through the even more radical establishment of a substantive fiscal union (notwithstanding the advocacy of important German public intellectuals such as Jürgen Habermas). The notion that a Banking Union could be developed to ensure risk sharing in the European banking system has also been viewed with suspicion in Germany. More substantive reforms to finance therefore look unlikely in this context. More generally, concerns around so-called moral hazard—the notion that burden sharing of various kinds will remove incentives for the economically irresponsible to become more 'responsible'—are, while in many respects built on misconceptions, acutely felt and effectively instrumentalized by opinion-makers in Germany (Newman 2015).

At the time of writing in mid-2017, the status quo looked politically unsustainable even as it at once looked politically unmovable. The imbalances that lay at the heart of the crisis and the core–periphery political and economic divisions it unleashed remained significant. In early 2017 Greece's economic woes continued and it remained an MoU country monitored by the 'troika' and with little to show by way of a sustainable economic recovery. Ireland, Spain and Portugal had all exited their programmes, and each had showed some signs of economic recovery from around 2015–2016. However, given the absence of broader structural changes in European policy it was difficult to see how these 'recoveries' might be sustainable. As a number of the authors of the chapters that follow argue, such upturns were based largely on the revival of, rather than reinvention of, the dysfunctional growth models that had proved so fragile when the crisis hit in 2009–2010. Moreover, it is important to emphasize that economic growth alone does not capture the hugely destructive distributional consequences that the crisis and austerity responses had embedded; consequences that only serve to reinforce internal political domestic divisions (Hopkin 2015).

As implied in the foregoing, other countries such as France and Italy were struggling economically in 2017, suggesting that the geographical scope and population size of what we here describe as the European 'periphery' was increasing vis-à-vis the 'core' at the time of writing. Such economic dynamics had domestic political implications throughout the periphery with the rise of new political parties including anti-European and far-right parties. Indeed, if the reduction of national monetary (and political) autonomy wrought by EMU had forced a convergence of pro-EU/euro mainstream parties in the political centre, then the crisis precipitated the filling of the 'void' that such convergence had established (Mair 2013). At the transnational level, political rifts were developing or intensifying not only between the core and GIPS, but also between Germany and France, with the re-emergence of longstanding tensions on the nature of economic governance. In relation to Greece, rifts were also emerging within the 'troika', with the IMF increasingly critiquing the EU's intransigence on the possibility of debt relief, while simultaneously calling for yet more cuts in public spending to make public finances sustainable in the absence of such relief.

At the same time, governments and populations in both core and periphery continued to offer at least some support to both the euro (Otero-Iglesias 2017) and the EU. And this support was reinforced in some national contexts as a consequence of first the Brexit vote and then Trump's election in 2016. European institutions such as the Commission showed signs of leniency in terms of the enforcement of austerity rules (Schmidt 2016; Parker and Pye 2017). And the election of Macron as French President in May 2017 increased the likelihood of the restoration of greater political unity between France and Germany, notwithstanding their divergent economic trajectories. In summary, at the time of writing (mid-2017) things were in considerable flux. It was extremely hard to predict whether the direction of travel would be one of 'muddling along' with the current status quo, disintegration or further integration (Borriello and Crespy 2016). Indeed, as the EU celebrated 60 years since the Rome Treaty in 2017, the ongoing effects of the Eurozone crisis fed a broader existential crisis that was yet to be resolved.

Chapter Overview

The first section of the book traces the origins of the economic crisis in GIPS and discusses the country-specific responses to it adopted by their governments. It allows for cross-country comparisons that reveal the commonalities as well as differences in the set of challenges faced in these contexts since the onset of the crisis as well as before it.

In Chap. 2, Seán Ó Riain analyses the case of Ireland and dispels the myth of the Irish economic miracle, both with respect to the pre-crisis period and in the context of the country's recent economic recovery and exit from its programme. Stressing the replacement of Ireland's earlier 'activist' liberalism with a post-2000 'aggressive' liberalism, he points to the inherent contradictions of Irish political economy that left it vulnerable to an abrupt slowdown and full-blown crisis by the time of the GFC. He argues that the 'Irish model' remains vulnerable, and the celebratory tones recently adopted by EU and Irish officials may yet prove to be premature (see also, Ó Riain, 2014).

Luis Buendia shows a similar logic at play in Spain. In Chap. 3, he argues that the much-praised 'Spanish miracle' was structurally linked to the country's place in the European division of labour, sustaining and reinforcing the core–periphery dichotomy ingrained in the Eurozone's setup discussed above. At the same time, Buendia points to the important role of agency, namely of Spanish political and economic elites, whose policy choices exacerbated the crisis and worsened the economic predicament of labouring classes in particular.

In Chap. 4, Neil Dooley highlights that, as in our other case studies, the vulnerability of the Portuguese economy predates the outbreak of the crisis. He traces the origins of Portugal's crisis and subsequent bailouts to the adoption of 'structural reforms' in the 1980s, which were facilitated by, if not a direct consequence of, its EU membership. Dooley points to the perverse effect of those reforms: a debt-led growth model was adopted over the next two decades and, combined with global economic pressures, led to the paradox of overheating *without* an acceleration of GDP growth.

Greece, the Eurozone's most vulnerable member, and the only one still subject to a bailout programme at the time of writing in 2017, is the focus of Chap. 5. Pavlos Gkasis pointedly spells out the inherent weaknesses of Greece's political economy, which fostered a problematic growth and development trajectory even before EU and Eurozone accession. At the same time, he draws our attention to the inadequacies and contradictions of the bailout programmes chosen for Greece, and the systemic factors that have made internal devaluation a recipe for further economic misery since 2010.

The second section of the book discusses the politics of the crisis. It considers in each country case the ways in which the economic crisis was framed politically, traces the political (and social) effects of the crisis and reflects upon the deeper political cultures and histories that allow us to understand the particularities of those effects.

Chapter 6 by Nicholas Kiersey on Ireland explores the way in which austerity was, far from simply an external imposition, successfully legitimated by a problematic domestic discursive politics that emphasized that the country and its people had lived beyond their means and would consequently need to pay for their excesses. This was problematic to the extent that it neglected the role of broader structural factors (enunciated in this Introduction), among which the EU was key, not only in terms of the single currency, but also in terms of the liberalization of the financial sector associated with the single market project. He also suggests that such a discourse neglects or effaces the way in which particular right-wing elites have historically dominated the management of the Irish political economy. Finally, he demonstrates that the popular acceptability of this problematic narrative of self-blame has been eroded in recent years, as reflected in increasing public protest and the shifting fortunes of formerly marginal political parties.

Mònica Clua-Losada's contribution in Chap. 7 outlines the political fallout from the economic crisis in Spain, highlighting the rise of new social movements (particularly the so-called 15-M movement in 2011), the strengthening of the Catalan independence cause and a growing number of 'institutional assaults' on the status quo by new political formations at both local and national levels. This is framed not only in terms of the economic crisis, but also in the context of the (problematic) constitutional settlement that emerged in the 1970s following the Franco dictatorship. Preoccupied with stability, that settlement delimited the formal possibilities for political opposition and goes some way to explaining the informal and spontaneous nature of the political responses to the crisis in Spain.

In Chap. 8, Isabel David argues that the Portuguese case is distinct among GIPS for two principal reasons. On the one hand, the crisis resulted in the implementation of a new political experiment, whereby the Socialist Party governs in alliance with the Communists and the Left. She notes that there are signs of consistent attempts by the new government to redress some of the harsh austerity measures of its predecessors. On the other hand, David points out that the crisis has not led to any major realignment of party politics in the country, despite the fact that the Social Democratic Party (centre-right) has not shied away from adopting an explicit, pro-austerity discourse.

Finally, Chap. 9 by Alexandra Prodromidou focuses on Greece, revealing a sharp contrast with the Portuguese case. Greek politics has been transformed since 2010, not least in terms of the collapse of the erstwhile dominant Socialist Party (PASOK), the emergence of the far-right (Golden Dawn) and the meteoric rise of the left-wing SYRIZA as a governing party.

What remains uncertain, however, is the sustainability of this change, and the answer is largely dependent on the extent to which the country manages to exit the bailout programmes with a semblance of socio-economic stability. Populist and clientelist governance, Prodromidou asserts, is largely an inherent feature of the country's party political scene, making optimistic predictions difficult.

Finally, our conclusion draws some comparative lessons from the country cases. While in different ways and to different extents, the cases show that there is some margin for domestic resistance to the neoliberal status quo sketched in this chapter, we suggest that ultimately both domestic and European (and, indeed, international) reforms will also dictate the degree to which those resistance movements—formal or informal—are able to gain significant and enduring traction. Thus, collective action locally, nationally and at EU level will need to work in tandem if a genuinely progressive challenge that successfully preserves the European project is to be realized.

Notes

1. Others were pointing out, however, that over time a currency union would by itself create the conditions necessary for it to work successfully (Frankel and Rose 1997).
2. Indeed one could argue that only the Greek case is unquestionably one of ballooning public debt levels prior to the onset of the crisis.
3. As it became clear in late 2010 that Greece would not be the only effected state, the EU and IMF put together a larger support mechanism that had three components: the European Financial Stability Facility (EFSF), backed by member states, was authorized to raise €440 billion; the European Financial Stabilization Mechanism (EFSM), backed by the EU budget, was able to raise €60 billion; and the IMF was to provide a further €250 billion. In 2012 this was replaced by a permanent institution, the European Stability Mechanism (ESM), which was agreed by treaty with a lending capacity of up to €500 billion.

References

Baldwin, R., and F. Giavazzi, eds. 2015. *The Eurozone Crisis: A Consensus View on the Causes and a Few Possible Remedies.* London: CEPR Press.

Bauer, M.W., and S. Becker. 2014. The Unexpected Winner of the Crisis: The European Commission's Strengthened Role in Economic Governance. *Journal of European Integration* 36 (3): 213–229.

Begg, I. 2011. *Fiscal Union for the Euro Area: An Overdue and Necessary Scenario?* Bertelsmann Stiftung. Available at: http://www.bertelsmann-stiftung.de/fileadmin/files/BSt/Presse/imported/downloads/xcms_bst_dms_34969_34970_2.pdf.

Bengtsson, E., and M. Ryner. 2015. The (International) Political Economy of Falling Wage Shares: Situating Working Class Agency. *New Political Economy* 20 (3): 406–430.

Bibow, J. 2013. The Euroland Crisis and Germany's Euro Trilemma. *International Review of Applied Economics* 27 (3): 360–385.

Blanchard, O., and F. Giavazzi. 2002. Current Account Deficits in the Euro Area: The End of the Feldstein-Horioka Puzzle? *Brookings Papers on Economic Activity* 33 (2): 147–210.

Blyth, M. 2013. *Austerity: The History of a Dangerous Idea.* New York: Oxford University Press.

Bohle, D., and B. Greskovits. 2012. *Capitalist Diversity on Europe's Periphery.* Ithaca/London: Cornell University Press.

Borriello, A., and A. Crespy. 2016. The EU Is at a Crossroads Between Federalism and Political Disintegration. *LSE Blogs.* Available at: http://blogs.lse.ac.uk/brexit/2016/01/19/the-eu-is-at-a-crossroads-between-federalism-and-political-disintegration/.

Bulmer, S., and W.E. Paterson. 2013. Germany as the EU's Reluctant Hegemon? Of Economic Strength and Political Constraints. *Journal of European Public Policy* 20 (10): 1387–1405.

Cohen, B.J. 2012. The Future of the Euro: Let's Get Real. *Review of International Political Economy* 19 (4): 689–700.

Darvas, Z.M., and Á. Leandro. 2015. *The Limitations of Policy Coordination in the Euro Area Under the European Semester,* No. 2015/19. Bruegel Policy Contribution.

De Grauwe, P. 2012. The Governance of a Fragile Eurozone. *The Australian Economic Review* 45 (3): 255–268.

———. 2013. *Design Failures in the Eurozone: Can They Be Fixed?* LEQS Paper No. 57. Available at SSRN: https://ssrn.com/abstract=2215762 or https://doi.org/10.2139/ssrn.2215762.

Der Spiegel. 2011. *Merkel Says EU Must Be Bound Closer Together*, September 7. Available at: http://www.spiegel.de/international/germany/if-the-euro-fails-europe-fails-merkel-says-eu-must-be-bound-closer-together-a-784953.html.

———. 2012. *German High Court OKs Permanent Bailout Fund with Reservations*, September 12. Available at: http://www.spiegel.de/international/germany/german-high-court-oks-permanent-bailout-fund-with-reservations-a-855338.html.

Dyson, K. 2013. Sworn to Grim Necessity? Imperfections of European Economic Governance, Normative Political Theory, and Supreme Emergency. *Journal of European Integration* 35 (3): 207–222.

Feldstein, M. 2008. *Optimal Currency Areas.* ECB Fifth Central Banking Conference. Available at: http://www.nber.org/feldstein/Optimal%20Currency%20Areas.pdf.

———. 2012. The Failure of the Euro. *Foreign Affairs*, January/February 2012. Available at: http://www.nber.org/feldstein/fa121311.html.

Fishman, R.M. 2011. Portugal's Unnecessary Bailout. *The New York Times*, April 12.

Frankel, J.A., and A.K. Rose. 1997. Is EMU More Justifiable Ex Post than Ex Ante? *European Economic Review* 41 (3): 753–760.

Gill, S. 1998. European Governance and New Constitutionalism: Economic and Monetary Union and Alternatives to Disciplinary Neoliberalism in Europe. *New Political Economy* 3 (1): 5–26.

Hall, P.A. 2014. Varieties of Capitalism and the Euro Crisis. *West European Politics* 37 (6): 1223–1243.

Hall, P.A., and D. Soskice. 2001. *Varieties of Capitalism: The Institutional Foundations of Comparative Advantage.* Oxford: Oxford University Press.

Hopkin, J. 2015. The Troubled Southern Periphery: The Euro Experience in Italy and Spain. In *The Future of the Euro*, ed. M. Matthijs and M. Blyth. Oxford: Oxford University Press.

Johnston, A., and A. Regan. 2016. European Monetary Integration and the Incompatibility of National Varieties of Capitalism. *Journal of Common Market Studies* 54 (2): 318–336.

Jones, E. 2015. The Forgotten Financial Union. In *The Future of the Euro*, ed. M. Matthijs and M. Blyth. Oxford: Oxford University Press.

Kenen, P. 1969. The Theory of Optimum Currency Areas: An Eclectic View. In *Monetary Problems in the International Economy*, ed. R. Mundell and A. Swoboda. Chicago: University of Chicago Press.

Krugman, P. 2012. Revenge of the Optimum Currency Area. *Opinion Piece, The New York Times.* Available at: https://krugman.blogs.nytimes.com/2012/06/24/revenge-of-the-optimum-currency-area/?_r=1.

Lavery, S. 2017. Enduring Imbalances in the Eurozone. In *The Coming Crisis*, ed. C. Hay. Basingstoke: Palgrave.

Mair, P. 2013. *Ruling the Void: The Hollowing of Western Democracy.* London: Verso.

Marsh, D. 2013. *Europe's Deadlock: How the Euro Crisis Could Be Solved—And Why It Won't Happen.* Hampshire: Yale University Press.

Matthijs, M., and M. Blyth. 2015. Introduction. In *The Future of the Euro*, ed. M. Matthijs and M. Blyth. Oxford: Oxford University Press.

McNamara, K.R. 1998. *The Currency of Ideas: Monetary Politics in the European Union.* Ithaca: Cornell University Press.

———. 2006. Economic Governance, Ideas and EMU: What Currency Does Policy Consensus Have Today? *Journal of Common Market Studies* 44 (4): 803–821.

———. 2015. The Forgotten Problem of Embeddedness. In *The Future of the Euro*, ed. M. Matthijs and M. Blyth. Oxford: Oxford University Press.

Michaelides, A., and A. Orphanides, eds. 2016. *The Cyprus Bail-in: Policy Lessons from the Cyprus Economic Crisis.* London: Imperial College Press.

Moravcsik, A. 2012. Europe After the Crisis: How to Sustain a Common Currency. *Foreign Affairs* 91 (May/June): 54–68.

Mundell, R.A. 1961. A Theory of Optimum Currency Areas. *American Economic Review* 51: 657–664.

Newman, S. 2015. The Reluctant Leader. In *The Future of the Euro*, ed. M. Matthijs and M. Blyth. Oxford: Oxford University Press.

Ò Riain, S. 2014. *The Rise and Fall of Ireland's Celtic Tiger: Liberalism, Boom and Bust.* Cambridge: Cambridge University Press.

Otero-Iglesias, M. 2017. Why the Eurozone Still Backs Its Common Currency. *Foreign Affairs*, January.

Paterson, W.E. 2011. The Reluctant Hegemon? Germany Moves Centre Stage in the European Union. *Journal of Common Market Studies* 49 (1): 57–75.

Parker, O., and Pye, R. 2017. Mobilising social rights in EU economic governance: a pragmatic challenge to neoliberal Europe. *Comparative European Politics.* Online first: https://doi.org/10.1057/s41295-017-0102-1.

Regan, A. 2013. *Political Tensions in Euro-Varieties of Capitalism: The Crisis of the Democratic State in Europe*, EUI Working Paper, 2013/14.

Ryner, M., and A. Cafruny. 2017. *The European Union and Global Capitalism: Origins, Development, Crisis.* London: Palgrave Macmillan.

Sachi, R. 2015. Renzi's Resignation Sparks Talks to form New Italian Government. *Financial Times*, December 7. Available at: www.ft.com/content/b26e1aa2-bc8c-11e6-8b45-b8b81dd5d080.

Schmidt, V.A. 2011. Saving the Euro Will Mean Worse Trouble for Europe. *Foreign Affairs*, November.

———. 2016. Reinterpreting the Rules 'By Stealth' in Times of Crisis: A Discursive Institutionalist Analysis of the European Central Bank and the European Commission. *West European Politics* 39 (5): 1032–1052.

Schwartz, H. 2012. Euro-Crisis, American Lessons? *Review of International Political Economy* 19 (4): 701–708.

Stockhammer, E. 2016. Neoliberal Growth Models, Monetary Union and the Euro Crisis: A Post-Keynesian Perspective. *New Political Economy* 21 (4): 365–379.

Thompson, H. 2015. Germany and the Euro-Zone Crisis: The European Reformation of the German Banking Crisis and the Future of the Euro. *New Political Economy* 20 (6): 851–870.

Trimikliniotis, N. 2013. Cyprus: Is the Eurocrisis the Beginning of the End of the Eurozone? *Open Democracy*, March 25. Available at: descrier.co.uk/news/world/cyprus-is-the-eurocrisis-the-beginning-of-the-end-of-the-eurozone/.

Wallerstein, I. 1974. The Rise and Future Demise of the World Capitalist System: Concepts for Comparative Analysis. *Comparative Studies in Society and History* 16 (4): 387–415.

———. 1979. *The Capitalist World Economy*. Cambridge: Cambridge University Press.

Watt, A. 2013. The German Minimum Wage Debate: Lessons from an EU Comparison. *Social Europe Journal*. Available at: http://www.social-europe.eu/2013/10/the-german-minimum-wage-debate-lessons-from-an-eu-comparison/.

PART I

The Economic Dynamics of the Crisis

CHAPTER 2

Tracing Ireland's 'Liberal' Crisis and Recovery

Seán Ó Riain

Abstract Ireland's deep crisis after 2008 was most immediately produced by the bursting of a real estate and banking bubble combined with collapsing tax revenues. This was made possible by Ireland's continuing weakness in developing indigenous enterprise and investment, its limited social contract and emergent tensions in its historical external ties with the UK, the USA and Europe. More generally, the character of Ireland's crisis was rooted in its varied history of economic liberalism, and particularly in an aggressive liberalism of the 2000s that succeeded earlier periods of passive and activist liberalism. Finally, despite recent economic and employment growth, Ireland's recovery remains tenuous, given the re-emergence of historical patterns and the failure to address some key dilemmas in the 'Irish model'.

Keywords Ireland • Financialisation • European integration • Economic development • Liberalism • Social contract

S. Ó Riain (✉)
Department of Sociology, Maynooth University,
Maynooth, County Kildare, Ireland

O. Parker, D. Tsarouhas (eds.), *Crisis in the Eurozone Periphery*,
Building a Sustainable Political Economy: SPERI Research & Policy,
https://doi.org/10.1007/978-3-319-69721-5_2

Once celebrated as the 'Celtic Tiger', Ireland experienced one of the deepest and most sustained crises during the Great Recession in Europe and beyond. Five years of austerity and stagnation slowly turned to recovery, with economic and employment growth well established again by 2014. The recovery faced major challenges and uncertainties by 2017, as Brexit, a Trump presidency and a faltering European project challenged key planks of Ireland's development strategy. This uncertainty was only increased by Ireland's economic history, where the only feature more striking than its ability to recover from a series of crises is to just as quickly move from each recovery into a new form of crisis.

This chapter briefly describes the key features of Ireland's crisis and then explores how those features are rooted in longstanding processes within Irish political economy. In particular, the chapter argues that the character of Ireland's crisis was rooted in its varied history of economic liberalism, and particularly in an aggressive liberalism of the 2000s that succeeded earlier periods of passive and activist liberalism. Finally, the chapter argues that Ireland's recovery remains tenuous, given the re-emergence of historical patterns and the failure to address some key dilemmas in the 'Irish model'.

The origins of Ireland's economic crisis appear to be no mystery. The crisis was five-fold (NESC 2009). The core was a *financial* crisis—an unholy combination of property speculation by developers, reckless lending by bankers and lack of governmental oversight and regulation created a property and banking bubble that brought the Irish economy to its knees when the international financial system ran into trouble in 2008. The liabilities of these banks were guaranteed by the state in 2008, and developer loans and assets were taken under state management. A parallel *fiscal* crisis mushroomed as the public finances were burdened with the cost of bailing out failing banks but also with a growing deficit as tax revenues associated with the asset bubble disappeared. One of the largest austerity policies in recent history was undertaken in response (Whelan 2010).

Behind these proximate causes were two deeper crises. Closely connected to the financial crisis was an *economic* crisis. Thought of by many as a problem of competitiveness, more important was weak productive investment and collapsing domestic demand. The weakness of productive investment in Ireland crucially linked the financial and economic crises together and to the broader history of Ireland's political economy. Economic and fiscal collapse further drove a major *social* crisis based on negative equity and mortgage arrears, cutbacks in public services and disastrous rises in unemployment. This social crisis directly reinforced the fiscal crisis through the increased demand on services and benefits and a reduced tax take. More profoundly, Ireland's social model related strongly to the fiscal crisis as the tax base was narrow, levels of inequality were high and key aspects of the welfare system (e.g. housing, active labour market policy and pensions) were very weak. Overall, a financial and economic system that generated poor levels of productive investment and high rates of property speculation combined disastrously with a social and fiscal compact that generated high inequality, weak services and a narrow tax base.

Finally, Ireland faced an external *reputational* crisis, particularly evident in the reluctance of international lenders to finance government debt—culminating in a European Union–International Monetary Fund bailout in November 2010—but also in increasing difficulty in managing international relations with tensions around foreign investment, tax and trade.

These factors are in many respects well understood. But how could they emerge in such a disastrous combination? And, with signs that many of the same dynamics are once more in play, why are they so persistent? To answer these questions, the chapter traces the trajectories of each of these five dimensions of the crisis (financial, fiscal, economic, social and reputational/international) in Irish economic development.

These crises emerged from a system that is often called liberal. But what does 'liberal' mean in contemporary comparative political economy? In neoclassical approaches, 'the market' is taken as the baseline for all economic analysis. However, economic sociology and comparative political economy emphasise that markets are 'embedded' in social relations and social and political institutions and that what happens in markets is heavily affected by how those markets are organised, who has power and which kinds of market activity are rewarded and which are discouraged (Granovetter 1985; Polanyi 1944).

We adopt a strategy which combines close attention to the prevalence of markets within a society with an analysis of how those markets are shaped by the social relations and institutions of that society (for a fuller account, see Ó Riain 2014: Chap. 1). Recent analyses have shown that 'neoliberalism' can be very 'resilient' as powerful corporate actors constantly escape regulation of their market behaviour (Schmidt and Thatcher 2014; Jessop 2014). But social institutions also try to re-regulate markets—so that even neoliberal societies can take a variety of forms of economic liberalism, at different times and places.

More liberal economies—particularly the USA, UK and those linked to them through colonialism (including Ireland)—tend to share certain features. The financial sector has a greater degree of power than in other countries; they rely more heavily on private regulation of markets (e.g. stock markets, rating agencies); raise fewer taxes and tend to be more unequal; have politics that is more centralised and more short-termist; and are more likely to have volatile growth patterns and greater government debt. But all these features are also affected by each individual country's distinct features—its history of development, government policies, party politics, trade union organisation and so on (Ó Riain 2014).

Therefore, an account of liberalism in Ireland must take account of its varied character, how it is socially organised, how liberal projects interact with non-liberal projects and how social compromises are shaped by liberalism itself. In this chapter, I apply this approach to an account of Ireland's varying historical liberalisms—passive, activist and aggressive—and how they laid the conditions for Ireland's crisis and the possibility and dilemmas of its contemporary recovery.

From Passive Liberalism to State Activism Within Liberal Globalisation

When Ireland received its independence from Great Britain in 1922, it was left with a legacy of institutions and political economic structures that in many respects reflected those of its coloniser. Having largely missed out on the first and second industrial revolutions (Ó Riain 2016), independence brought the partition of the main industrial centre around Belfast from the new Free State. The primary patterns of trade were patterns of unequal exchange with the UK, mainly consisting of low-value agricultural exports, combined with significant labour migration enabled by free movement between the two countries. The system of public administration not surprisingly mirrored the Whitehall model, while the absence of a Parliament was soon rectified with the establishment of a system that in many important respects borrowed from the UK Westminster model. In addition, even at this early stage, Ireland's welfare state was significantly underdeveloped compared to other societies (Cusack et al. 2007). Other institutions too were borrowed from the UK, including a pluralist system of industrial relations where many of the unions themselves (especially craft unions) were English-based unions. In the decade after independence, Ireland only reinforced its liberal character, with the conservative Cumann na nGaedheal party pursuing policies of free trade and relative continuity with the British era.

Overall, the Irish political economy was characterised by a 'passive liberalism'—a system where the institutions of industrial policy, welfare state development and industrial relations were very weakly developed but where business played a relatively passive role in national affairs, where capitalist development was weak and where stock markets and other market governance mechanisms were marginal. Between the 1930s and the 1950s, economic policy was strongly protectionist—but this brought very little additional development of enterprise, finance or welfare policy. The late 1950s brought a significant change to export orientation from protection. However, even this was of a passive nature at first, with foreign investment in the 1960s coming mainly from the UK to serve the domestic market and little or no state action taken to protect or develop the domestic businesses that were decimated by trade and the new arrivals.

Economically, Ireland was weak but this combined with an inactive business and, especially, financial sector. Ireland's social compact was disastrously underdeveloped, but within a conservative fiscal approach, the safety valve for Ireland's politics was not budget deficits, but emigration (Mjoset 1992). Internationally, the key (practically the only) relationship was with the UK. Nonetheless, the 1960s and 1970s brought significant economic growth and some major social transformations—including the beginning of the 'modern' welfare state, the expansion of educational participation, changing family and gender relations and the entry of Ireland into the European Economic Community in 1973.

A new measure of state activism was evident throughout this period. Even the most obvious shift in Ireland's economy—the attraction of foreign investment—was a project driven by the state. The government's Industrial Development Authority (IDA) took on the role of 'hunter and gatherer' of foreign direct investment (FDI) and became unusually powerful within the national state system. Working closely with its foreign 'client companies', it provided a 'one stop shop' for meeting their tax and regulation needs within the country, often promoting new policy measures based on their conversations with managing directors of foreign firms (an increasing proportion of whom were Irish-born). Thus, the IDA combined planned targeting of key technology sectors with ongoing briefings from local managers of foreign firms. In addition to a general project of 'modernisation' from the 1960s (central to which was the provision of free secondary education in 1966), additional public investments were made in following decades in the expansion of high education and some expansion of research activity—driven, or at least made politically easier, by the demands of foreign investors.

Nonetheless, poor fiscal management in the late 1970s resulted in economic disaster in the 1980s. The government of the day borrowed heavily to pour money into the economy, only to see that new spending disappears out of the economy due to the weakness of the development of domestic enterprise. Ireland was left with ballooning government debt, soaring unemployment and mass emigration. Stabilised by a series of policy changes from 1987 onwards, supported by a series of 'social partnership' agreements, the Irish economy began to take off in the 1990s. At the core of this economic and employment performance was a boom in exports, driven largely by American foreign investments in high-tech sectors. Although foreign firms in Ireland engaged extensively in 'transfer pricing' and other forms of creative accounting, there was also a boom within the bubble. Employment in multinational companies in Ireland became more professionalised, and expenditure on R&D per employee increased quite significantly in a number of sectors, including in the growing, domestically owned software industry. Furthermore, beneath the veneer of a flowering of Irish entrepreneurialism was a great deal of state coordination. Agencies played a crucial role in supporting and promoting this upgrading, especially in the Irish-owned sectors through grant aid, soft supports, promoting associations and networking and providing and incentivising financing of businesses—working through a network of agencies to form a 'developmental network state' (Ó Riain 2004).

A system of neocorporatist social partnership was established, based around a series of formal agreements from 1987 to 2009. Darius Ornston (2012) has described Ireland as a case of competitive corporatism, focusing on reducing inflation and increased wage competitiveness. However, in many respects Ireland better fits Ornston's label for the Nordic economies of 'creative corporatism'. In the 1990s, Ireland delivered supports for active labour market policy, risk capital and (to a lesser extent) R&D that approached the levels provided in the Nordic economies and surpassed many continental European economies such as Belgium and Austria (Ó Riain 2014). Irish corporatism in the 1990s therefore was more creative than the competitive corporatism description allows for.

This was linked also to a changing international context. Ruane (2010) argued that while Ireland is certainly a semi-peripheral economy, the nature of its peripheral status has changed over time. In particular, he argues that Ireland has shifted from a 'simple periphery' of the UK to a 'multiple interface periphery' located between the UK, the USA and Europe. Ruane argues that this new peripheral position has been adopted strategically by the Irish State and has allowed Ireland greater opportunities to manoeuvre and re-position itself within a more diverse set of international connections—even if all of these connections are in themselves unequal. Famously, this strategy is based in part on the attractiveness of Ireland as a low tax location for US investors within the EU. Since the arrival of Digital to manufacture computers in Ireland in 1971, a series of waves of investment by US high tech had boosted Irish growth. However, the 1990s saw a huge increase in this investment, even as UK and European investment in Ireland declined. Ireland was established as a key hub for the European operations of US high tech (computers, semiconductors, medical devices, pharmaceuticals and software) and financial firms.

But there are other significant aspects to Ireland's international ties. In particular, in the 1990s, European public funds were part of an effort to promote convergence across European regions and ultimately funded a high proportion of Ireland's investment during this decade of development. Much of this funding was related to agriculture, but there were significant increases also in the total non-agricultural funds and in the European social funds that supported training and other measures for labour market inclusion. This increase persisted through the 1990s and only returned to the nominal levels of 1989 in 2007. Even in the booming late 1990s, EU funds accounted for over 15 per cent of Irish public capital expenditure (Ó Riain 2014).

The classic 'European model' of small economy growth involved heavy involvement in international trade, with strong social protection systems as a compensation for the risk from trade and high rates of business and social investment that facilitated success in international markets. Any tensions within this complex balancing act were negotiated through corporatist bargaining. An attenuated version of this European model of development was at the heart of the genuine development of the Irish economy in the 1990s—productive investment, enabled by enterprise policy; European investment in social and regional cohesion within a trading zone; and a set of 'creative corporatist' institutions that mobilised capital and labour as well as managing relations between them. While Ireland had built its development strategy on full participation in liberal globalisation, the period between the 1960s and the 1990s had seen the emergence of a new level of state activism in shaping Ireland's place within that international economy.

Nonetheless major gaps remained. Despite the boom of the 1990s, the financial system remained remarkably weak in its support for productive private investment—as Honohan (2006) notes, the role of finance in promoting growth during the Celtic Tiger years was minimal. The vast bulk of productive capital spending in the Irish economy during this period came from the public sector (White 2010)—including foreign public investors such as the EU and the Irish State (through direct grant aid and through seeding venture capital funds). Private productive investment in Ireland in these boom years was primarily driven by foreign investors such as multinational corporations. The domestic banks acted primarily as passive providers of working capital to domestic business. Economically, domestic enterprise was making progress, but foreign investment remained the primary driver of growth in exports and employment.

Socially, while significant social progress was made on employment and real wages, major structural weaknesses remained—a failure to provide a sustainable housing system; a reliance on cash transfers over high-quality services (combined with poor or unequal service provision); and especially a focus on providing tax breaks over public services in the partnership bargain (Ó Riain and O'Connell 2000). The core wage bargain was an agreement by unions to limit their wage increases, for which they were compensated by government reducing income taxes. Indeed, taxes of all kinds were typically low—including social security taxes which were reduced to boost small employers and corporate tax rates, which boosted large employers. Fiscally, while tax revenues were increasing rapidly, they were declining as a percentage of gross domestic product (GDP). Internationally, Ireland was managing its multiple interfaces but with looming tensions around taxation politics in particular.

Aggressive Liberalism and the Crisis

The response to these significant challenges in the midst of the boom of the late 1990s was to avoid them by employing a more aggressive form of economic liberalism in pursuit of an economic growth that would make it possible to sidestep these lurking problems. Where the activist globalisation of the 1990s was based on export-led improvements in local demand

and investment, the 2000s saw a boom in real estate and financial activity. Furthermore, this was combined with a significantly increased role for private capital in governing the economy. Fundamentally, the economy shifted from a state-managed process of facilitating and serving international productive capital towards governance by (often domestic) financial capital. For the first time in Irish history, domestic financial capital played a key role in the dynamics of the Irish economy. In many respects this was at the cost of making conditions for international capital worse. For instance, it meant increased costs as cheap money boosted demand very rapidly, the crowding out of productive investment and the misallocation of crucial resources reflected, for instance, in a decline in student applications to science degrees. But if this represented a dilemma in the 2000s, financialisation brought Ireland to full-blown crisis by 2008.

In some respects, Ireland's financial crisis was a very local crisis. The sub-prime mortgages and securitised mortgage products that were central to the triggering of the US crisis were much less important in the Irish case, where lending to developers and inflated property prices were much more significant (Connor et al. 2012). While mortgage lending practices loosened in the 2000s, the crisis was not caused by mortgage defaults (although these became significant elements of the evolving crisis) but by developers failing to repay loans to banks when liquidity suddenly dried up in 2008.

However, other features of the Irish crisis were shared more broadly. Ireland's financial expansion was only one leg of a 'triple financialisation', also including Anglo-American financial systems and the financialisation associated with European integration and the euro in the 2000s. While the USA was always more financialised than the European core, that gap widened significantly over the 1990s, and financialisation is most closely associated with 'liberal market economies' (Hall and Soskice 2001) such as the USA, the UK and Ireland. Nonetheless, the EU economies closed the gap somewhat from 2001 onwards—with France and Germany showing a surge in the 2002–2004 period (Ó Riain 2014).

This financialisation was both a driving force in economic liberalisation and also enabled by 'liberal' policies in the state itself. The key 'liberal' element in Ireland's policy regime during these years was the faith in the ability of private capital to allocate investment resources effectively in the economy. Crucially, the new government's budget of 1998 reduced capital gains tax from 40 per cent to 20 per cent with a view to releasing pent up capital into the economy. This goal was rapidly achieved—in the decade after the reduction of capital gains tax to 20 per cent in 1998, bank lending in the economy grew 466 per cent. However, that capital flowed primarily and rapidly into property investment. Together, domestic banks and a small group of residential and commercial property developers misallocated capital in Ireland on a grand scale. A lending and investment coalition focused on domestic property was able to secure the lion's share of available capital, to the cost of competing sectors (most notably the medium and high-tech sectors). Construction and real estate lending increased from 7 per cent to 28 per cent of total lending over the period. In contrast, the high-profile high-tech sectors attracted less than 2.5 per cent of credit (Ó Riain 2014). This was reflected in investment, where although non-construction investment increased, the vast bulk of the capital available for investment in the economy went into construction (see Fig. 2.1).

Furthermore, in addition to this changing dynamic of economic activity, economic governance was also distinctly 'liberal'—with a state-facilitated process of handing over key control levers to private capital. With an institutionally and personally weak Financial Regulator, finance in

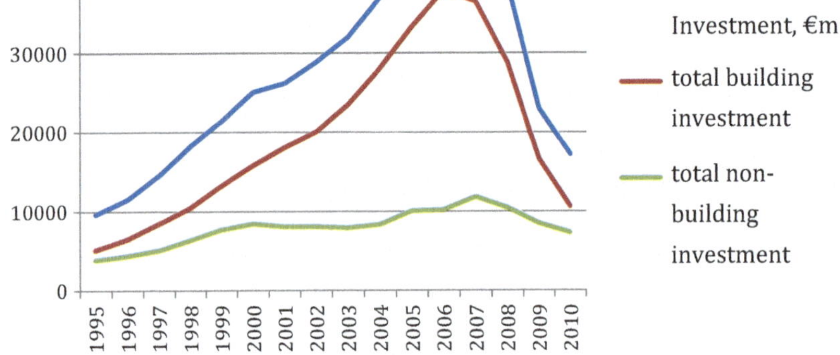

Fig 2.1 Capital availability and investment in Ireland, 1995–2010 (Source: CSO, National Accounts—Institutional Sectors)

Ireland was to be a liberal experiment based on governance by a set of market mechanisms. Unfortunately, these mechanisms failed to provide the necessary controls. Most basically, competition between the banks appears to have been a factor in 'crowding in' the two leading banks, Allied Irish Banks (AIB) and Bank of Ireland, into 'irrational' property lending. A much smaller bank called Anglo Irish Bank (Anglo) was the bank infamously most closely associated with reckless property lending in the 2000s. This saw a surge in profits at Anglo to the point where it had significantly closed the gap with Bank of Ireland and AIB by 2007. Executive compensation followed suit—including, as became apparent in 2008, secret loans to executives and directors of as much as €70 million. AIB, Ireland's most profitable bank, responded to the Anglo surge with a shift into real estate and development lending, with a corresponding boost in profits. But these rising profits masked a very fragile financial system, built on property—and very rapidly leading to disastrous collapse.

If market competition did not provide the discipline required, perhaps managerial authority could. In practice, however, the centralisation of executive authority in the banks reinforced the convergence of optimistic assessments of asset quality, capital position and economic growth (Ó Riain 2014). Bank executives faced few challenges to their perspectives. Authority within the banks was highly centralised, as the Anglo report of 2006 notes: 'The Bank's centralised business model enables quick decision making, ensuring consistent delivery of service to our customers and effective management of risk. It also allows us to operate in an efficient and streamlined manner, as reflected by our cost to income ratio of 27 per cent.' Senior bank executive salaries rose rapidly in all banks through the 2000s, with bonuses that were in practice increased by corporate strategies that inflated the bubble (TASC 2010).

Shareholders were the other candidates for providing sufficient external oversight from within the private sector as a 'market for governance' (Davis 2011). However, the stock market itself reinforced the tendencies towards financialisation. Ó Riain (2014) examined trends in a variety of Irish Stock Market Indices from 1995 to 2005. The General Index showed strong growth in the late 1990s but dipped from 2001 to 2003 and only recovered by 2005. However, the financial stocks surged from 2000 onwards, after strong growth in the 1990s. The stock market was also a weak mechanism for distributing investment to the productive and innovative, rather than speculative, sectors. The technology-based index never recovered subsequent to the dot.com bubble bursting in 2001, while the financial stocks increased rapidly in value. The stock market rewarded the lending patterns that were ultimately to crash the economy.

Nor did an increasing engagement with international financial institutions have the required effect. A crucial role here was played by the credit-rating agencies, private regulatory organisations that provide ratings of the quality of a wide variety of financial instruments, linked both to private and sovereign issuers. These agencies provided increasingly positive ratings of Ireland's banks, including for Anglo Irish Bank—which in turn was given a series of international accolades by consulting firms (Ó Riain 2014). The market institutions which were to provide a regulatory function to market actors and actions failed disastrously to limit the financialisation of Ireland's economy and in practice facilitated and rewarded the dangerous expansion of the financial sector to a scale that would ultimately produce Ireland's dramatic austerity.

Disastrously, this financialisation of business and households also found its way into the public finances through the structure of taxation and levels of public spending. As the bargains struck through social partnership and through partisan politics expanded in their scale through the 2000s, they relied most heavily on the return of after tax income to citizens across the income distribution. With social security taxes and corporate taxes already low entering the Celtic Tiger years, the period from 1998 to 2002 saw major cuts in income tax with the top rate dropping from 48 per cent to 41 per cent.

This focus on income tax reductions was reinforced by the structure of the Irish welfare regime which placed a particularly strong emphasis on providing households with more after tax income rather than significantly expanding the social services available to citizens. The structure of the Irish welfare state itself, in common with other liberal and Mediterranean welfare states, relied more heavily on transfer payments (cash payments such as Unemployment Benefit) than on the direct provision of social services. Indeed, the major policy report on the welfare state in the 2000s—the National Economic and Social Council report on the 'developmental welfare state'—argued for both a re-balancing of income transfers, social services and active measures, and a more flexible system of supports across the life course (NESC 2005). This notion found little support in the government, and welfare improvements in the 2000s emphasised not an expansion of services but increases in payments and expanded access to those payment with changing eligibility rules (e.g. subsidies for childcare rather than growing a public system of childcare provision). A welfare state that focused on cash payments rather than universal public services undermined public support for protecting social services.

By the eve of the financial crisis of 2008, the developmental network state had not disappeared but was under internal attack from a new centralism and market orientation and was competing forlornly for resources with a speculative juggernaut of finance and property. In the 2000s, partisan politics and in particular the politics of the electoral cycle came to dominate the political landscape once more. As the bargains struck through social partnership and through partisan politics expanded in their scale through the 2000s, the temptation was always that political exchange would focus on negotiating as large a cash benefit as possible, before the rapid growth slowed. However, the fiscal and political foundations of a broader 'creative corporatist' social contract were increasingly hollowed out (Ó Riain 2014).

The combination of low tax and spending always rendered Ireland's fiscal model vulnerable (Ó Riain 2004, 2009). While many economists worried aloud about increased public spending through the 2000s and, in particular, increases in public sector wages, the factor that turned these structural weaknesses into an acute crisis was the increased dependency of the state on the 'bubble taxes' from capital gains and real estate sales. The financial and fiscal crises were tightly linked together through the property bubble, the core of the banks' business model and the source of the state's surging but vulnerable tax revenue. The flaw at the heart of Ireland's social contract was expressed in the reliance on bubble taxes—the increased spending of the 2000s was financed to an unsustainable degree by the bubble. When the financial crisis hit, those tax revenues disappeared and the weakness of the social contract was disastrously exposed. Overall, even as creative corporatism was eroded in the 2000s, so too was the prudent fiscal management of the late 1990s.

Internationally, the European dimension now was decisive for the first time in Ireland's history. However, Ireland's relationship with Europe changed significantly in the 2000s as the character of the European economic project itself shifted. The proportion of Irish banks' liabilities derived from foreign sources grew dramatically in the 2000s, from around 20 per cent to over 75 per cent within five years (Lane 2011). During this period, the EU Structural Funds were reduced significantly in newly wealthy Ireland (see Fig. 2.2).

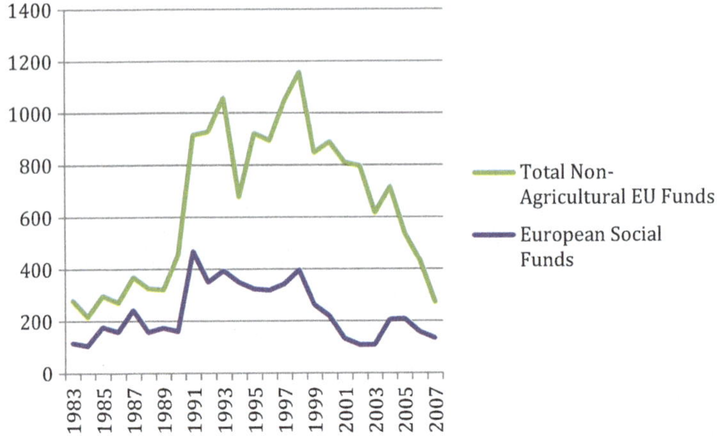

Fig. 2.2 EU funds in Ireland, 1983–2007

Behind these trends was a deeper shift in governance and in economic model. In the 1990s, Ireland benefited from a policy that incorporated strong elements of public developmentalism, in the form of regional, cohesion and research funds, within a trading union, which allowed a measure of negotiated coordination of the different trajectories of member states. However, in the 2000s, this was supplanted by a system dominated by private financialisation, as financial flows within the EU drove resource allocation, in a monetary union, where governance rested heavily on the responsibility of the European Central Bank to enforce relatively narrow economic orthodoxies. Under this regime, the triangle of Irish banks, international funders and credit ratings agencies connected the Irish financial world based on personalised property development lending to the international trade in securitised financial instruments through the standardising effects of credit ratings. In the process, it further weakened the ties between financial and industrial capitals in both the European periphery and the core.

This financialisation was linked to the long-term twin project of monetary union and increased financial integration. Capital liberalisation could support Germany's industrial competitiveness through laying the foundations for a single currency, the euro. Financial integration and monetary union had the potential to deliver a variety of benefits for Europe's core countries, and particularly Germany's export model. First, the euro has been a significant subsidy for German exports, relative to the deutschmark which, had it continued, would have been a much stronger currency and would have made German exports much more expensive. In that sense, some of the advantages of the euro depended on the weakness of the periphery. Second, in a world where an increasing share of profits (although not necessarily employment) was in the financial sector, the banking sector itself became an important export sector in Germany (as it did in more liberal economies such as the UK and Ireland). While capital liberalisation meant a significant shift away from the bank-centred 'hausbank' system that had underpinned much of German industrial growth by providing long-term investment loans to German industrial firms, it could still be seen as a strategy to boost the competitiveness of German exports in the new services sectors.

However, it was at the macroeconomic level that the benefits of the euro were expected to be greatest, providing stability and external market discipline. Indeed, the liberalisation of finance was seen by key German policy makers as providing the external market discipline on public finances that was to be crucial to the European project (Ó Riain 2014). The financialisation of European economies was linked to a broader project of apparently managed economic integration and in particular the monetary union of the 2000s. However, ultimately, it was the role of the financial system itself in managing the flows of finance that undermined the very stability and discipline it was supposed to provide. The financial integration that the euro facilitated was politically significant in shifting the balance of the different 'models of capitalism' within the European Union as the greatest threat to social democratic strategies came less from trade integration than from the danger posed by financialisation to governments' ability to mobilise capital for productive investment (Scharpf 1991). In the process, the European economy became badly unbalanced as where this financialisation took off most dramatically (i.e. in the European periphery), it was funded through external financial systems.

Where once Europe had invested heavily in the future, it now speculated on it. Ruane warns that 'a structurally weak peripheral state may be tempted to abandon the arduous task of monitoring and managing the external-internal interface and decide instead to go with the international flow' (2016: 103). In the 2000s, Ireland's economic model rode that international wave of speculative capital. This was a response to the overall restructuring of the relationship between the core and the periphery of

Europe in this period, which had culminated in the creation of major structural imbalances (described in the Introduction).

Ireland's Persistent Dilemmas

What then of Ireland's recovery? Ireland appears to have emerged alone from the economic wreckage of the European periphery, with rapid economic growth and, more significantly, substantial employment growth. Assessing the Irish recovery is made difficult by the usual issues that plague the observer of Irish economic fortunes—data on growth, trade and productivity are exceptionally difficult to understand given the distortions introduced by the accounting practices of foreign firms located in Ireland (indeed, even Gross National Product (GNP)—once a trusted figure—has been rendered suspicious in recent years) (Bailey and Barry 2016). However, it is clear that there has been an improvement in the Irish economy's fortunes—most reliably observable in an improved employment performance.

Ireland has seen exceptionally strong employment growth since 2012, the low point after the disastrous collapse in employment after the crisis. While there are controversial aspects to the figures, the large majority of this employment growth is real—and, after early growth in part-time, temporary and flexible hour work, nearly all of the growth since 2013 has been in full-time, non-temporary employment. This has been concentrated in three key sectors that have led the recovery—industry and information and communications technology (forming an export-oriented growth cluster); construction (primarily of commercial buildings, in a state-promoted process) and accommodation and food. Furthermore, investment in the Irish economy has shifted from the crisis era, with investment in dwellings collapsing and growing investment in R&D and software now outstripping non-residential building and roads, respectively (Ó Riain forthcoming). Indeed, a major problem in Ireland today is the major underinvestment in dwellings.

While macroeconomic stabilisation no doubt played a role in Ireland's employment recovery, an explanation focused on 'internal devaluation' (wage cuts) is incomplete at best. Looking at the three drivers of growth we have examined, wages grew in information and communications technology, were largely stable in construction and declined somewhat in accommodation and food. While a moderated approach to wage growth certainly helped competitiveness, there is little evidence that it was central to the major part of Ireland's employment growth—the employment growth that is now slowly boosting private demand and income tax revenues. More crucial were two other factors—the weakening of the distorting factors that sucked resources into financialised speculation in the 2000s and the role of public action in promoting the export, construction and tourism sectors.

Nonetheless, Ireland's 'multiple interface periphery' strategy is unravelling fast. The UK vote to leave the EU has created numerous difficulties for Ireland's relationship to the UK and the EU, notably around the Northern Ireland border and the free travel area with the UK (potentially producing a historic reconfiguration of the post-colonial arrangements solidified in the first half of the twentieth century). For our purposes, it has different implications for the foreign and domestic sectors. Brexit may offer opportunities to the IDA to attract foreign investors away from one of its major competitors for mobile US investment—and Ireland has already begun to court technology firms and London-based financial firms away from the UK. However, the implications for Irish firms are much more damaging, given their greater reliance on the UK market.

Meanwhile, Ireland's strategy for attracting foreign investment faces a twin threat from the promises of the US President-Elect to pressure US firms to reduce their global activities and movements in the EU and the Organization for Economic Cooperation and Development (OECD) to develop a consolidated shared method of calculating corporate revenues for taxation purposes. It is clear that a presence in Ireland has facilitated a large number of (primarily US) companies in avoiding tax, an issue which has attracted increasing global attention in light of the EU Commission's finding that Apple owes €13 billion in taxes to Ireland (a finding contested by the Irish government who fear alienating foreign investors more than they desire the additional funds). However, it is less clear how much of that investment would leave if Ireland is forced to re-construct its regime in order to leave this network of locations that together enable the stockpiling of lightly taxed cash by high-tech companies and financial institutions. Nonetheless, it is clear that Ireland will have to place increased emphasis on its other advantages in attracting investment—ironically potentially directing it towards more productive investments in the medium term.

Ireland certainly faces a more complex political context, with the loss of the UK as a supporter in the EU, pressures from EU countries around taxation and a potentially hostile US regime. As Ruane argues, 'multiple interface peripheries in general – and Ireland particularly – [tend to be] structurally vulnerable and crisis-prone' (2016: 104). Ireland's political economy may now come, ironically, to depend even more on its national conditions and strategies. In contemporary debates, this is typically taken to mean that greater attention should be paid to fiscal prudence as growth resumes and public finances improve. However, the question goes deeper. Ireland's most intractable contemporary economic and political dilemmas remain and are evident in debates that seem unable to address the core of the issue, let alone resolve it.

Let us briefly note four of these dilemmas. First, financially, while Ireland brings in significant monies from the international economy, its ability to turn this to productive investment is weak, weakening the current account balance over time—this is largely due to the relative weakness of domestic enterprise. Second, fiscally, Ireland's public finances rest on a narrow base with employer contributions exceptionally low, while an unusually high percentage of workers are outside the tax net. Yet both these poorer households and the smaller firms have realistic difficulties in paying these contributions. Third, economic debates are caught in a bind between the need to increase a wide band of relatively mediocre wages while improving competitiveness—emphasising the need for enhanced productive investment and greater innovation. Fourth, socially, distributional politics are caught between a persistent inequality in market incomes and an effective but controversial redistribution using cash transfers—Ireland's comparatively high inequality in market incomes means there is a 'missing middle' in the income distribution. These dilemmas promise to remain intractable without further progress on Ireland's developmental project, and not just enhanced competitiveness.

Despite the strengths underlying the recovery, Ireland's ability to move forward is still threatened by the same trends that contributed to its crash. While banks are not lending as recklessly as they once did, they have provided little credit to productive businesses. Both finance and property are once again being boosted as growth sectors, and rising rents and prices are putting pressure on households and small businesses. Key investments in education, training, enterprise development, infrastructure and more are being threatened by the very significant cutbacks of recent years. A rush to promise tax cuts undermines the ability to make the investments that will be essential to avoiding the mistakes made at the end of the 1990s, when society was taken down a path of speculation rather than the sustained egalitarian investment that would have put Ireland in a quite different position in 2008, and today. Resolving these dilemmas will involve very significant challenges to the liberalism of Ireland's political economy, whether passive, active or aggressive.

Acknowledgment Research for this chapter was supported by a Starting Investigator Grant of the European Resesarch Council to the 'New Deals in the New Economy' project.

References

Bailey, D., and J. Barry. 2016. The Hollowness of GDP: The Case of Ireland. *SPERI Comment*. http://speri.dept.shef.ac.uk/2016/09/22/the-hollowness-of-gdp-the-case-of-ireland/.

Connor, G., T. Flavin, and B. Kelly. 2012. The U.S. and Irish Credit Crises: Their Distinctive Differences and Common Features. *Journal of International Money and Finance* 31: 60–79.

Cusack, Thomas, Torben Iversen, and David Soskice. 2007. Economic Interests and the Origins of Electoral Institutions. *American Political Science Review* 101 (3): 373–391.

Davis, G. 2011. *Managed by the Markets*. Oxford: Oxford University Press.

Granovetter, M. 1985. Economic Action and Social Structure: The Problem of Embeddedness. *American Journal of Sociology* 91 (3): 481–510.

Hall, P.A., and D.W. Soskice, eds. 2001. *Varieties of Capitalism: The Institutional Foundations of Comparative Advantage*. Oxford: Oxford University Press.

Honohan, P. 2006. To What Extent Has Finance Been a Driver of Ireland's Economic Success? *ESRI Quarterly Economic Commentary* 2006 (4): 59–72.

Jessop, B. 2014. A Spectre Is Haunting Europe: A Neoliberal Phantasmagoria. *Critical Policy Studies* 8 (3): 352–355.

Lane, P.R. 2011. *The Irish Crisis*, IIIS Discussion Paper No. 356, IIIS: TCD.

Mjøset, L. 1992. *The Irish Economy in a Comparative Institutional Perspective*. Dublin: National Economic and Social Council.

NESC. 2005. *The Developmental Welfare State*. Dublin: NESC.

———. 2009. *Ireland's Five-Part Crisis: An Integrated National Response*. Dublin: NESC.

Ó Riain, S. 2004. *The Politics of High Tech Growth: Developmental Network States in the Global Economy*, Structural Analysis in the Social Sciences 23. New York/Cambridge: Cambridge University Press.

———. 2009. Addicted to Growth: Developmental Statism and Neoliberalism in the Celtic Tiger. In *The Nation-State in Transformation: The Governance, Growth and Cohesion of Small States Under Globalisation*, ed. M. Bøss. Aarhus: Aarhus University Press.

———. 2014. *The Rise and Fall of Ireland's Celtic Tiger*. Cambridge: Cambridge University Press.

———. 2016. The Shifting Politics of Innovation and State Developmentalism in Ireland. *Stato e Mercato* 2016 (1): 41–68.

———. forthcoming. Ireland's Recovery: Explanation, Potential and Pitfalls. In *Debating Austerity*, ed. E. Heffernan, J. MacHale, and N. Moore-Cherry. Dublin: Royal Irish Academy.

Ó Riain, S., and P. O'Connell. 2000. Chapter 16: The Role of the State in Growth and Welfare. In *Bust to Boom? The Irish Experience of Growth and Inequality*, ed. B. Nolan, P. O'Connell, and C. Whelan. Dublin: Economic and Social Research Institute/Institute for Public Administration.

Ornston, D. 2012. *When Small States Make Big Leaps: Institutional Innovation and High-Tech Competition in Western Europe*. Ithaca: Cornell University Press.

Polanyi, K. 1957/1944. *The Great Transformation*. Boston: Free Press.

Ruane, J. 2010. Ireland's Multiple Interface-Periphery Development Model: Achievements and Limits. In *The Nation-State in Transformation: The Governance, Growth and Cohesion of Small States under Globalisation*, ed. M. Bøss. Aarhus: Aarhus University Press.

———. 2016. Modelling Ireland's Crises. In *Dynamics of Political Change*, ed. N. Ó Dochartaigh, K. Hayward, and E. Meehan. London: Routledge.

Scharpf, F. 1991. *Crisis and Choice in European Social Democracy*. Ithaca: Cornell University Press.

Schmidt, V., and M. Thatcher. 2014. Why Are Neoliberal Ideas So Resilient in Europe's Political Economy? *Critical Policy Studies* 8 (3): 340–347.

TASC. 2010. *Mapping the Golden Circle*. Dublin: TASC.

Whelan, K. 2010. Policy Lessons from Ireland's Latest Depression. *Economic and Social Review* 41: 225–254.

White, R. 2010. *Years of High Income Largely Wasted*. Dublin: Davy Stockbrokers.

CHAPTER 3

The Spanish Economic 'Miracle' That Never Was

Luis Buendía

Abstract The expansive phase experienced by the Spanish economy had long been praised, described in the early 2000s as an 'economic miracle'. However, the crisis that struck in the late 2000s would become the deepest that the country had endured since at least the 1970s, leading to the general conclusion that its prior success had been a mirage rather than miracle. Using a political economy approach, this chapter identifies and analyses the factors that allow us to understand the Spanish model, including the role played by Spain in the European division of labour; the institutional framework of the domestic economy; and the key agents that have been central to the configuration of the whole model. Finally, it considers the distributive effects and consequences of the model.

Keywords Political economy • Spanish growth model • Distributive struggle • 2008 crisis

---

L. Buendía (✉)
Department of Economics and Statistics, University of León, León, Spain

O. Parker, D. Tsarouhas (eds.), *Crisis in the Eurozone Periphery*,
Building a Sustainable Political Economy: SPERI Research & Policy,
https://doi.org/10.1007/978-3-319-69721-5_3

At the beginning of the current crisis, there was a debate in the economics profession concerning the policies that countries should adopt in order to grow again. Those debates hinged on two prominent positions. On the one hand, there were those economists who—in an apparent endorsement of Mariano Rajoy's statement that 'we have lived beyond our own means'—argued for austerity policies. This was the position of the International Monetary Fund (IMF) and the European Commission, which considered that only through austerity could countries in crisis recover (see, for instance, European Commission 2011; and Weisbrot and Jorgensen 2013, for an overview of IMF recommendations to European Union [EU] countries).[1] On the other hand, there were those who argued for expansive policies to enable countries under strain to re-establish economic growth. Authors including Lapavitsas and Munevar (2014) for the Greek case and Navarro et al. (2011) for Spain have attempted to show the inadequacies of austerity in the crisis context.

To ascertain the appropriate medicine for a sick economy, we need first to correctly diagnose the sickness. This chapter will attempt to do so in the six sections that follow. The first section introduces the political economy of the so-called Spanish miracle; the second analyses the pattern of growth followed by Spain, both from the supply side and the demand side; and the third section focuses on the role of Spain in the European division of labour in order to understand some of the contradictions in its economic model. The fourth and the fifth sections are devoted to the roles played respectively by the financial sector and the public sector, and the sixth section provides a general view of how income was distributed throughout the period. Finally, the chapter considers the impact and consequences of the crisis and offers some concluding remarks.

The Political Economy of the 'Spanish Miracle'

Spain was, before the crisis, widely admired by economists and others for embodying what was termed the 'Spanish miracle'.[2] 'España va bien' (Spain is doing well) was the well-known description given by José María Aznar, the prime minister between 1996 and 2004. But, was it so? Can we speak of a miracle? Before we focus on the economic variables that will allow us to answer this question, we will first consider the political-economic aspects of the expansive phase (1995–2007), which provides the framework inside which the policy-making decisions were made. Three sets of interrelated actors were central to this story: the two major political parties, the financial sector and the construction sector.

Two parties, the conservative PP (Partido Popular) and the social democratic PSOE (Partido Socialista Obrero Español), have governed the country for almost all of its democratic period (with just one exception[3]). The differences between them have always been notable. The PSOE, formed in 1879, has always been a member of the Second International and the representative of social democracy in Spain. The PP, in contrast, was created in 1976 by former Francoist ministers, and is the main conservative party in the country. However, just as in the rest of Europe, as social democracy chose a road of 'accommodation to global finance' under the Third Way (Ryner 2010), the differences in economic policy-making became less marked. As early as the 1980s, the PSOE had abandoned any attempt to implement Keynesian countercyclical policies (Pérez 1999: 671), and both the PP and the PSOE accepted the monetarist consensus to prioritize inflation as the key economic policy goal and later the adjustment process during the 1990s on the road towards European Monetary Union. Particularly noteworthy in the 1995–2007 period was a political consensus around the centrality of the construction sector. When in power, both parties refused to accept the reality of a real-estate bubble, their denial incentivized by ongoing rapid job creation and extraordinary public revenues that allowed for popular tax cuts throughout the period.

The financial sector of Spain has traditionally been made up of three types of institution: commercial banks, savings banks and credit unions. The first two account for over 95 per cent of deposits in Spain. Before the 1980s, savings banks—conceived as quasi-public institutions—specialized in the household sector, whereas banks specialized in the corporate sector, but these differences have since been eroded. The degree of concentration has traditionally been high: five institutions (three commercial and two savings banks) owned on average half the assets of the whole financial sector and this concentration was not reduced by the neoliberal reforms introduced in the 1980s. The power of these institutions was such that the policies applied even by social democratic governments were designed not to harm their position, even if the upshot was damage to the industrial and public sectors (Pérez 1999). During the expansive phase of 1995–2007, both commercial and savings banks increased their profit margins as interest rates went down as a consequence of EU membership and demand for mortgages was buoyant. The peculiar role played by the two political parties in the management of savings banks was also significant, leading to the financing of unsustainable 'white elephant' projects including airports and amusement parks, moves apparently aimed at electoral gain.[4]

The third key actor during this expansive phase was the construction sector, which was at the centre of a model driven by rapid growth in residential property and large-scale public infrastructure projects. A group formed by six construction firms with close links to political power has long dominated the sector (see Recio et al. 2006; López and Rodríguez 2010: 323–331).[5] Those firms benefitted not only from investment in infrastructure but also from residential investment as the latter became the main growth engine.

This triangle of actors (see Fig. 3.1) was central to the growth model that constituted the so-called Spanish miracle and able to successfully block alternative paths. They did so with the apparent endorsement of an electorate that felt the wealth effects of this ostensible miracle. However, as we will see below, the key driver of that effect was credit-driven consumption.

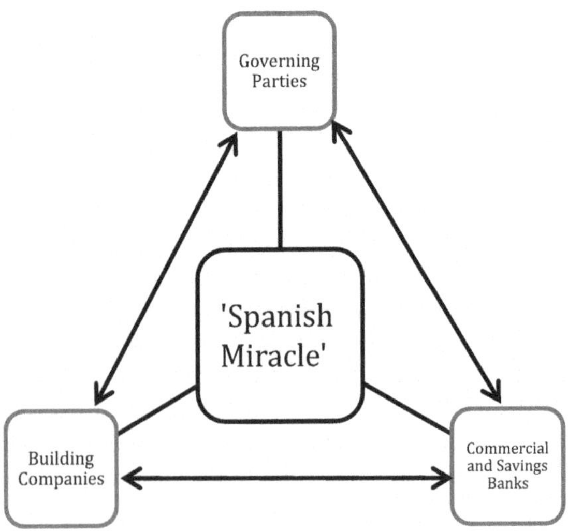

Fig. 3.1 The actors at the centre of the 'Spanish miracle'

An Extensive Pattern of Growth

The Spanish growth model can be usefully analysed through both the supply and the demand sides. The supply side of an economy refers to the factors upon which its growth has relied, the efficiency with which those factors have been used and the economic sectors that have been predominant. There are two ways in which an economy might grow: increased efficiency (measured as each factor's productivity) or augmenting the volume of factors in use.

Table 3.1 shows that economic growth (*Y*) was high throughout the expansive phase: for instance, whereas in the 1996–2007 period it was 3.7 per cent, the corresponding figure for the euro area was 2.3 per cent. This growth was based on the accumulation of factors (either work, *L*, measured in persons, or capital, *K*), rather than in the increase in their productivity. In contrast, labour productivity (*Y/L*) grew at very low rates in both periods. Considering labour productivity as a relationship between *K/L*, which shows how productive factors have been combined, and *K/Y*, which is the degree of capitalization of production, we can observe that between 1996 and 2000 employment grew faster than capital, leading to a decrease in the capitalization of the economy. However, this trend was reversed during the period after 2001, when the use of capital grew faster than the use of labour as means of production and the economy was highly capitalized. Capital accumulation reached a rate of 4.5 per cent per year in the period 2001–2007, while the productivity of that capital, as seen in the inverse of the ratio *K/Y*, was negative in the same period, which means that employers had diminishing returns, in terms of value added, per each unit of capital used in the production process.

As regards the use of factors, there was an increase in the use of labour in Spain that was greater than in other countries in the euro zone, but we can also observe a greater increase in residential capital than in productive capital, reflecting the construction-oriented growth model. Data from the

Table 3.1 Yearly average growth, several variables. 1996–2007

	Y	*L*	*Y/L*	*K*	*K/L*	*K/Y*
1996–2007	3.7	3.3	0.4	4.1	0.8	0.4
1996–2000	4.1	3.9	0.2	3.6	−0.3	−0.5
2001–2007	3.4	2.9	0.5	4.5	1.5	1.0

Source: Own elaboration with data from INE (Spanish Statistical Office)

Spanish Statistical Office (INE) illustrate the increase in the share of the construction sector in the whole economy, such that from 1995 to 2007, its share of the GDP in real terms went from 8.8 per cent to 12.3 per cent. Data from the European Commission's Annual Macro-economic database (AMECO) show that in 2007 the share of construction in total value added was much higher in Spain (11.2 per cent) than the equivalent in France (6.1), Germany (3.9), Italy (6.0) or the UK (6.9). The growth in this sector was due to (1) the public policies that were implemented; (2) the inflow of a new population attracted to a labour-intensive economy (that, in turn, demanded homes to live in); (3) the purchase of apartments (by Spaniards and Europeans) on the Spanish coast; (4) improved financing conditions linked to the euro; and (5) the existence of a speculative bubble, that drained money from other sectors.

At the same time as this boom, the industrial and energy sectors declined, down from 20.3 to 15.6 per cent in the 1995–2007 period. And within industry, high-tech manufacturing was well below the EU average, and its weight declined during the expansion period. In 2007, Spain invested 1.23 per cent of its GDP in R&D, while the average in the euro area was 1.81 per cent and patent applications to the European Patent Office per million inhabitants made by Spanish researchers were 30.95, compared with 146.88 in the euro area (all data from Eurostat). In short, Spain became a European leader in the construction sector, but to the detriment of other sectors.

This pattern of specialization helps explain the evolution of productivity. On the one hand, while productivity was greater in industry and agriculture, these were sectors whose importance diminished during the boom years. On the other hand, as Mateo and Montanyà (2014) show with data from AMECO, of the 12 years between 1996 and 2007 (inclusive), only in three did construction contribute positively to the increase in productivity in the economy. Considering the economic weight of that sector, it is no surprise how overall productivity evolved.

Regarding demand, it should be emphasized that domestic demand was key to understanding the growth model adopted by Spain. Both consumption and investment played an important role in the macroeconomic development of the economy, but concretely the performance of investment was outstanding. According to data from INE, Gross Fixed Capital Formation (GFCF) reached yearly growth rates that averaged 6.1 per cent in the whole period, and 7.2 per cent between 1996 and 2000. This is closely related to the rate at which the economy accumulated capital, as noted above. As a consequence, this part of domestic demand represented 21.4 per cent of GDP in 1996 and 30.7 per cent in 2007. As a result, the share of residential investment was substantial and grew during the period: in 1996, it accounted for 32.6 per cent of investment and 40 per cent in 2007. On the other hand, investment in machinery accounted for 21.3 per cent in 1996 and 16 per cent in 2007 (all data from FBBVA 2014). In accord with these trends, prices in this sector increased much more than they did in the rest of the economy (Mateo and Montanyà 2014).

The Role of Spain in the European Division of Labour

As consumption grew in Spain, the current account deficit increased due to increasing imports. Those deficits in the balance of goods had been traditionally financed by the surplus in the balance of services, particularly due to tourism. However, from the end of the 1990s, the surplus in services was increasingly inadequate to compensate as consumption increased more quickly and tourism lost its dynamism due to increasing competition. A net lender in 1997, Spain had become a net borrower by 2007, with a net borrowing position worth 9.6 per cent of GDP (CES 2012). This became an important source of vulnerability. Two main factors account for this evolution: on the one hand, increasing domestic demand driven by cheap credit and, on the other hand, a weak position in the European division of labour. Spain has traditionally had a lower share of exports in its GDP compared to its European neighbours. In addition, the Spanish economy specializes in goods with lower technological content (as a consequence of the growth model we have discussed above) that are less competitive. Indeed, in the case of intra-industry trade (which amounts to up to 70 per cent of all trade), it is notable that the economy imports components that are more advanced than those that it exports, negatively contributing to the current account balance of the economy.

Over 60 per cent of Spain's trade takes place with other EU partners (a figure which is similar for other EU countries). Following Luengo and Álvarez (2011) we can say that Continental and Anglo-Saxon countries experienced trade surpluses in the years under study, whereas Southern and Enlargement countries experienced structural trade deficits. According to their analysis, enlargements, first towards Southern Europe, and then towards Eastern Europe, led to the formation of a complex and diverse economic structure that paved the way for the creation of imbalances, both within and between countries. To offer one example, consider the current account balance of Spain and Germany during these years. The difference between them (see Fig. 3.2) is the result of different patterns of specialization, with Germany specializing in goods with higher value added and greater technological content (Luengo and Álvarez 2011; Garzón 2013).

If trade could not be used to finance Spain's external imbalances, a new source had to be found. Before monetary union, devaluation of the national currency (the Spanish peseta) was a viable way to balance the economy. Within that union financing relied increasingly on direct investment and borrowing, either issuing financial instruments or applying for loans. Membership in the Economic and Monetary Union (EMU) helped Spain to raise those funds (see Parker and Tsarouhas, Chap. 1, this volume). Spain's share of global inward foreign direct investment (FDI) stock almost tripled between the 1980s and the 1990s,[6] but since the mid-1990s the main source of financing has been from borrowing and issuing financial instruments (Garzón 2013). Since the end of the 1990s investment has relied increasingly on private debt (Garzón 2014), while public debt fell. By 2009, total debt was estimated at 502 per cent of GDP (Lapavitsas et al. 2010). Thirteen per cent of this was held by the public sector, 17 per cent by households and the remaining 70 per cent by corporations, both financial (31 per cent) and non-financial (39 per cent). Data from the Bank of Spain (taken from Sanabria and Medialdea 2014) suggest that private debt was just under 90 per cent of GDP in 1994 but 311.5 per cent in 2007.

Spain was among those countries that based their growth model on debt in order to solve the dilemma of having an economy in which internal demand is crucial but wages are relatively stagnant. As we can see in Fig. 3.3, there is a stark difference between the path followed by Germany (an export-led country) and Spain (a debt-led country) (Álvarez et al. 2013). In Spain high rates of investment were financed with funds from abroad, in a context of low interest rates. Debt-led growth was increasingly dependent on increasing housing prices—a bubble—which sooner or later would burst.

Channelling the Funds: The Financial Sector

While the funds that made the 'Spanish miracle' possible came from abroad, the domestic financial institutions discussed above were key in channelling those funds to certain sectors. Concretely, 'Spanish banks [...]

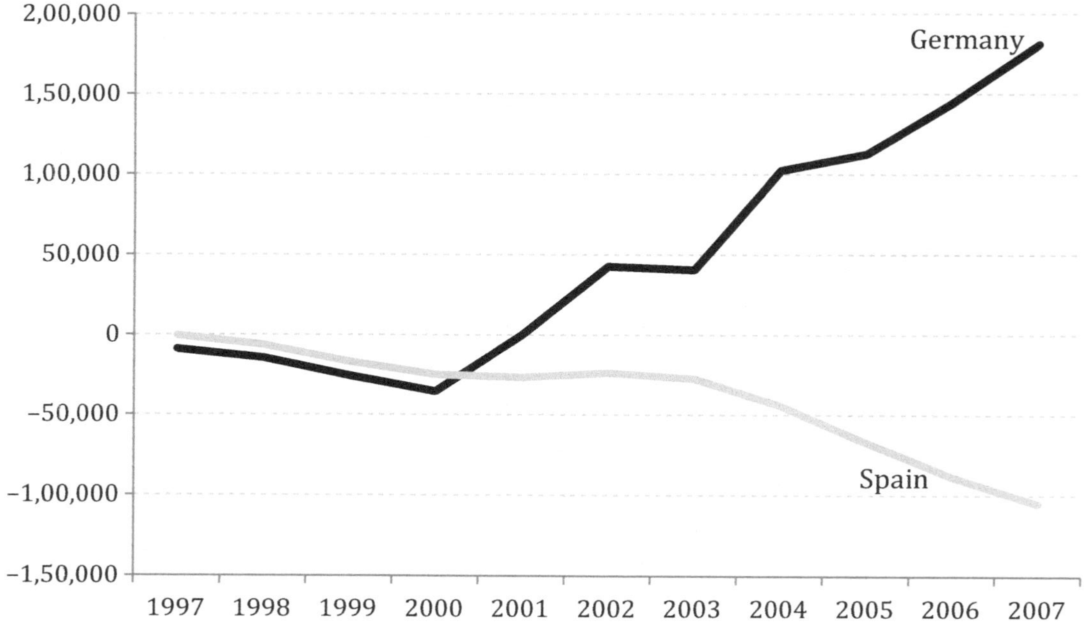

Fig. 3.2 Current account balance of Germany and Spain, 1997–2007 (Source: Own elaboration with data from Eurostat)

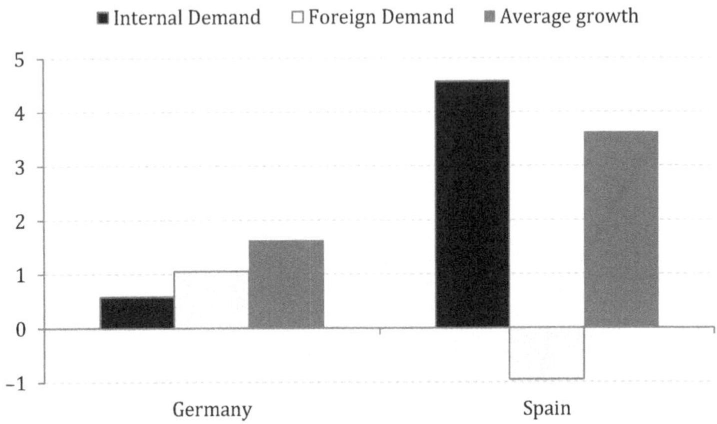

Fig. 3.3 Contribution to growth of internal and foreign demand, 2000–2007 (Source: Álvarez et al. 2013: Chap. 4)

were borrowing over a quarter of their balance sheets in the interbank lending market from their German and Dutch competitors' (Fernández-Villaverde and Ohanian 2010: 10). Spain has not been an exception in the global trend of financialization. Between 1985 and 2000, financial assets grew from 424 per cent to 700 per cent of GDP (Garrido 2013). Financial institutions increased credit provision at an annual rate that reached 30 per cent per year at the end of the expansive phase (data from INE and Bank of Spain), much of it funded by borrowing in international markets (given that savings were low in Spain during the period). This increase in credit went hand in hand with a rapid increase in the number of bank offices and employees (particularly in the case of savings banks).

While savings banks were supposed to contribute to the implementation of the industrial policy designed by the government, the absence of any such policy allowed them to allocate credit according to other interests (Santos Castroviejo 2013). Credit from abroad was consequently channelled by both commercial and savings banks to the aforementioned construction and real-estate sectors (Molero 2014). When the crisis started, these were the sectors in which credit delinquency was highest. The financial sector was therefore completely functional to the development of the pattern of specialization. Government deregulation (which increased notably during the period, see Abiad et al. 2008) contributed to this by making financial institutions less reluctant to lend, particularly in the case of savings banks. This deregulation process, however, did not reduce concentration in the financial sector. By 2008, the asset base of Banco Santander (the biggest bank) was only 20 per cent less than that of JPMorgan Chase (the biggest US bank), with BBVA, the second financial institution in Spain, not far behind (Fernández-Villaverde and Ohanian 2010: 19).

The Public Sector

The public sector played a crucial role in the processes described up to this point. During the democratic period, the public sector grew, but never reached the EMU average. In the case of expenditures, Spain got closer to that average, but in the case of revenues, the gap was never lower than four percentage points (see Fig. 3.4).

As early as the 1980s the PSOE government made an active choice to privilege the interests of the financial sector, *inter alia*, through the appointment of government officials in the Ministry of Finance with close links to that sector (Pérez 1999). This protection harmed the industrial sector (in the form of higher financial costs) in such a way that not only did governments reject any attempt to implement an active industrial policy, but contributed to the de-industrialization process that the economy experienced after entering the European Economic Community in 1986. The retreat of the state was reflected also in extensive privatizations from the early 1990s. More generally, both the PP and the PSOE sought to reduce the public sector as a matter of policy, and this was linked in part at least to efforts to meet the EMU's Maastricht criteria, which required a reduction in public deficit and debt. It is worth noting that—contrary to certain myths with respect to the profligacy of periphery governments—during these years, public expenditure as a percentage of GDP fell even below the level of government revenues and Spain became one of the EU countries with the lowest public debt to GDP ratio.

As to tax revenues (where, as Fig. 3.4 shows, the gap with the euro area is bigger) nominal tax rates in Spain are among the highest in the EU, but effective taxes are well below the average, due to tax avoidance and evasion (BBVA Research 2013; Lagares et al. 2014). Tax reforms introduced during the expansive phase did nothing to address this problem; on the contrary, they made the tax system more dependent on revenue from the real estate and construction sectors. Indeed, increases in government revenue during the expansive phase were due to activities linked to that sec-

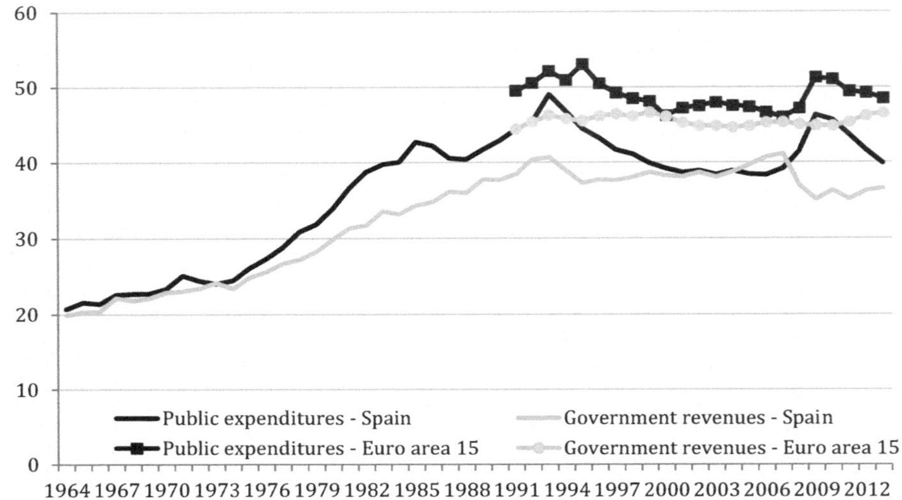

Fig. 3.4 Public sector expenditures and revenues, 1964–2013 (Source: Own elaboration with data from Eurostat)

tor, and tax cuts implemented in 1999 and 2003 were possible only because of such revenue (Zack et al. 2013). The shared desire of the two main political parties to cut taxes in the period was indicative of the abovementioned (neoliberal) ideological convergence.[7] A reliance on construction for revenue created incentives for the authorities to remove barriers to the expansion of the sector. For instance, the labour market reform in 1997 reduced employers' layoff costs (Ruiz Galacho 2006: 17; see also Molero and Murillo 2014: 4 and ff.), while in 1998, new legislation granted easier access to building permits and permitted construction almost anywhere. In parallel, the stock of public housing was reduced, which was offset by tax relief measures for home-buying while a 'lax environmental policy' granted 'subsidies for squandering energy and water on inefficient property developments' (López and Rodríguez 2011b: 14).

In short, the increase in revenues during the expansive phase was not used to improve or reinforce a welfare state that was below EU-15 standards. Although some universal features were expanded, simultaneous cutbacks and privatizations were applied as part of the consolidation process of public expenditures (Rodríguez Cabrero 2011; Moreno 2012). Retrenchment was applied in Spain before it had developed a comprehensive and generous welfare state (Muñoz de Bustillo and Antón 2014) with significant social consequences.

Who Owns What?

Although one out of three jobs created in Europe during the period under study were created in Spain, those jobs were mainly low-skilled (attracting both migrants and early school leavers), with the vast majority closely linked to construction and real estate. Such jobs were precarious and often temporary jobs—one third of contracts took this form during the expansive phase (Recio and Banyuls 2004)—whereby average wages were approximately worth two-thirds of permanent employees (Murillo 2008). Therefore, despite the narrative of prosperity associated with the years of economic growth, the reality of working poor remained. In 2004 the in-work at-risk-of-poverty rate was 10.8, while in 2007 it was 10.2 (increasing thereafter), and the incidence of such poverty was 2.3 percentage points higher than in the EU-15 (Eurostat).

While real wages grew slowly—even below the low rates of productivity growth—other sources of income increased much faster, as shown in Fig. 3.5. In particular, the value of financial assets and real-estate assets

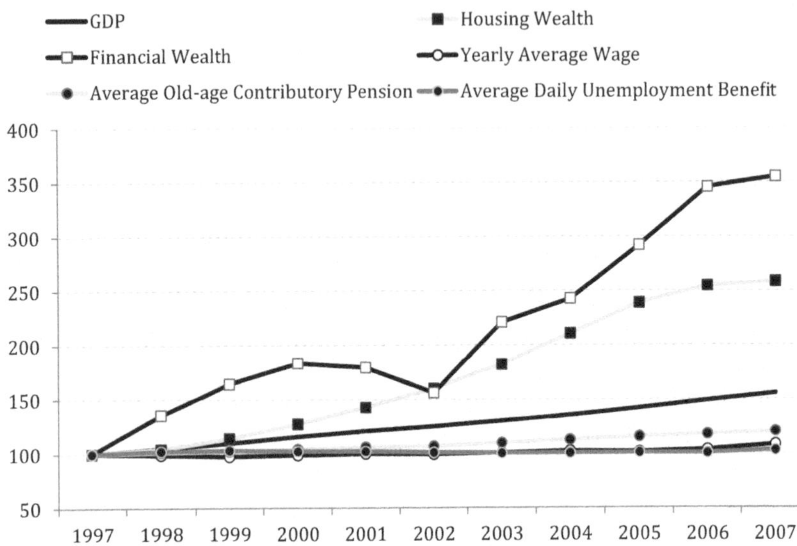

Fig. 3.5 GDP and different sources of income. Spain, 1997–2007 (Source: Own elaboration with data from Barómetro Social de España, www.barometrosocial.es)

increased by 150 per cent and 250 per cent respectively. It is not surprising then that the share of income obtained by the richest 1 per cent of the population increased from 8.3 per cent of national income in 1996 to 12.7 per cent in 2006.[8]

The implications of these trends for understanding the political economy of the 'Spanish miracle' are not trivial. As explained above, the growth model was dependent, from the demand side, on consumption and investment, but those rates of consumption growth can hardly be sustained with such meagre wage growth alone. Thus, in the country with the highest home-ownership rate in Europe (López and Rodríguez 2011a: 50) individuals used their homes as collateral to finance consumption. This was possible only because of increasing house prices. Such a context permitted easy access to debt, which became a substitute for welfare in a process that has been paralleled elsewhere (see, e.g., Soederberg 2014; Montgomerie (coord.) 2014). As states retreat in the provision of social protection, debt enters the scene; in the case of Spain, through the real-estate sector. As elsewhere, indebtedness was a necessary solution to fuel the economic engine (Lavoie and Stockhammer 2013; García 2014) given that the incomes of the majority of the population were not enough to drive the internal demand required for growth in the context of Spain's position in the international—especially European—context.

The 'Miracle' Was a Mirage

For Spain, the crisis moment arose when debt stopped renewing itself. In Spain, the credit crunch was preceded by two exogenous factors: on the one hand, the bankruptcy of Lehman Brothers in 2008 dried up international credit channels; on the other, the increase in interest rates (from 0.25 per cent to 4.25 per cent in July 2008) made the situation harder. However, the excessive reliance of the model on debt underpinned the crisis (Sanabria and Medialdea 2016: 205). When the financial sources of the current growth model failed, its engine, the construction sector, was heavily damaged. The collapse of this sector contributed to the largest destruction of jobs in the euro zone: 3.4 million between 2007 and 2013 (and the figure in 2015 was still 2.7 million lower than it was then).

The broader social and economic consequences of the crisis have been enormous. The public accounts were hit hard. Of all EU-28 countries, Spain's revenues experienced the greatest fall at the onset of the crisis: 6 percentage points of GDP. And in 2015, public revenues were still 2.7 points below the 2007 level and almost 7 points below the EU-28 average. While there was a surplus in the public sector accounts worth 2 per cent of GDP by 2007, in 2009 it had become an 11 per cent deficit and was still 5.1 per cent in 2015 (data from Eurostat). This collapse in public finances was the result of a two-fold process. First, public expenditure went up as a consequence of automatic stabilizers (particularly due to the boost in unemployment-benefits recipients), bank bailouts and, to a lesser extent, the implementation of expansionary policies by the PSOE at the beginning of the crisis. Second, public revenues sank due to the aforementioned reliance on the (now ailing) construction sector.

At the same time, an austerity programme was introduced that made matters worse. While endorsed by the government, this programme, whose measures were gradually toughened, was also the result of pressures coming from the EU (see Parker and Tsarouhas, Chap. 1, this volume): first in the form of (stringent) recommendations and later—when the government encountered difficulties in refinancing its debt in the financial markets—as a condition for European Central Bank (ECB) intervention (Pavolini et al. 2016). The programme hinged upon three main goals (all rooted in supply-side economics). First, to decrease labour costs to improve the country's competitiveness and facilitate deleveraging (so-called internal devaluation). Second, to reduce the size of the public sector, thereby mitigating the role of the state in the economy (which, in an inversion of the actual causality, was blamed for the crisis through the 'fiscal crisis'). And, third, to replace welfare with workfare (which, implicitly, and sometimes explicitly, presents the unemployed and those in need of social protection as responsible for their situation).

With respect to internal devaluation, both the PSOE and the PP passed labour market reforms (notably, in 2010 and 2012). The reforms have, *inter alia*, made dismissal cheaper (from 45 days per year worked to 33 days per year) and easier; promoted the decentralization of collective bargaining (by introducing the opting out clause for firms not to apply sectoral collective agreements); and reduced unemployment benefits (after the sixth month) (Banyuls and Recio 2015). These reforms paralleled the huge increase in unemployment.

Between 2007 and 2009 alone, the number of people receiving unemployment benefit doubled, those receiving social assistance increased by 50 per cent and those claiming old-age pensions increased by 3 per cent (OECD 2012). The government tried to curb the subsequent increase in public expenditure through measures that included: a wage freeze and layoffs in the public sector; a (gradual) increase in retirement age from 65 to 67; an increase in the years of contribution required to access the maximum old-age pension (from 35 to 37); the augmentation of the years used to calculate pensions (from the last 15 to the last 25 years); a hardening in the requirements to access voluntary early retirement; a shift, from 2013, to a defined-contribution pension system, from a defined-benefit system; a reduction in the range of medicines eligible for public subsidy; the outsourcing of several services in the healthcare sector and the erosion of its universalism (by restricting the access of undocumented immigrants); an increase in the price of childcare services; a reduction in, or the elimination of, certain educational services (such as those focused on students with special needs); an increase in the pupil/teacher ratio; an increase in tuition fees and cuts to grants; and privatization in several sectors (such as airports and lotteries) (see Banyuls and Recio 2015). Finally, under German and French pressure in 2011, the parliamentary support of both the PP and the PSOE allowed for a reform of the Constitution in order to prioritize the repayment of debt over any other goal.

The consequences of these adjustment programmes have been grave. After an initial increase in annual wages between 2007 and 2009—which was mainly due to the destruction of temporary employment linked to construction—in 2014 wages were still 7 per cent lower than in 2009 in real terms (OECD 2012). The at-risk-of-poverty rate for those in work was in 2015 higher than ever (13.1 per cent compared to 10.2 per cent in 2007). The risk for the population as a whole was 28.6 in 2015 (after it decreased 0.6 points from the previous year) and 23.3 in 2007. Finally, inequality, measured through the Gini coefficient, was at the same levels as in the mid-1990s, after rising from 0.319 to 0.346 in the 2007–2015 period. According to Eurostat (the source of this data), Spain was in 2014 (the last year with available comparable data) the most unequal EU-15 country, and the sixth most unequal EU-28 country. Mortgage foreclosures increased from 25,943 in 2007 to a peak of 93,636 in 2010 (and in 2015, there were still 68,135) (data from the General Council of the Judiciary). Data from the Bank of Spain (collated from financial institutions) show that 110,140 repossessions of foreclosed dwellings took place between 2012 and 2014 (the only period currently available).

Meanwhile, the government facilitated the restructuring of the financial sector, promoting a greater concentration and transforming savings banks into commercial banks, as well as bailing them out when necessary (either by acquiring their bad debts or by offering blanket guarantees). Construction firms in turn also underwent a concentration process, but given that the sector was experiencing problems, the main actors chose to reinforce their internationalization strategy.

From 2014, the Spanish economy began to grow again. It benefitted from the ECB's low-interest-rate policy, the decrease in international energy prices and a push from the public sector in the electoral year of 2015 (including a cut in taxes and an increase in expenditures). As a result, exports were, in 2016–2017, more dynamic than they had been. However, if inflation rates increase again (as data suggested they were at the time of writing), this will affect real wages. And if the ECB increases interest rates to curb inflationary pressures, it will damage consumption, which once again will only be supported by debt. Moreover, the kind of employment that has been created and the increase in inequality pose a permanent threat to internal-demand-driven economic growth, not to mention poverty and unemployment levels, which in 2017 remained well above their pre-crisis levels. At the same time, given the kind of specialization that we have shown above, the Spanish share in world exports is unlikely to substantially increase. Thus, we should be extremely circumspect with respect to the strength and length of the so-called recovery.[9]

Conclusion

This chapter provides a picture of how the Spanish economy evolved, why it was particularly vulnerable to crisis and the consequences of that crisis. As highlighted at the outset, Spain was considered the outstanding student in the European classroom as a consequence of its astonishing growth path between 1995 and 2007. We have seen though that all that glittered was not gold, and the growth model suffered from several inherent and interrelated problems that were for too long ignored. In the context of imbalances inside the EU—whereby certain countries lend too much to countries that borrow too much—Spain was clearly a debt-led economy. Unable to produce the required resources to finance its growth model, Spain had to rely on debt, which was borrowed by its private sector cheaply—as a consequence of the low interest rates that accompanied euro membership—and invested in the construction and real-estate sectors at the expense of other sectors of the economy. This indebtedness was at the heart of the crisis.

The government and public sector facilitated the emergence of such a model through its support and protection of the increasingly interwoven finance and construction sectors. Such a model enjoyed popular support to the extent that the wealth effects of a housing bubble could compensate for stagnant wage growth. Following the crisis, the government came to the aid of its finance sector (supported by the EU) and unleashed a series of socially and economically damaging austerity programmes that were well attuned to the broader EU response.

Notes

1. Muñoz de Bustillo (2014) provides an excellent analysis of the theory and evidence of the so-called myth of expansionary austerity.
2. Liberal economists and those linked to the parties in government tended to base this statement on the high rates of economic growth in the context of the 'Great Moderation' (see, e.g., Bernaldo and Martínez 2005). Moreover,

within the European Commission Spain was presented in the mid-2000s as a model to follow (see the newspaper article 'El milagro económico español', *El país*, 22 March 2007).

3. Only during the first years of democracy in Spain can we find another governing party, UCD, Unión de Centro Democrático, but since 1982, PSOE's governments have alternated with PP governments, sometimes with the support of other regional parties, namely from Catalonia and the Basque Country.
4. There are many examples, but the most widely known are those related to the airports in Ciudad Real and Castellón, as well as the amusement park 'Terra Mítica' in Alicante.
5. These firms are ACS, Acciona, Ferrovial, Fomento de Construcciones, OHL and Sacyr Vallehermoso. It is worth noting that, on the shoulders of the state, these same companies have become international champions in infrastructure building (Government of Spain 2014).
6. Data extracted from UNCTADstat (http://unctadstat.unctad.org/EN/) in 2013.
7. As an example of the ideological convergence of the PP and the PSOE concerning the public sector, it is worth mentioning that José Luis Rodriguez Zapatero, 'the would-be premier of the social democratic government in the period 2004–2011, [declared] "I think that the idea of lowering taxes is leftist"' (quoted in Muñoz de Bustillo and Antón 2014 from *El País*, 1 September 2000).
8. World Wealth & Income Database, wid.world, 1981–2012.
9. This assessment is in contrast with reporting in financial newspapers: see, for instance, *Financial Times*, 6 April 2017, 'Spain: Boom to bust and back again'.

References

Abiad, A., E. Detragiache, and T. Tressel. 2008. *A New Database of Financial Reforms*, IMF Working Paper WP/08/266. Washington: IMF.

Álvarez, I., F. Luengo, and J. Uxó. 2013. *Fracturas y crisis en Europa*. Madrid: Eudeba.

Banyuls, J., and A. Recio. 2015. Crisis dentro de la crisis: España bajo el neoliberalismo conservador. In *El triunfo de las ideas fracasadas. Modelos de capitalismo europeo en la crisis*, ed. S. Lehndorff, 39–69. Madrid: La catarata.

BBVA Research. 2013. Gasto e ingresos públicos: expansión, crisis y consolidación. *Observatorio Económico*, November 21.

Bernaldo de Quirós, L., and R. Martínez Rico. 2005. *El modelo económico español. 1996–2004: una revolución silenciosa*. Madrid: Instituto de Estudios Económicos.

Consejo Económico y Social (CES). 2012. *La internacionalización de la empresa española como factor de competitividad.* Madrid: CES.

European Commission. 2011. *Quarterly Report on the Euro Area.* Vol. 10, Issue 1, April. Brussels: European Commission.

Fernández-Villaverde, J., and L. Ohanian. 2010. *The Spanish Crisis from a Global Perspective*, Documentos de trabajo (FEDEA), N°. 3.

Fundación Banco Bilbao Vizcaya Argentaria (FBBVA). 2014. *El stock y los servicios del capital en España y su distribución territorial y sectorial (1964–2012)*, Database. Available from: http://www.fbbva.es/TLFU/microsites/stock09/fbbva_stock08_index.html. Accessed 14 Dec 2016.

García, N. 2014. Las causas de la doble recesión de España en 2008–2013. In *Qué ha pasado con la economía española*, coords. Norberto García and Santos M. Ruesga, 29–54. Madrid: Pirámide.

Garrido, A. 2013. Sistema financiero. In *Lecciones de economía española*, ed. J.L. García Delgado and R. Myro. Navarra: Aranzadi.

Garzón, A. 2013. El capitalismo español en el siglo XXI. ¿Qué lugar en la economía mundial. *Pensar desde abajo* 2: 11–39.

Garzón, E. 2014. El déficit público es necesario para que las familias y empresas puedan ahorrar, *Saque de esquina*, November 14. Available at: http://eduardogarzon.net/el-deficit-publico-es-necesario-para-que-las-familias-y-empresas-puedan-ahorrar/. Accessed 21 July 2015.

Government of Spain. 2014. *Spanish Firms Build the World.* Madrid: Ministerio de Asuntos Exteriores y de Cooperación.

Lagares, M., et al. 2014. *Informe de la comisión de expertos para la reforma del sistema tributario español.* Madrid: Ministerio de Hacienda y Administraciones Públicas.

Lapavitsas, C., and D. Munevar. 2014. *Greece Needs a Deep Debt Write-Off*, Research on Money and Finance Occasional Policy Papers, No. 10. London: Research on Money and Finance.

Lapavitsas, C., A. Kaltenbrunner, G. Lambrinidis, D. Lindo, J. Meadway, J. Michell, J.P. Painceira, E. Pires, J. Powell, A. Stenfors, and N. Teles. 2010. *The Eurozone Between Austerity and Default.* London: Research on Money and Finance.

Lavoie, M., and E. Stockhammer. 2013. *Wage-led Growth. An Equitable Strategy for Economic Recovery.* Houndmills: ILO-Palgrave Macmillan.

López, I., and E. Rodríguez. 2010. *Fin de ciclo. Financiarización, territorio y sociedad de propietarios en la onda larga del capitalismo hispano (1959–2010).* Madrid: Traficantes de Sueños.

———. 2011a. Del auge al colapso. El modelo financiero-inmobiliario. *Revista de Economía Crítica* 12: 39–63.

———. 2011b. The Spanish Model. *New Left Review* 69 (May–June): 5–28.

Luengo, F., and N. Álvarez. 2011. Desde los desequilibrios comerciales a la crisis económica en la Unión Europea. In *Economía política de la crisis*, ed. P.J. Gómez, 145–160. Madrid: Editorial Complutense.

Mateo, J.P., and M. Montanyà. 2014. *Acumulación de capital y burbuja inmobiliaria en España*. Paper Presented to XIV Jornadas de Economía Crítica, Valladolid.

Molero, R. 2014. *La desigualdad de la renta en el modelo de crecimiento de la economía española. Alternativas a las políticas de ajuste*, Estudios de Progreso 82/2014. Madrid: Fundación Alternativas.

Molero, R., and F.J. Murillo 2014. *La distribución de la renta en la economía española durante los periodos pre y post-crisis. La profundización del ajuste salarial*. Paper Presented to XIV Jornadas de Economía Crítica, Valladolid.

Montgomerie, J. (Coord.). 2014. *The Politics of Indebtedness in the UK. A Public Interest Report*. London: Goldsmiths University of London.

Moreno, L. 2012. *La Europa asocial. Crisis y estado de bienestar*. Barcelona: Península.

Muñoz de Bustillo, R. 2014. Questioning the Myth of Expansionary Austerity: European Macroeconomic Policy During the Crisis and Its Aftermath. In *Public Sector Shock: The Impact of Policy Retrenchment in Europe*, ed. Javier Bilbao, 511–542. Cheltenham: Edward Elgar.

Muñoz de Bustillo, R., and J.I. Antón. 2014. Turning Back Before Arriving: the Dismantling of the Spanish Welfare State. In *Dismantling the European Social Model: Europe Losing Its Soul*, ed. Daniel Vaughan-Whitehead, 341–381. Cheltenham: Edward Elgar.

Murillo, F.J. 2008. *El proceso de acumulación en España (1973–2005): ¿Progreso material para todos?* Paper Presented to XI Jornadas de Economía Crítica, Bilbao.

Navarro, V., J. Torres, and A. Garzón. 2011. *Hay alternativas. Propuestas para crear empleo y bienestar social en España*. Madrid: Sequitur.

OECD. 2012. *Social Spending During the Crisis*. Paris: OECD.

Pavolini, E., M. León, A.M. Guillén, and U. Ascoli. 2016. From Austerity to Permanent Strain? The EU and Welfare State Reform in Italy and Spain. In *The Sovereign Debt Crisis, the EU and Welfare State Reform*, ed. C. De La Porte and E. Heins, 131–158. London: Palgrave Macmillan.

Pérez, S. 1999. From Labor to Finance Understanding the Failure of Socialist Economic Policies in Spain. *Comparative Political Studies 32* (6): 659–689.

Recio, A., and J. Banyuls. 2004. *¿Crecimiento del empleo sin tecnología? La paradoja del mercado de trabajo en España*. Paper Presented to IX Jornadas de Economía Crítica, Madrid.

Recio, A., R. de Alós-Moner, and I. Olivares. 2006. *Construction in Spain*, QUIT Working Paper No. 13. Available at: http://quit.uab.es. Accessed 21 May 2016.

Rodríguez Cabrero, G. 2011. The Consolidation of the Spanish Welfare State (1975–2010). In *The Spanish Welfare State in European Context*, ed. A.M. Guillén and M. León, 17–38. Surrey: Ashgate Publishing.

Ruiz Galacho, E. 2006. Las reformas laborales en España (1977–2002). *Laberinto* 20: 7–22.

Ryner, M. 2010. An Obituary for the Third Way. *Eurozine*, April 27. Available at http://www.eurozine.com/articles/2010-04-27-ryner-en.html. Accessed 10 June 2016.

Sanabria, A., and B. Medialdea. 2014. La crisis de la deuda en España: elementos básicos y alternativas. In *Análisis y perspectivas 2014: Precariedad y Cohesión Social*, ed. FOESSA, 63–70. Madrid: FOESSA.

Sanabria, A., and B. Medialdea. 2016. Lending Calling. Recession by Over-Indebtedness: Description and Specific Features of the Spanish Case. *Panoeconomicus* 63 (2, Special Issue): 195–210.

Santos Castroviejo, I. 2013. *Elites del poder económico en España en 2013. Transformaciones en las redes de gobierno empresarial durante la crisis*. Vigo/Pontevedra: Universidade de Vigo.

Soederberg, S. 2014. *Debtfare States and the Poverty Industry. Money, Discipline and the Surplus Population*. New York: Routledge.

Weisbrot, M., and H. Jorgensen. 2013. *Macroeconomic Policy Advice and the Article IV Consultations: A European Union Case Study*. Washington, DC: Centre for Economic and Policy Research (CEPR).

Zack, G., P. Poncela, E. Senra, and D. Sotelsek. 2013. *Towards an Effective Structural Budget Balance for Economic Stability*, Documentos de Trabajo UC-CIFF-IELAT No. 13, June. Alcalá de Henares: University of Alcalá de Henares.

CHAPTER 4

Portugal's Economic Crisis: Overheating Without Accelerating

Neil Dooley

Abstract Portugal's economic crisis was characterised by the experience of 'all of the signs of overheating … without any acceleration of GDP' (Deutsche Bank 2010). This chapter traces how the introduction of European Community/European Union (EU) facilitated 'structural reforms' throughout the 1980s and 1990s contributed to the development of new and dangerous patterns of debt-led growth. In the 1990s, a rejuvenated private banking sector drove the expansion of economic growth in Portugal's non-tradable sector, damaging the country's competitiveness and creating some of the highest levels of private debt in the EU. This trajectory of economic growth contributed to a decade of recession in the 2000s, ensuring that Portugal was particularly vulnerable to contagion from the Greek and Irish crises from 2010 onwards.

Keywords Political economy • Europeanisation • Debt-led growth • Structural reforms

N. Dooley (✉)
Department of Politics and Sussex European Institute, University of Sussex, Brighton, UK

O. Parker, D. Tsarouhas (eds.), *Crisis in the Eurozone Periphery*, Building a Sustainable Political Economy: SPERI Research & Policy, https://doi.org/10.1007/978-3-319-69721-5_4

In April 2011, Portugal requested a bailout of €78 billion from the European Union (EU) and IMF. Following the Greek crisis in 2009, successive Portuguese governments introduced numerous austerity programmes to reduce the country's budget deficit and public borrowing, and to send positive signals to the international community. But such measures were unable to alleviate market nervousness (Fishman 2011; Brazys and Hardiman 2013; Mody 2014). By 2010, risk premiums on Portuguese bonds hit record highs as credit ratings agencies downgraded the country's sovereign bond rating, and Portugal had little choice but to seek help.

With all of the (much unwanted) attention Greece receives, the story of Portugal's economic crisis is perhaps less familiar. For many, Portugal's crisis is a simple case of contagion (see Fishman 2011; Arghyrou and Kontonikas 2012; Kalbaska and Gątkowski 2012), while for others the country's 'chronic fiscal misbehaviour' and long-standing productivity problems echo the Greek crisis (see Blanchard 2007; Pereira and Wemans 2012; Royo 2012; Soares 2012; OECD 2013; and for a critique, Dooley 2014). Yet for many others, the Portuguese crisis is more complex and difficult to explain (Krugman 2011; Rodrigues and Reis 2012; Reis 2013; Serra 2014). On the eve of its bailout, Paul Krugman suggested that the 'difficult' Portuguese macro story is harder to tell than those of Greece, Spain, and Ireland:

> Greece was excessive government borrowing; Ireland and Spain, housing bubbles. Portugal, by contrast, wasn't all that bad fiscally—debt/GDP on the eve of the crisis roughly comparable to Germany. But it also didn't have surging house prices. There was a lot of private-sector borrowing, but it's not that easy to explain exactly why. (Krugman 2011)

More puzzling still, while Greece and Ireland were booming post-Euro membership, Portugal's economy stagnated. As a 2010 Deutsche Bank report put it, Portugal exhibited all of the signs of overheating but without the growth. It quickly becomes clear that we are dealing with a very different crisis to that afflicting Greece. Portugal is not just out of sync with 'core Europe', it is out of sync with the rest of the periphery (Lourtie 2011: 5).

In this chapter, I shed some light on the 'difficult story' of Portugal's economic crisis over three chronological sections. In the first section I show that the story of Portugal's difficulties begins with the fallout from its democratic revolution in 1974. The nascent Portuguese democracy sought to overcome the economic and political turmoil of the revolution (Maxwell 1995) by introducing a number of 'structural reforms', which were made and legitimised with specific reference to joining the European Community (EC) by 1986. The second section shows how these structural reforms generated brand new patterns of economic growth during the 1990s. Yet behind this growth, the Portuguese economy had transformed into something quite fragile, into an economy driven by 'debt-led domestic demand' growth (Lagoa et al. 2014). The third and final section explores how debt-led growth caused serious difficulties in the 2000s. I show that the stagnant growth during this period is a direct legacy of domestic and EU-driven reforms from the 1980s. I conclude by showing how this economic downturn ensured Portugal was particularly vulnerable in the context of the Eurozone crisis.

Revolution and Structural Reform: Portugal 1974–1990s

The story of Portugal's economic crisis begins with a period of revolutionary turbulence. On the 25 April 1974, the 'Carnation Revolution' overthrew the 40-year-old dictatorship of Olivier Salazar's *Estado Novo*.[1] The revolution began as a bloodless military coup but quickly turned into a full-scale revolution, leading to years of political uncertainty and revolutionary change. The revolutionary period (typically understood as from 1974 to 1979, see Morrison 1981) was characterised by 'political turmoil, social upheaval and military factionalism' (Maxwell 1995: 157). The institutional structure that was emerging during this time leaned towards the radical left and included such policies as the constitutionally 'irreversible' nationalisations of banking and industry (Macedo 1990: 311). However, institutional construction during this period was a highly fluid and unstable process, and the socialist vision ultimately failed to take root. The authority of the state during the revolutionary period was frequently in question, with successive short-lived and unstable governments 'barely having enough time to introduce their programs and nominate their ministers' (Maxwell 1995: 163).

This political crisis was to be punctuated by severe economic instability. By the spring of 1975, an economic crisis emerged that had so far been postponed by the US $2.8 billion of gold and foreign-currency reserves left behind by the Salazar dictatorship (Maxwell 1995: 139). Socialist governments since 1974 had pursued large-scale borrowing, expensive nationalisations, and expansionary fiscal policies aimed at redistribution. These policies quickly dried up the *Estado Novo* reserves by as early as 1975. As a consequence, Portugal had accumulated massive debts, balance of payments deficits, and inflation was out of control (Macedo 1990: 324). 'Revolutionary' austerity and two IMF bailouts followed, creating strong electoral pressure for a new, non-socialist direction by the early 1980s (Maxwell 1995: 164).

This is where the story of Portugal's 2011 economic crisis begins. From the 1979 legislative election onwards, the centre-right Social Democratic Party (PSD) began to form and then lead successive governments (forming a grand coalition with the Socialist Party in 1983, and leading a minority government in 1985). This party, which was founded two weeks after the Carnation Revolution in May 1974, began to introduce a new institutional infrastructure, which was to be defined against the turmoil of the 1970s, and made possible through deepening European integration. In these years, the more radical elements of the 1974 revolutionary state were dismantled. The military-dominated Council of the Revolution was abolished in 1982, and in the same year, a Constitutional Review weakened the powers of the president by restricting the ability of the office to veto legislation and dismiss Parliament. Another major reform was reversing the supposedly constitutionally 'irreversible' nationalisations of banking and industry in a second Constitutional Review in 1989.

The major turning point came after the legislative election of 6 October 1985 when, under the leadership of Aníbal Cavaco Silva, a new minority government of the PSD was formed with the support of the Democratic Renewal Party (PRD), a new party founded in July of the same year. The economic situation began to improve shortly afterwards, bolstered by pre-accession EC aid (Magone 1997: 32). Accession to the EC in 1986 rapidly restored international confidence in the Portuguese market. Cavaco Silva and the PSD consolidated this popularity with a programme for economic and political stability in 1987, when they formed the Third Republic's first majority government (Magone 1997: 32–33). This government saw Portugal into the EC, and the accession coincided with the adoption of the Single European Act and progress towards the Single Market (Magone 1997: 34). It was these governments that implemented the structural reforms that were to characterise Portugal's new economic trajectory in the following decades.

The popularity and success of the PSD structural reforms was helped by the fact that they appeared to be working well. By 1986, all indications suggested that Portugal was on the road to recovery. Rising growth, increasing domestic demand, falling unemployment, and a positive balance of payments all served as evidence of the apparent success of PSD policies. It's important to note that Portugal's accession to the EC took place at precisely the moment the European project was undergoing its 're-launch' with the Single European Act (Teixeira 2012: 25). As such, PSD reforms were closely linked to the introduction of various EC/EU reforms after 1986. These EU/PSD structural reforms were to have dramatic consequences for the Portuguese economy.

Structural Reform and 'Debt-Led' Growth: Portugal 1990–2000

By the mid-1990s, a mere 20 years after the revolution, Portugal's democracy and economy appeared stable, which was no mean feat considering the relatively recent turbulence of the late 1970s. Political and economic instabilities no longer constituted existential threats. In fact, the economy was actually growing, leading to a short but substantial boom in the 1990s. However, this economic growth was to prove precarious as it represented the growing importance of new economic sectors in Portugal, mainly the financial and non-tradable sectors.

Two important transformations to Portugal's economy during the 1990s are important to understand. First, as a result of structural reforms relating to banking and finance, driven by the PSD and the EU, private indebtedness rose dramatically during the 1990s, paving the way for stagnant levels of economic growth in the early 2000s. Second, investment was redirected to the domestic, non-tradable sector of the economy, damaging the country's competitiveness and generating a particularly fragile pattern of growth for the country that had not existed before.

Structural Reforms and the Growth of Private Indebtedness

For Portugal, the 1990s were a decade of accelerated modernisation, which was to have a clear transformative impact on the structure of its economy (Teixeira 2012: 25). It was during this decade that the Portuguese economy experienced the third fastest growth rate among the EU15 countries, falling behind only Ireland and Luxemburg, with GDP increasing at an average annual rate of 4.1 per cent (Lagoa et al. 2014: 6; IMF 2002).[2] Unemployment fell to a record low of 4 per cent in 2000, and inflation was brought down to just over 2 per cent in 1999 (Royo 2012: 187; Cardoso 2005). Growth during the 1990s was impressive, but the second half of the 1980s saw Portugal registering particularly high rates of growth (see Fig. 4.1). This early growth is largely attributable to the implementation of the European Single Market programme across Europe, but also to Portugal's accession to the European Economic Community (EEC) in 1986, which brought massive inflows of Foreign Direct Investment (FDI) and European structural funds along with it (Leao et al. 2013: 8).

Portugal continued to grow until the early 2000s, but in a damaging way. The structural reforms of the 1980s had significant effects for banking and finance in the country. The Portuguese banking sector was rejuvenated and the restructuring of the financial sector produced a 'very competitive and innovative market highly suitable for absorbing the rapid increase in credit demand and for sustaining its dynamism' (European Commission Directorate-General for Economic and Financial Affairs 2004: 11; Banco de Portugal 2009: xxi). In anticipation of joining the Single Market and Economic and Monetary Union (EMU), reforms took place in terms of liberalisation of regulatory frameworks, privatisation, and

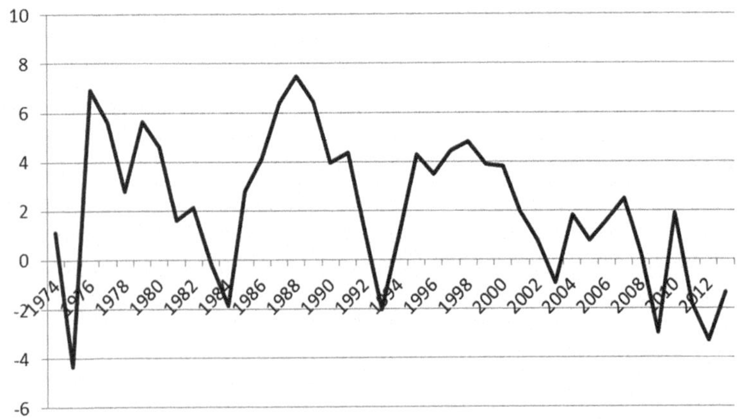

Fig. 4.1 GDP growth in Portugal, 1974–2014 (Source: World Bank—World Development Indicators)

the freeing of international capital movements (Decressin and Mauro 1998: 5; Leao et al. 2013: 6).

Privatised, liberalised, and deregulated banking and finance sectors represented a dramatic turning point for Portugal's economy. It is important to remember that in the wake of the 1974 revolution, the Portuguese banking system was characterised by pervasive public intervention and tight controls. All interest rates were fixed and there were even subsidised rates for eligible projects in agriculture, housing, and exports. This all began to change in 1983 when the PSD helped form their first government of that decade. Key reforms were implemented that reversed state controls and the banking system was opened to private, foreign, and domestic entries and authorised commercial banks to engage in medium-term operations (e.g. housing credit), blurring a previous distinction between commercial and investment banks. Following EC accession, there was a wide-ranging overhaul of the financial system (see Decressin and Mauro 1998: 7 for a detailed summary of these measures), propelled by various EU Banking Directives and other measures. Among the most important were the EU's Second Banking Directive of 1993, the EU's Capital Adequacy Directive (91/121/EEC), as well as Directives on the components of banks' capital (89/299/EEC), on the Bank for International Settlements (BIS) solvency ratio (89/647/EEC), and on consolidated supervision (89/30/EEC) (Decressin and Mauro 1998: 7–9).

The upshot of many of these reforms was the raising of banks' opportunities to take on more risk, to provide new products, and to access new sources of financing. Interest rates were deregulated and credit ceilings were abolished. All restrictions in consumer credit were abolished in 1995 following the completion of the Single Market. Privatisations also played an important role in this changing landscape (see Decressin and Mauro 1998: 10 for a list of selloffs). By the 1990s the banking and financial systems in Portugal were completely transformed within a very short period (Honohan 1999; Dooley 2015).[3]

The consequence of all of this was that credit-fuelled consumer spending became a significant driver of economic growth during the 1990s (see Table 4.1). During this decade, household savings decreased and household indebtedness tripled to just over 120 per cent of disposable income between 1994 and 2004, which as Cardoso (2005) notes was well above the Euro area average of 80 per cent. Incredibly, private consumption was responsible for 70 per cent of GDP growth in the period (Lagoa et al. 2014: 7; italics added).

Table 4.1 GDP growth and contributions of the main demand components in 1995–2000 (annual average, at 2005 prices)

1995–2000				
GDP growth	*Contribution of:*			
	Private consumption	*Public consumption*	*Gross fixed capital formation*	*Net exports*
3.6%	2.4%	0.7%	1.8%	−0.9%

Source: Reproduced from Lagoa et al. (2014: 9)

Credit growth in Portugal during the 1990s was truly remarkable. It accelerated (in real terms) from close to 0 per cent in 1990 to more than 25 per cent in 1998. The result of this dramatic growth in credit was that by 2002, household debt approached 71 per cent of GDP in 2002—up from just 15 per cent in 1990 (European Commission Directorate-General for Economic and Financial Affairs 2004: 57; see also Lagoa et al. 2014: 17).

All of this meant that household spending and household indebtedness rose dramatically during the 1990s. A 2004 European Commission report noted that the indebtedness of the household sector and non-financial sector more than doubled between 1995 and 2002 (European Commission Directorate-General for Economic and Financial Affairs 2004: 12; Banco de Portugal 2009: xxi). Lagoa et al. similarly note that outstanding loans to households and non-financial firms increased from 50 per cent to 93 per cent of GDP, and that almost three fifths of this growth was directed at households, three quarters of which were mortgage loans (Lagoa et al. 2014: 10). None of this would have been possible without the structural reforms of the 1980s. In other words, the EU/PSD reforms are strongly implicated in the transformation of Portugal into a 'debt-led domestic demand' model of economic growth during the 1990s (Lagoa et al. 2014: 16). For Portugal, 'Europeanisation' meant debt-led growth.

Damaging Competitiveness

These reforms didn't just lead to an explosion in private debt. They also helped overheat particular sectors of the Portuguese economy in ways that severely damaged competitiveness. As a result of the newly liberalised banking and finance sectors, investment and capital inflows were attracted to inward-looking, non-tradable sectors, including construction, retail, and privatised utilities. These sectors were relatively more profitable than manufacturing as they were less exposed to foreign competition (Rodrigues and Reis 2012: 197). As Leão et al. (2013: 12) note, the financial sector itself began to grow as a result of this capital inflow.

David Corkill stresses how Portugal became gripped by 'construction fever' during the 1990s as a result of credit being directed to the sector (2002: 44–46). Lower interest rates and greater supply of credit created a situation where the construction industry was growing at four times the rate of the economy as a whole (Corkill 2002: 43). A 2013 IMF report notes how a liberalised financial sector combined with increased bank competition to direct a surge in capital flows into the non-tradable sector, which contributed to growing macroeconomic imbalances (IMF 2013: 8). The Portuguese economy, following EU membership, tended to favour domestic demand over exports—especially in sectors such as construction, real estate, and wholesale/retail trade. These were all sectors where, as the IMF notes, productivity was lagging (IMF 2013: 8).

The poor performance of the manufacturing sector in Portugal, concentrated mainly in 'traditional sectors' such as clothing, textiles, and footwear, also contributed to the emergence of the debt-led model in the 1990s. Leão et al. (2013: 18) argue that in the period 1993–2007, it is clear that the newly liberalised and privatised banking system had given far more credit to construction, real estate, and other non-tradable activities than to manufacturing, and that this difficulty for the latter in obtaining credit was partially due to the reality that banks assess manufacturing as a higher risk sector, 'exposed to competitive pressures from abroad' (Decressin and Mauro 1998). During the 1990s, but especially during the 2000s, there was clear competitive pressure from abroad, which threatened the Portuguese manufacturing-for-export sector. Because this sector suffered from low productivity and due to (warranted, as it turned out) fears about its future growth prospects, economic activity during the 1990s and 2000s was redirected towards the non-tradable sector.

Over the course of the 1990s, the Portuguese economy was transformed into an economy mainly driven by domestic consumption, seeing the growth of the financial and non-tradable sectors, and the expansion of their activity. It was EU/PSD-led reforms that created the conditions for a new type of economic growth. As such, Portugal's participation in the project of European integration since the 1980s set in motion a new form of economic growth. This new model emerged directly as a result of

Portugal's adjustment to the Single Market and its preparations for the Euro. It was about to hit a wall, and would lead Portugal directly to its 2011 bailout.

Economic Stagnation and Crisis: Portugal in the 2000s

The fortunes of the Portuguese economy turned just before the 2000s when the country entered a prolonged period of stagnant economic growth. In stark contrast to the impressive and above average growth rates of the 1990s, between 2000 and 2013 economic growth stagnated to an average rate of 0.1 per cent of GDP, the second lowest in the entire EU (only Italy's growth rate was lower) (Lagoa et al. 2014: 6) (see Fig. 4.2). The causes of the economic downturn in the 2000s are crucial to understanding the difficulties that Portugal found itself in on the eve of its troika bailout in 2011. It was during this period that rising public and private debt coincided with dramatically low prospects of GDP growth. All of these factors led to falling investor confidence in Portugal after the 2008 crisis.

Portugal's downturn has its origins in the vigorous fuelling of credit-led growth of the 1990s. Portugal was heavily indebted by 2000, to an extent that was not the case for Greece or Ireland at that stage (Lourtie 2011). By the end of the 1990s, consumers 're-assessed their income expectations amid high indebtedness and a rebound of interest rates, as well as a gloomier outlook with the Portuguese economy', leading to a

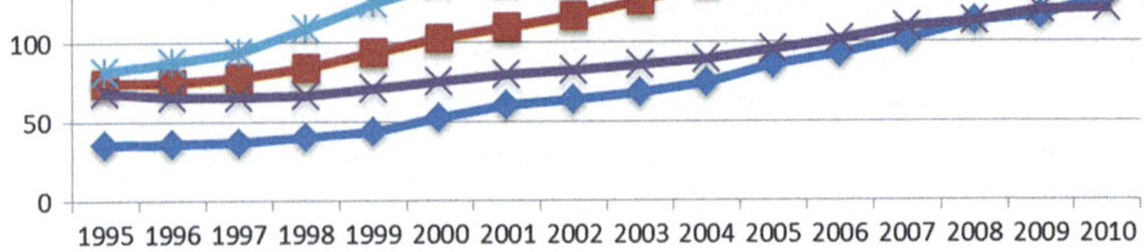

Fig. 4.2 Private sector debt, consolidated—percentage of GDP (Source: Eurostat)

dramatic fall in consumption (Cardoso 2005). Falling consumption during the 2000s is clearly evident when looking at the construction sector, in which, significantly, Portugal was the only European country to record a decline in investment in construction from 2002 until 2011 (Lourtie 2011: 6).

Similarly, because Portuguese companies tended to favour cheap debt over equity financing in the run-up to Euro membership, corporate indebtedness stunted investment growth in Portugal, which having peaked in 1997, gradually declined to eventually turn negative, in line with increasing leverage (IMF 2013: 9; Selassie 2012: 5–7). Interestingly, Portugal's experience from the mid-1980s to the 2010s is the reverse of the one experienced by Greece and Ireland. It already had private indebtedness levels that were too high by the turn of the century, whereas Greece and Ireland only really began to accelerate their levels of debt after the 2000s (Lagoa et al. 2014: 6).

This was to prove a difficulty for Portugal when, in response to signs of overheating in the Eurozone, the European Central Bank (ECB) raised its key interest rate from 0.25 per cent in early 1999 to 4.5 per cent in late 2000 (Lagoa et al. 2014: 12). This had a significant impact on domestic demand in Portugal—to an extent that it didn't in Greece and Ireland, where such high levels of private indebtedness did not exist around that time. Rising interest rates also had a negative impact on the Portuguese public deficit and debt levels, which became more expensive to service, leading to Portugal's breach of the Excessive Deficit Procedure in 2001. As a result, the country was obliged to follow a pro-cyclical, contractionary fiscal policy, which further contributed to falling GDP (Lagoa et al. 2014: 12). As a consequence, economic policy during the 2000s was characterised by austerity, improving competitiveness and productivity (see Abreu 2006; Lourtie 2011; Royo 2012), which further dampened demand and economic growth. Unlike Spain, Ireland, and Greece, Portugal was bailed out after a decade of stagnation, not overheating.

Portugal's economic downturn in the 2000s has clear origins in the model of 'debt-led domestic demand growth' that emerged in the 1990s. As the European Commission Directorate-General for Economic and Financial Affairs reported, 'since 2001, private agents and public authorities alike have started to readjust their balance sheets, bringing spending more in line with incomes/revenues' (2004: 7). Portugal's economic success since the 1980s had been premised on the inflation of domestic demand. As this declined during the 2000s, the economy stagnated.

Declining Export Competitiveness: The Rise of China and the CEECs

Adding insult to injury, Portugal's export sector encountered serious problems around the same time as the decline of its debt-led sector. Portugal's unemployment rate began to rise from 5.1 per cent in 2000 to 9.2 per cent in 2009, and to 17.5 per cent in 2011. Aside from the steep rise after 2009, much of this unemployment can be attributed to declining export competitiveness and difficulties faced by the manufacturing sector. Between 2000 and 2007 Portugal lost jobs in manufacturing at an average annual rate of 2 per cent, 'one of the fastest rates of deindustrialisation in the EU' (Lagoa et al. 2014: 13). Additionally, the increased indebtedness of non-financial corporations led to declining investment in Portuguese enterprises, because it may have increased the difficulty of their getting additional funding (Lagoa et al. 2014: 47).

It is important to understand that Portugal's exports have historically been concentrated in 'traditional sectors', especially in textiles, clothing, and footwear. This industry has been contracting across Europe since the 1970s in the face of fierce competition from low-cost manufacturers in East Asia, North Africa, Eastern Europe, and elsewhere (Corkill 2002: 158; Lains 2003). Portugal was threatened also, but due to its own low wages and integration in Europe. By 1999, textile and clothing was still a major industry, accounting for one third of manufacturing employment and some 20 per cent of the value of manufacturing output. It comprised some 30 per cent of total exports, 22 per cent of which were destined for the EU market (Corkill 2002: 158–159). Corkill, writing in 2002, estimated that one million people depended on the textile and clothing industry (p. 159). The industry has typically been characterised by a large number of small- and medium-sized firms—'only a little over 10 percent of cotton textile plants have more than 500 workers' (Corkill 2002: 159). During the 1990s boom, the sector accumulated problems of low productivity and a lack of capital investment. This was to become more problematic in the 2000s.

Portugal's international competitiveness became threatened by China's entry into the World Trade Organization (WTO), the ending of the Multi-Fibre Arrangement in 2005,[4] and the prospect of EU enlargements to Central and Eastern Europe (CEE) (Serra 2014: 43). Due to this decline in international competitiveness, economic growth became more and more dependent on domestic demand (ibid. 2014: 43). As a result of participation in the Single Market, but also to more general processes of trade liberalisation happening on a global level, Portugal became affected by its traditional productive sectors being exposed to 'wider and more aggressive foreign competition' (Serra 2014: 43). Portugal encountered difficulties in world trade markets, because of its specialisation in low-wage and low-value-added goods, which were especially hurt by competition from CEE states and China (Mamede 2012; Royo 2012: 205–213; Reis 2013: 148; Ministry of the Environment 2013: 18; Lane 2012: 10). The accession of the latter to the WTO in 2001 introduced a fierce competitor for Portuguese exports, one that, like Portugal, specialised in exploiting its low wages relative to more prosperous EU countries (Reis 2013: 154). The ending of the Multi-Fibre Arrangement in 2005 ended restrictions on the quantities of textiles and clothing that could be exported from developing economies to developed economies, further damaging Portuguese competitiveness, especially as so much of its exports went to Europe. It is important to note that the EU gave enthusiastic support to China's accession to the WTO (Sales Marques 2013: 33), to the dismay of Portugal (Amado Mendes 2010: 238). In an important respect, the EU's sponsoring of China further cemented the peripheral status of the beleaguered Portuguese economy.[5]

Additionally, attempts at developing a more advanced export sector in medium-tech manufacturing (including some emblematic projects such as a large car plant—see European Commission Directorate-General for Economic and Financial Affairs 2004: 24) were stunted by the prospect of EU enlargement and competition from CEE states. As such, in the second half of the 1990s, inflows of FDI into Portugal fell below EU average. In addition, Portugal's preparation for the Euro led to the appreciation of Portugal's former currency, the Escudo, during the 1990s, which further damaged export competitiveness, and promoted the redirection of economic activity to domestic demand. Portuguese exports of medium-to-high-tech products like vehicles and electrical machines also lost market share over the 2000s, mainly to CEE states, which have benefitted from a combination of lower wages and a more skilled labour force (Leão and Palacio-Vera 2011: 12). Anticipating the EU's Eastern Enlargement in 2004, a number of multinational corporations in automotive and related industries relocated their productive capacity from Portugal to the new member states (Mamede 2012). As a result, over the last decade CEE states have attracted large flows of FDI into medium-to-high-tech sectors, which had formerly headed towards southern Europe, including Portugal (Leão and Palacio-Vera 2011: 12).

The consequences for the Portuguese manufacturing sector were significant (Serra 2014: 43). Because the composition of Portuguese exports is almost twice as high in terms of 'low-tech' goods as compared to the rest of the Eurozone countries, it seems obvious that their exports are likely to be more directly associated with competition from China and East Asia (Leão and Palacio-Vera 2011: 7). As Lourtie (2011) notes, the textile sector represented 33 per cent of total Portuguese exports in 1990. It accounted for only 13 per cent in 2006. In addition, the market share of Portuguese exports in the EU15, the main destination for Portuguese exports (having accounted for 71 per cent of total in 2008), declined by 33 per cent between 2003 and 2009, mainly in favour of China and the CEE states. This led to more imports in the Portuguese market, and the skewing of the economic model towards services and non-tradables (Leão and Palacio-Vera 2011: 11).

This changing international economic environment contributed to consolidating the redirection of economic activity in Portugal. Economic growth became increasingly inward looking (Serra 2014: 43), contributing to the continued widening of Portugal's current account deficit. The competitiveness of China and other East Asian economies meant that the Portuguese economy was unable, under these conditions, to attract significant amounts of capital to its manufacturing and export sectors. Instead, investment tended to become redirected to non-tradable sectors. Portugal's economy transformed in precarious ways during the 1990s as a result of the EU/PSD structural reforms. Yet, it is also important to note the role of the EU in contributing to Portugal's competitiveness woes during the 2000s, not only through CEE Enlargement but also through its enthusiastic sponsoring of China into the WTO.

Portugal followed a unique path to crisis. In contrast to the experience of Ireland, Greece, and Spain, unemployment and public and private indebtedness increased as GDP growth stagnated. Portugal's public deficits and debt rose during membership of the Euro, but they were nowhere close to Greece's levels and, in fact, its public debt did not exceed 60 per cent of GDP until 2007 (see Fig. 4.3) (Baer and Nogueira Leite 2003: 3). Germany's government debt exceeded 60 per cent this year also, and in fact, Portugal's public debt was lower than Germany's from 1996 until 2007. It was not until after the eruption of the Eurozone crisis that Portugal's longer-term structural fault lines began to mark it as a target for international financial market anxiety.

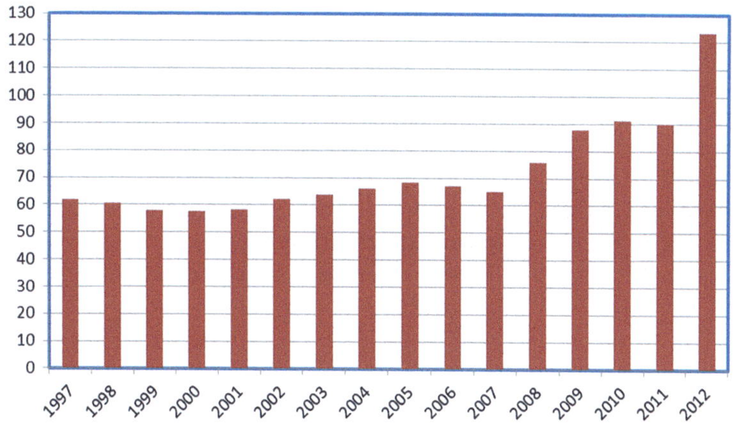

Fig. 4.3 Portugal's annual central government debt, total (percentage of GDP), 1997–2012, not seasonally adjusted (Source: World Bank, retrieved from FRED, Federal Reserve Bank of St. Louis)

From 2009, the deficit increased dramatically as it did in most European economies during this time, to 9.3 per cent of GDP from 2.7 per cent in 2008 (Lourtie 2011: 14). Portuguese governments responded to international market pressure following the Greek and Irish bailouts by introducing new austerity programmes (Lourtie 2011: 20). Nevertheless, as the Eurozone continued to drift from crisis summit to crisis summit during 2010, Portuguese borrowing costs soared. As Lourtie notes, for Portugal in 2010 and 2011:

> Even the agreement reached late in the evening of Friday, 29 October, between the Portuguese government and the main opposition party (PSD) on the strong austerity 2011 budget, after very difficult and tense negotiations, had no positive effect on bond prices. It was clear by then that good news at national level could always be trumped by bad ones at European level. (Lourtie 2011: 20)

Although Portugal was, to an important extent, a victim of contagion during this time, this contagion fed off the longer-term structural vulnerabilities of the Portuguese economic trajectory. This chapter has traced the emergence of these vulnerabilities since 1974. It argued that it was Portugal's transformation into a 'debt-led domestic demand' model of growth as a result of adapting to centre-right policies of the PSD and underpinned by European integration during the mid-1980s and 1990s that can account for its crisis. It has shown how the 'Europeanisation' of Portugal contributed in clear ways to the precarious divergence of its economy. Today, despite years of painful reforms and exiting its bailout agreement, Portugal's economy is still highly vulnerable. Its experience demonstrates nothing less than the complex *problematique* of a late developing peripheral European state attempting to catch up, via Europeanisation, with its Western European neighbours.

Notes

1. That is despite the fact that Salazar had resigned in August 1968 due to health problems, and it was his successor Marcelo Caetano who was to be the last prime minister of the *Estado Novo* regime.
2. Figures cover the period from 1986 to 2000.
3. The discussion of this paragraph draws on the detailed account of Decressin and Mauro (1998, see especially pages 5–10).
4. The Multi-Fibre Arrangement was an international trade agreement on textile and clothing, which imposed quotas on the amount that developing countries could export to developed countries.
5. The EU adopted an active role as a broker, and critical momentum was created by various EU proposals in the late 1990s, which granted China transition periods for certain conditions, as well as the EU–China agreement of 2001 which helped lay important groundwork for formal accession (Mortensen 2009: 86).

References

Abreu, O. 2006. Portugal's Boom and Bust: Lessons for Euro Newcomers. *ECFIN Country Focus* 3 (16): 1–6.

Amado Mendes, C. 2010. The Significance of the PCA in Sino-European Relations. A Step Forward or a Stumbling Block? In *Prospects and Challenges for EU-China Relations in the 21st Century: The Partnership and Cooperation Agreement*, ed. J. Men and G. Balducci. Brussels: European Interuniversity Press.

Arghyrou, M.G., and A. Kontonikas. 2012. The EMU Sovereign-Debt Crisis: Fundamentals, Expectations and Contagion. *Journal of International Financial Markets Institutions and Money* 22 (4): 658–677.

Baer, W., and A. Nogueira Leite. 2003. The Economy of Portugal Within the European Union: 1990–2002. *The Quarterly Review of Economics and Finance* 43 (5): 738–754.

Banco de Portugal. 2009. *The Portuguese Economy in the Context of Economic, Financial and Monetary Integration*. Lisbon: Banco de Portugal. https://www.bportugal.pt/en-US/BdP%20Publications%20Research/AllItems.aspx. Accessed 5 Apr 2017.

Blanchard, O. 2007. Adjustment Within the Euro. The Difficult Case of Portugal. *Portuguese Economic Journal* 6 (1): 1–21.

Brazys, S., and N. Hardiman. 2013. *From Tiger to PIIGS: Ireland and the Use of Heuristics in Comparative Political Economy*, Working Paper, University College Dublin, Geary Institute. http://researchrepository.ucd.ie/handle/10197/4928. Accessed 15 Feb 2017.

Cardoso, P.L. 2005. *Household Behaviour in a Monetary Union: What Can We Learn from the Case of Portugal?* Country Focus. Brussels: European Commission Directorate General for Economic and Financial Affairs. http://ec.europa.eu/economy_finance/publications/publication_summary1353_en.htm. Accessed 7 Jan 2016.

Corkill, D. 2002. *The Development of the Portuguese Economy a Case of Europeanization*. London/New York: Routledge.

Decressin, J., and P. Mauro. 1998. *The Portuguese Banking System: Feeling Its Pulse on the Eve of EMU Membership*, 98/127, IMF Country Report.

Deutsche Bank. 2010. Portugal's Difficulties Come from Afar. *Global Markets Research*. Frankfurt am Main, March 10.

Dooley, N. 2014. Growing Pains? Rethinking the "Immaturity" of the European Periphery. *Millennium—Journal of International Studies* 42 (3): 936–946.

———. 2015. Bad Things Can Still Happen to Good Pupils in the Eurozone. *SPERI*, December 9. http://speri.dept.shef.ac.uk/2015/12/09/bad-things-can-still-happen-to-good-pupils-in-the-eurozone/. Accessed 23 Jan 2016.

European Commission Directorate-General for Economic and Financial Affairs. 2004. *The Portuguese Economy After the Boom*, Occasional Papers No. 8. Brussels: European Commission. http://ec.europa.eu/economy_finance/publications/publication1000_en.pdf. Accessed 30 Nov 2016.

Fishman, R.M. 2011. Portugal's Unnecessary Bailout. *The New York Times*, April 12. http://www.nytimes.com/2011/04/13/opinion/13fishman.html. Accessed 7 Mar 2017.

Honohan, P. 1999. *Consequences for Greece and Portugal of the Opening-up of the European Banking Market*. Washington, DC: World Bank. http://documents.worldbank.org/curated/en/1999/04/5146052/consequences-greece-portugal-opening-up-european-banking-market. Accessed 25 Apr 2017.

IMF. 2002. *Selected Euro-Area Countries: The Determinants of Growth: The Experience in the Southern European Economies of Greece and Portugal*, Country Report. Washington, DC: IMF.

IMF. 2013. *Portugal: Selected Issues Paper*, 13/19, Country Report. Washington, DC: IMF.

Kalbaska, A., and M. Gatkowski. 2012. Eurozone Sovereign Contagion: Evidence from the CDS Market (2005–2010). *Journal of Economic Behavior & Organization* 83 (3): 657–673.

Krugman, P. 2011. Portugal? O Nao! *The New York Times*, January 10. http://krugman.blogs.nytimes.com/2011/01/10/portugal-o-nao/. Accessed 30 Sept 2016.

Lagoa, S., E. Leão, R. Mamede, and R. Barradas. 2014. *Financialisation and the Financial and Economic Crises: The Case of Portugal*, Working Paper 24. Studies in Financial Systems. Financialisation, Economy, Society and Sustainable Development (FESSUD). https://www.google.co.uk/url?sa=t&rct=j&q=&esrc=s&source=web&cd=2&ved=0CCsQFjABahUKEwjp6r6I5pbIAhUSDRoKHf1KCGo&url=http%3A%2F%2Ffessud.eu%2Fwp-content%2Fuploads%2F2012%2F08%2FFESSUD-STUDY-WP3-Country-study-Portugal-final-study-24.pdf&usg=AFQjCNFndT4YQOcktPrUVR0F9KGcisrahw&bvm=bv.103388427,d.d24&cad=rja. Accessed 20 Mar 2017.

Lains, P. 2003. Catching Up to the European Core: Portuguese Economic Growth, 1910–1990. *Explorations in Economic History* 40 (4): 369–386.

Lane, P.R. 2012. The European Sovereign Debt Crisis. *Journal of Economic Perspectives* 26 (3): 49–68.

Leão, P., and A. Palacio-Vera. 2011. *Can Portugal Escape Stagnation Without Opting Out from the Eurozone?* Rochester: Social Science Research Network.

Leao, E., R. Barradas, R. Mamede, and S. Lagoa. 2013. Financialisation in the European Periphery and the Sovereign Debt Crisis: The Portuguese Case. In *FESSUD*. Oporto. http://fessud.eu/?p=2297. Accessed 23 Nov 2016.

Lourtie, P. 2011. *Understanding Portugal in the Context of the Euro Crisis*. Chantilly: Peterson Institute for International Economics.

Macedo, J.B.D. 1990. External Liberalization with Ambiguous Public Response: The Experience of Portugal. In *Unity with Diversity in the European Economy: The Community's Southern Frontier*, ed. J.B.D. Macedo and C.J. Bliss. Cambridge: Cambridge University Press.

Magone, J.M. 1997. *European Portugal*. New York: Palgrave Macmillan.

Mamede, R. 2012. *Causes, Consequences, and Ways Out of the Crisis: A Perspective from the EU's Periphery*, June. http://citation.allacademic.com/meta/p_mla_apa_research_citation/5/6/7/7/7/p567770_index.html?phpsessid=ai8bkj6c63tvjbahj3d32imji0. Accessed 25 June 2016.

Maxwell, K. 1995. *The Making of Portuguese Democracy*. Cambridge: Cambridge University Press.

Ministry of the Environment. 2013. *National Strategic Reference Framework 2007–2013 Portugal*. http://www.qren.pt/np4/file/1354/2_NSRF_National_Strategic_Reference_Fram.pdf. Accessed 11 June 2017.

Mody, A. 2014. The Ghost of Deauville. *Bruegel Opinion*, January 13. http://bruegel.org/2014/01/the-ghost-of-deauville/. Accessed 25 May 2017.

Morrison, R.J. 1981. *Portugal, Revolutionary Change in an Open Economy*. Boston: Auburn House Pub. Co.

Mortensen, J.L. 2009. The World Trade Organisation and the European Union. In *The European Union and International Organizations*, ed. K.E. Jørgensen. London: Routledge.

OECD. 2013. *Portugal: Reforming the State to Promote Growth*. Paris: OECD.

Pereira, P.T., and L. Wemans. 2012. *Portugal and the Global Financial Crisis—Short-Sighted Politics, Deteriorating Public Finances and the Bailout Imperative*, Working Papers Department of Economics 2012/26. ISEG—School of Economics and Management, University of Lisbon. http://econpapers.repec.org/paper/iseisegwp/wp262012.htm. Accessed 12 July 2016.

Reis, R. 2013. *The Portuguese Slump-Crash and the Euro-Crisis*, Brookings Papers on Economic Activity. http://www.brookings.edu/~/media/Projects/BPEA/Spring%202013/2013a_reis.pdf. Accessed 23 Feb 2016.

Rodrigues, J., and J. Reis. 2012. The Asymmetries of European Integration and the Crisis of Capitalism in Portugal. *Competition and Change* 16 (3): 188–205.

Royo, S. 2012. *Portugal in the Twenty-First Century: Politics, Society, and Economics*. Lanham: Lexington Books.

Sales Marques, J.L. 2013. The Rise of China and the European Crisis: Their Effect on the Future of China-Europe Relations. In *East and West: China Portugal: Five Hundred Years*, ed. R. Whitfield. EWIAS Viewpoints. http://www.ewias.org/?page_id=752. Accessed 10 Apr 2016.

Selassie, A.A. 2012. Portugal's Economic Crisis: Diagnostics and Remedies. Presented at the Ordem dos Economistas – Presentation for the IMF, Lisbon. https://www.imf.org/external/country/PRT/rr/2012/121212.pdf.

Serra, N. 2014. Debt and Financialisation: The Portuguese Example. *Green European Journal* 7: 41–45.

Soares, Goucha A. 2012. Portugal: An Incomplete Europeanization. In *Portugal in the Twenty-First Century: Politics, Society, and Economics*, ed. S. Royo. Lanham: Lexington Books.

Teixeira, N.S. 2012. Introduction: Portugal and European Integration, 1974–2010. In *The Europeanization of Portuguese Democracy*, ed. A. Costa Pinto and N. Severiano Teixeira, 7–26. New York: Columbia University Press.

CHAPTER 5

Greece and European Monetary Union: The Road to the Demise of the Greek Economy

Pavlos Gkasis

Abstract Even prior to the crisis, the Greek economy had been plagued by structural inefficiencies, which were responsible for the gradual decline of its economic performance. At the same time, the structural inefficiencies of both modern capitalism in general and the architecture of European Monetary Union in particular have worsened conditions for the country after the global financial meltdown of the 2007–2008 period. This chapter identifies major factors behind the build-up to the crisis that Greece has been facing, pointing to domestic inefficiencies and externally imposed rigidities. Their combination has led to an inability to escape the current death spiral.

Keywords Greek crisis • Political economy • Economic and Monetary Union • Structural reforms • Debt

P. Gkasis (✉)
Department of Business Administration and Economics,
The International Faculty of the University of Sheffield-CITY College,
Thessaloniki, Greece

O. Parker, D. Tsarouhas (eds.), *Crisis in the Eurozone Periphery*,
Building a Sustainable Political Economy: SPERI Research & Policy,
https://doi.org/10.1007/978-3-319-69721-5_5

After close to a decade since the start of what would become known as the Eurozone crisis, Greece, the first state to be hit by that crisis, remained in the doldrums, reliant on external financial support and a supplicant to external supervision by 'the Troika' of European Commission (EC), European Central Bank (ECB), and International Monetary Fund (IMF). This chapter seeks to make sense of the crisis with reference to the particularities of the Greek context. It emphasises both the domestic causes of the crisis, to be found in the inherent deficiencies of the Greek state, and the external causes, in particular an improperly functioning European Monetary Union (EMU). Politically motivated domestic mismanagement of the economy, on the one hand, and the faulty tools used in European economic integration, on the other, have led to long-term economic suffocation. At the time of writing, successive bailout packages and the corresponding Memoranda of Understanding, along with the sovereign debt restructuring of 2012, have proven to be non-remedies and have failed to offer any viable solution with respect to securing the long-term sustainability of the Greek debt and the creation of a sustainable growth potential for the country.

This chapter examines the Greek economy's growth pattern over the past decades and considers the ways in which this evolved, with a focus on the period after Greece's EMU participation. It considers the extent to which Greece's crisis originates primarily in its exposure to European Union (EU) membership and the foundation and operation of EMU, or in domestic failings. The chapter also identifies the main economic agents that led to the demise of the Greek economy through the framework of an uneven economic development process that took place during the preparation phase for EMU participation. Interest rate policy has been the most important driver in this respect.

The chapter is structured as follows. The first section describes the process of Greece's integration into the EU and the second section presents the build-up to the Greek crisis and the reasons behind the demise of the Greek economy, identifying both internal and external structural factors. The third section addresses the response to the crisis and the solutions put forth to alleviate it, while the final section concludes by discussing relevant policy options as to a viable way forward.

Greece's Integration with the EU

The 1980–1990 Period

Greece has historically utilised external conditionality as a driver for reform efforts in its political economy.[1] Conditionality has played a crucial role in Greek reform efforts in the past, and this became evident during the country's preparatory phase for EMU accession. Further, Greece's efforts to join today's EU and then European Economic Community (EEC) have been mostly grounded on the potential advantages emanating from the common market, lower trade barriers, the increased mobility of capital, and the economic support associated with EU membership. Another major reason was the attempt of Greek foreign policy to form a common defence umbrella with the rest of the EU as a protective web to the perceived threat emanating from other countries of the region.

What Greek governments failed to identify is that the top-down approach followed under external conditionality would never be fruitful if not accompanied by a bottom-up approach, or more appropriately, a 'circular Europeanisation' process (Saurugger 2014), instead of a horizontal Europeanisation process. A prerequisite for every modern state is for it to formulate coherent growth and developmental goals by taking into consideration the intricacies that it faces. In the Greek case these intricacies include crony capitalism, various forms of corruption, inefficient public operations, state monopolies, and geo-strategic concerns, just to name a few (Tsoukalis 2012). As reported by Featherstone (2011, 2015) and Transparency International (2010), Greece is in the worst position in terms of corruption compared to the other South European countries of the EU. Featherstone (2011) based on Crozier (1964) also stresses that the Greek state can be characterised as a 'blocked society', or *une société bloquée*. Overall, the inconsistencies in the functioning of Greek governments have created significant bottlenecks in the proper application of governmental policies through the years.

Greece's accession to the EU in 1981 was a well-embedded goal of almost every Greek government, since it was considered a means to achieve a multitude of goals. The first was to become officially a member, thus gaining direct and participatory access to the project of European integration. The second was for Greece to use the argument of converting its own borders to EU borders and thus effectively protect itself from foreign threats, while the final was to gain access to EU structural funds. The implicit assumption here was that following the lead of the core EU countries would allow for higher and better growth potential. At the same time though, the implementation of structural reforms was also much needed for Greece, and this was overlooked. Almost all Greek governments, afraid of the political cost that they would potentially incur, failed to undertake these structural reforms, which were mostly linked with restructuring failing parts of the domestic economy such as the public pension scheme, the inefficient and sluggish public sector, labour relations, privatisations, and the reform of the educational system, among others.

During the 1980s Greece was experiencing very high inflation rates and the Central Bank (Bank of Greece) was targeting inflation through the liberalisation of the financial sector, which was then used as a driver to achieve monetary stability and economic integration with the EU (Pagoulatos 2014). This gradually changed perceptions in society and politics, as financial markets became 'a strategic ally in the central bank's effort to rid itself of inflationary government encroachment in its conduct of monetary policy' (Pagoulatos 2014: 456). During this liberalisation process the Central Bank started using extensively the tools offered by the modern financial system to exert control and affect the level of interest rates, while at the same time the private sector started playing a central role in the financing of public debt which was the heritage of the troubled, in terms of fiscal adjustment and inflation targeting, 1980s. By the end of the 1980s and as Greece was gradually reforming its institutional framework in terms of the openness of the market and the increasing liberalisation of the financial sector, with the banking sector being the pioneer in this process (Pagoulatos 2014), Greece was following the direction of economic integration with the EU.

Towards the end of the 1980s interest rates were approximately 20 per cent while inflation was also high, being close to 18 per cent and being decreased to about 11 per cent by the end of the decade (Bank of Greece 1998). Another important characteristic of the economy was the constant increase in private consumption targeted towards the retail sector and more specifically in import-oriented sectors of the economy such as the car industry, imported food and beverages, consumer electronics, and consumer goods. With respect to GDP, Table 5.1 depicts the instability in its growth fluctuation from 1986 to 1993. The Greek growth rate was erratic throughout the pre-Maastricht phase and also during the first two years that followed its ratification. This fact, along with data presented in Table 5.2, further accentuates the structural weaknesses of the Greek

Table 5.1 Greek GDP growth, 1986–1993

Year	*GDP growth*
1986	2.6
1987	−0.6
1988	4.7
1989	3.5
1990	−0.4
1991	3.2
1992	0.8
1993	−0.5

Source: OECD (1986, 1991, 1995)

economy, which, evidently, could not maintain its impetus for a series of years due to the maladies of the domestic economy.

By contrasting selected two-year periods on the country's main economic indicators (1984–1985, 1989–1990, and 2008–2009), Table 5.2 vividly displays some of the main indicators that underline the inherent dysfunctions of the Greek economy. Starting from 1984, we observe a deteriorating current account balance, which before the advent of the crisis reaches −14.9 and −11.1 per cent for 2008 and 2009, respectively. Net borrowing does not change significantly through the last 25 years, while public debt rises steeply, reaching 180 per cent of GDP by 2016. Unemployment was also rather stable in the region of 7–8 per cent, but as of 2016 it had climbed above 24 per cent. Inflation, on the other hand, is one of the few indices that performed well between the 1980s and the 2000s, since Greece's accession to EMU. This, though, leads to the final three measures, which are probably the most striking findings, depicting the effect of cheap credit to borrowing. Private sector debt in 1984 and 1985 was approximately 50 per cent of GDP, while just before the outbreak of the crisis it had risen to 107.7 per cent. Household debt in 1984 was not more than 6.8 per cent of GDP, ending up being more than seven times higher in 2009 at 51.6 per cent of GDP. Finally, household debt as a percentage of gross disposable income grew from 8.1 to 86 per cent of GDP in the same period.

The 1990–2001 Period

In an attempt to take the benefits of EU membership a step further, Greece formulated an economic model based on the goal of a common

Table 5.2 Selected main economic indicators (two-year periods)

Indicator	1984	1985	1989	1990	2008	2009
Current Account Balance as % of GDP	-6.5	-9.8	-4.7	-5.4	-14.9	-11.1
Net Borrowing as % of GDP	-15.4	-17.9	-14.5	-15.1	-7.4	-14.1
Public Debt as % of GDP	33.5	42.5	34.1	33.4	113.0	129.4
Unemployment as % of Labour Force	7.4	7.4	7.4	7.7	7.2	8.9
Consumer Price Index, %	18.5	19.3	13.7	20.4	4.2	1.2
Private Sector Debt as % of GDP	50.3	49.3	45.3	43.1	103.9	107.7
Household Debt as % of GDP	6.8	6.6	7.0	6.9	50.3	51.6
Household Debt as % of gross disposable income	**8.1**	**7.8**	**7.9**	**7.8**	**83.7**	**86.0**

Source: OECD (1986, 1991, 2011b)

economic policy centrally controlled by the institutions of EMU. By tying its economic policy to the goals set by the Maastricht Treaty, Greece proclaimed its willingness to undertake economic and financial reforms, which had as their main goal EMU accession. During the same period though, reform efforts seem to have been nearly absent and policies that followed

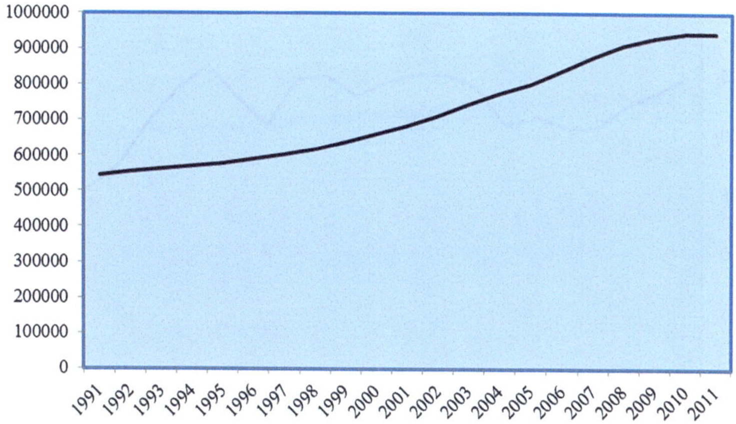

Fig. 5.1 Greek capital stock, 1991–2011 (in millions of US$, 2005 parity) (Source: Penn World Tables 2015)

were fragmented, failing to construct the sound economic, political, and financial environment that would attract foreign investment and promote private investment from domestic agents.

In Figs. 5.1 and 5.2 an overview of Greek capital stock (in millions US$) and of gross fixed capital formation as a percentage of GDP for the period 1991–2011 is presented. This shows that the rate of growth of capital stock has been significantly low. It also depicts in great detail the sluggish growth of Greek capital stock through the period 1991–2011. What can be derived from this is that the de-industrialisation process that took place in Greece in the previous decades (1970–1980) seriously damaged the productive basis of the economy, which, following the trend of most countries in the Western world had started focusing more towards consumption and less towards investment.

Another important index is gross fixed capital formation. In Fig. 5.2 we observe the plummeting of the index immediately after 2007, when from 25.7 per cent it fell to 11.2 by 2013. This demonstrates that as the country was paving its way for its accession to the EMU, it was at the same time rapidly losing its productive capacity. The conclusion that can be drawn from the aforementioned data is that a country such as Greece, plagued by de-industrialisation and the lack of a proper developmental paradigm, will face significant difficulties in the future as it reformulates its productive

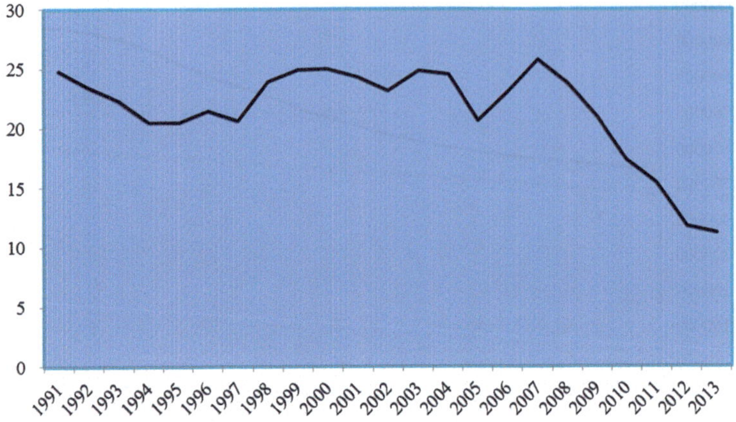

Fig. 5.2 Gross fixed capital formation, 1991–2013 (per cent of GDP) (Source: Penn World Tables 2015)

paradigm in order to become resilient to internal and external shocks in the future.

What the above points to is an economy that cannot create the capacity to grow by itself through more capital and expansion of its infrastructure. It is well established in the relevant literature that new capital formation is vital for the creation of growth momentum. In the Greek case though, this mechanism has failed due to inconsistent policies followed by successive Greek governments throughout the 1980s and the 1990s, making it unlikely that it will gain momentum any time soon.

Greece in EMU: The Build-Up to the Greek Crisis

Greece moved closer to the fulfilment of the Maastricht Treaty's criteria at the start of the 2000s, mostly with respect to achieving low inflation and interest rates. In a pattern repeated elsewhere in Southern Europe and beyond, access to cheap borrowing led to higher public and private debt levels (Philippopoulos 2014; Parker and Tsarouhas, Chap. 1 of this volume). The policies followed by the ECB with respect to lowering interest rates played a significant role in the creation of a housing bubble in the Greek economy, with a large part of the population focused on acquiring their own residence through (mostly subprime) mortgage loans.

As stated explicitly by the OECD (2011a, b), in the previous years, there have been numerous innovations in the mortgage markets that had not been regulated properly. The ECB followed suit and continued decreasing the interest rates during the second half of the 2000s, leading a large part of the Greek population to over-borrow based on debt collateralised by mortgages. Has this been the result of a 'one size fits all' ECB/EMU approach? Following low interest rates policies was probably the correct approach for some EMU members but not for many others. As has been pointed out by Gibson et al. (2014) though, such approaches pose significant threats when asymmetric shocks appear in different economies (see also Parker and Tsarouhas, Chap. 10 of this volume).

Taking advantage of the policies followed by the ECB, the banking sector during the first years of the 2000s followed aggressive policies that favoured loan provision in the form of mortgage loans and credit card issuance along with other types of non-collateralised credit. This had a multiplying effect as it led to increased aggregate consumption (Paparsenos 2014). The construction sector was experiencing a boom, and banks were offering subprime mortgage loans to consumers that would never be able to acquire a loan had the selection criteria of the banks been more rational and strict.

As discussed by Pagoulatos (2014) and Streeck (2011, 2014), low interest rates achieved inside EMU allowed Greece to finance government budget deficits and practically 'sweep under the carpet' the inherent predicaments of the Greek economy. The myopic behaviour of indebtedness led the country into a deep crisis created by the unfolding of three main crises: a balance of payments crisis, a debt crisis, and a banking crisis (Tsoukalis 2012). The problems of the Greek state, such as high tax evasion levels, corruption in connection with patronage and nepotism, and lack of political will to confront the above meant that the necessary steps to reform the economy in order to comply with the Maastricht criteria, such as the restructuring and rationalisation of the public sector, were never implemented. With the gradual decrease of interest rates and, as Greece started moving steadily towards the fulfilment of the Maastricht criteria, money was becoming cheaper and was mostly used for imports while export capacity remained stagnant. This then led to growing trade deficits and growing dependence.

At the beginning of the 2000s inflation continued its downward trend prior to the adoption of the common currency (2002). Greece was steadily growing with GDP growth accelerating (not least in the context of the Olympic Games' preparations), unemployment being under control (around 10 per cent) and public deficit and public debt decreasing (Bank of Greece 1999, 2000, 2001, 2004). What continued to grow, however, was the trade deficit, which was further fuelled by continuing falls in interest rates.

During the period 2004–2006, the main economic indices remained at the same level, depicting rather steady economic conditions throughout the economy (Bank of Greece 2004, 2005). GDP growth decreased marginally, unemployment remained steady at about 10 per cent, and inflation hovered around 3 per cent. The alarming index was the increasing proportion of loans to households compared to loans provided to firms. This signalled a significant lack of investment effort in an economy that was forming a culture of consumerism, and one that followed an economic model characterised by short-termism.

Another important aspect of the unfolding situation was the cost of servicing loans, which started to become a significant burden for most indebted households as the ECB started increasing interest rates. With the ECB continuing to increase interest rates in the 2005–2008 period, Greek households gradually became unable to service their loans in an already inflated housing market while higher interest rates put extra pressure on investors seeking to acquire funding by banks to support their businesses (Bank of Greece 2006, 2007, 2008). This created a vicious circle of over-borrowing and over-indebtedness through the non-servicing of loans, which became a hindrance in credit offered by banks as demand from households fell significantly. Finally, the lower supply of loans to firms led to lower levels of consumption, investment, and GDP (Paparsenos 2014).

Consumption decreased heavily, while the same happened with investment levels and inflation. For the first time in many years deflation emerged, with the rate of change of the aggregate price level being constantly negative (Bank of Greece 2009, 2010). Government debt rose to unprecedented levels (more than 179 per cent of GDP in 2016) while exports of goods and exports of services as a percentage of GDP rose only slightly throughout the 2010–2013 period (Bank of Greece 2011, 2012, 2013, 2014). This undermined the argument (put forth mostly by Greece's creditors) that the austerity programmes implemented during this period were helping the economy become more competitive. The reason is that with the magnitude of deflation the Greek economy had been reporting the benefits ought to have been reaped at a much faster pace.

Figure 5.3 presents clearly the damage inflicted on the Greek economy in terms of the unemployment rate. During the period 2008–2014

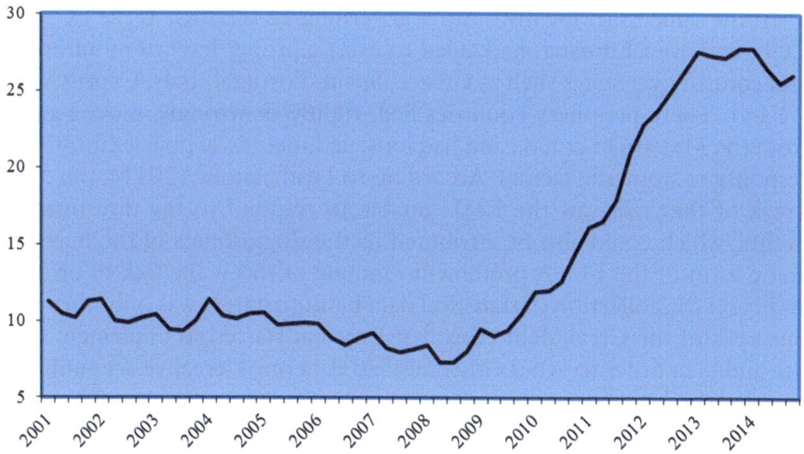

Fig. 5.3 Unemployment rate, 2001–2014 (Source: Bank of Greece 2014)

unemployment steadily increased reaching heights of more than 27 per cent at the crisis' peak and having slightly declined since. The rising unemployment rate after 2009 underlines the gradual disintegration of growth potential which has been a blow to the productive basis of the country and one that will cast its shadow on its growth efforts for many years to come.

Following the collapse of Lehman Brothers and the ensuing chaos in the US subprime mortgage market, Greece was one of the first countries to face significant pressure from international financial markets as well as speculators. The structural weaknesses of the economy combined with its heavy dependence on imports, and the shift of its economic activity from the primary and secondary sectors to the tertiary sector of the economy played an important role in making the country vulnerable to the advent of the global financial crisis. Furthermore, the crisis has revealed the limits to the effectiveness of EU/EMU institutions and raised serious questions about the direction taken by the EU, as well as the EU's capacity to deal with the crisis (Gibson et al. 2014). The EU failed to respond to the crisis in a timely manner and even when it did the imposition of harsh austerity measures dragged southern Europe into a deeper recession and caused further economic, political, and social crises. Such crises have become evident in recent years with the rise in populism throughout Europe being a perfect example (Tsoukalis 2012; see also other chapters in this volume).

At the same time, the institutions governing EMU, such as the EC, the ECB, and even Eurostat, had failed to exert a proper level of monitoring and control over states such as Greece, Spain, Portugal, Italy, Cyprus, and Ireland. These periphery countries had, rightly or wrongly, moved away from the Maastricht criteria and had loosened their fiscal policies mostly in response to domestic factors. According to Featherstone (2011), the outbreak of the crisis saw the EMU unable to respond to the dire turn of events, which could also be attributed to the sluggishness of the bureaucratic form of the EU. A prominent example of this is the lack of on-site audits on the collection of statistical data by Eurostat. It was only after the outbreak of the Greek debt crisis that Eurostat started to implement on-site audits in order to avoid either falsified data or of 'creative accounting' practices in the future.

There is an ongoing debate in the literature, associated with issues surrounding the Greek crisis, mainly revolving around the binary of ill-functioning institutions and regulations of the Greek state, as well as the improper application of the Maastricht Treaty terms (Featherstone 2011). As identified by Featherstone (2011), there has been an obvious 'moral hazard' issue in the case of Greece. Being in the safe harbour of the EMU led many Greek governments to become hesitant and unwilling to proceed with important and much needed structural reforms, being afraid of the associated political cost. The recession that the global economy entered after the collapse of Lehman Brothers and the decision of the US government not to intervene (at least in the beginning), a decision that proved a lot costlier afterwards, also played a significant role in the worsening and deepening of the Greek debt crisis (Rogers and Vasilopoulou 2012). The above accentuates the fact that the problems faced by Greece can be attributed to two distinct sources. The first is the inherent, chronic deficiencies of the Greek state that predate its EU and EMU participation, and the second is the improper functioning of EU and EMU supervision institutions as well as their institutional setup. The latter revealed the limits of the Maastricht architecture and contributed to the deepening of a crisis that hit the Eurozone's periphery particularly hard.

Response to the Crisis

Following the outbreak of the crisis in 2010 and the significant exposure of many European banks to Greece, the issue of contagion was high on European policy-makers' agenda. Many member states feared that a default of the Greek economy without their banks being fully prepared and protected could have devastating effects for their financial sector. There is an opposing view though, which is presented by Mink and de Haan (2013) claiming that it was mostly Greek banks that would face severe difficulties in case of a default, since they were more entangled with the domestic economy.

The main scenarios that were put forth to face the crisis were the default and exit of Greece from the Eurozone, the use of a double currency, and the restructuring of the debt with a simultaneous implementation of austerity measures. There had, at the time of writing, been no definitive answer as to which might offer the best route forward. A default and subsequent exit from the Eurozone would probably have devastating effects for the Greek economy in the short and medium term. As has been seen in the case of Argentina in the past, the economy would need a respectable amount of time to regain its momentum. As stated explicitly by Philippopoulos (2014) a Greek exit from EMU would add a premium of risk for the Greek economy, which is particularly small in size and heavily dependent on imports, given that its primary and secondary sectors have been continuously shrinking since the 1950s. The problem that a country such as Greece faces is a lack of resources in minimising its dependence on foreign imports, most of which are vital for many areas of economic activity and for the daily needs of the majority of the population.

An alternative proposal is a dual-currency regime. As analysed by Kasimati and Veraros (2013), the dual currency would have a positive effect on smoothing the recession, thus, helping the economy through a milder devaluation of the domestic currency.[2] This, however, would eventually lead to inflation, which would then be detrimental for Greek exports. This is crucial because export orientation for an economy like Greece's is of great importance if the country wants to regain its momentum by using mostly tourism and a niche that is starting to appear in the premium segment of the food and beverages sector. Of course, as the authors also state, if the economy is indeed making a turn towards the above-mentioned niches, it should do this following a long-term strategy of product innovation and development, instead of a short-term and myopic strategy of internal or external devaluation.

The approach finally followed for Greece—and pushed by 'the Troika' (EU, ECB, and IMF)—has been to perform a major restructuring of the domestic economy by passing laws that attempt to make the economy more effective. Additionally, the debt has undergone a significant 'haircut' of 53.5 per cent through a Private Sector Involvement (PSI). The PSI was the policy agreed by the then coalition government comprising the centre-right New Democracy, the socialist PASOK, and the right-wing nationalist LAOS under the leadership of Lucas Papademos, former Governor of the Bank of Greece during the accession phase of Greece to the EMU. According to the terms of the PSI, holders of Greek debt agreed to restructure the Greek debt held by international institutions and mostly foreign banking institutions. The PSI has been one of the 'economic patchworks' identified above, since the logic behind it was to help foreign investors get rid of 'toxic' Greek debt, which was then sold to pension funds and Greek institutions. In that sense, it provided a short-term solution for foreign investors, crippling at the same time Greek pension funds. In the long term, though, it will pose a severe threat to the Greek polity since it is just postponing the inevitable, that is, a clash between society and the country's economic and political elites, to the extent that the crisis is further prolonged and much needed economic development remains elusive.

Following its recapitalisation, the Greek banking sector suffers from a 'credit crunch' and an introverted approach towards securing its assets. At the same time it also lacks the ability to create new financial products or provide the private sector with additional credit due to the high degree of non-serviced loans which lock-in a large part of banks' reserves. It is very difficult for any economy, including the Greek one, to achieve growth through 'creditless recovery', since it lacks the necessary infrastructure and is only recently attempting to put in place efficient structures and institutions to create a proper export-oriented culture. These will potentially attract more foreign direct investment (FDI) inflows in the country thus providing the economy with additional and productive foreign funds.

A fundamental problem with all of the options considered as potential responses is that they take for granted that the only solution that can be reached emanates from the already ineffective 'toolkit' of modern financialised capitalism. The solutions provided in recent years are all in accordance with the prevailing logic of trying to find alternative solutions that do not alter the essence of contemporary capitalism but are somewhat 'economic patchworks' which are used to smoothen, mostly in the short term, the inherent problems of the ***modus operandi*** of capitalism. As suggested by Streeck (2014) the debate on how the modern economic system should operate is not one that will try to provide a substitute for capitalism but one that poses and accentuates capitalism's inherent fallacies paving the way for alternative approaches to re-establish democracy, and disentangle the interests of elites from the right of states towards reclaiming a meaningful sense of sovereignty.

The global economic recession triggered by the collapse of the Lehman Brothers hit Greece the hardest in the Eurozone. Fear of contagion to other member states led to the subsequent bailout programmes leading Greece towards an internal devaluation process in order for the country's economy to 'regain competitiveness'. The move on behalf of the EU and the IMF to choose this specific solution instead of a Greek exit from the EMU or an adoption by the Greek state of a dual-currency regime might have seemed the best option both for Greece and the other Eurozone and EU members, as their financial institutions were exposed to the Greek economy. However, this was neither without error nor without cost.

The Greek state is inherently weak due to its institutional and structural deficiencies, and its obsolete business laws and regulations. Therefore, the country is more in need of structural reforms rather than to make its economy 'more competitive' through a process of internal devaluation. The 'one size fits all' mind-set of the IMF, together with the serious mistakes on behalf of the Fund, like the notorious case of the mistaken fiscal multiplier that was implemented for the model estimations in the case of Greece, had a grave effect on the real economy, spiralling the continuous devaluation of the economy and augmenting unemployment.[3]

What, at the time of writing, could be a way forward for the Greek economy, given its current predicament? Initially, Greek governments need to exert pressure on EMU member states and the IMF for a further restructuring of Greek debt through the extension of the maturity of the loans, the further decrease of the interest rates, and the lowering of the goal for primary surpluses from 3.5 per cent[4] to 1.5 per cent, or with the inclusion of a clause for growth. This has been central in the deliberations of the last few years between Greece, led by the left-wing SYRIZA government, and its creditors, but moral hazard issues have made the main actors involved rather reluctant. Still, such an agreement would help significantly the Greek economy. A second policy prescription relates to the continuation of the current quantitative easing (QE) programme of the ECB, and the participation of Greece, which will help the country overcome the lack of liquidity that is evident in the economy and the ongoing 'credit crunch'. Thirdly, the efforts for structural reforms need to continue. There are inherent predicaments in the Greek political economy that need to be addressed once and for all, with the current state of the economy making this an imperative if Greece wants to return to a sustainable growth path.

Should the aforementioned policies be followed it is highly likely that gradually growth will pick up and this can lead to normalisation in the socio-political landscape of the country and a re-establishment of the Greek peoples' faith in state institutions. The expected result would be to have more stable governments with fewer abnormalities in electoral behaviour and less social upheaval. This stability would then feed into the investment climate in the country.

The final point that needs to be made, which is probably the most important, is for economic actors at a global scale to realise that the problem is not just with Greece. If there is no re-adjustment and restructuring of the theoretical models underlying financialised, quick profit capitalism it will not be long before other countries take the place of Greece. Should there be no change in the way the global economy is structured and is operating there will soon be a need for further tools to be invented in order to provide, yet again, short-term solutions to states in need, EMU or not.

Notes

1. Conditionality is one of the policy tools employed by the EU in the pre-accession process of candidate countries. It is based on a carrot and stick approach to stimulate policy reform by candidates to achieve convergence with EU practices.
2. According to Kasimati and Veraros (2013), the dual-currency regime would be applied with the introduction of a new currency for the domestic economy (e.g., drachma) while the public debt would be denominated in Euro. The government would then be aiming to collect adequate amounts of Euro through exports and other activities to proceed with interest payments on its outstanding debt, while it would cover all other expenses in drachma. This would not be sustainable in the long-run though, since it would mean a devaluation of the currency and imported inflation through the more expensive imports due to the weak currency.
3. It remains to be seen whether the example of Greece will act as pressure on the EU and the IMF to improve their social model and Economic Adjustment Programmes in order to ensure economic, social, and political stability in the Eurozone.

4. The goal in the past had reached 4.5 per cent. At the time of writing the precise goal for the 2018–2022 period has yet to be set.

References

Bank of Greece. 1998–2014. *Governor's Annual Reports 1998–2014*. Athens: Bank of Greece.

Crozier, M. 1964. *The Bureaucratic Phenomenon*. London: Tavistock.

Featherstone, K. 2011. The Greek Sovereign Debt Crisis and EMU: A Failing State in a Skewed Regime. *Journal of Common Market Studies* 49 (2): 193–217.

———. 2015. External Conditionality and the Debt Crisis: The 'Troika' and Public Administration Reform in Greece. *Journal of European Public Policy* 22 (3): 295–314.

Feenstra, R.C., R. Inklaar, and M.P. Timmer. 2015. The Next Generation of the Penn World Table. *American Economic Review* 105 (10): 3150–3182.

Gibson, H.B., T. Palivos, and G.S. Tavlas. 2014. The Crisis in the Euro Area: An Analytic Overview. *Journal of Macroeconomics* 39: 233–239.

Kasimati, E., and N. Veraros. 2013. Should Greece Adopt a Dual-currency Regime to Resolve Its Economic Crisis? *Journal of Policy Modelling* 35 (4): 588–600.

Mink, M., and J. de Haan. 2013. Contagion During the Greek Sovereign Debt Crisis. *Journal of International Money and Finance* 34: 102–113.

Organisation for Economic Co-operation and Development. 1986. *OECD Economic Surveys: Greece 1986*. Paris: OECD.

———. 1991. *OECD Economic Surveys: Greece 1991*. Paris: OECD.

———. 1995. *OECD Economic Surveys: Greece 1995*. Paris: OECD.

———. 2011a. *Economic Policy Reforms: Going for Growth*. Paris: OECD.

———. 2011b. *OECD Economic Surveys: Greece 2011*. Paris: OECD.

Pagoulatos, G. 2014. State-Driven in Boom and Bust: Structural Limitations of Financial Power in Greece. *Government and Opposition* 49 (3): 452–482.

Paparsenos, A. 2014. *Greece: New Financial Structure and Ample Funding of the Private Sector as the Keys Towards Economic Growth*. Paper Presented at the Conference: 'The Greek Economy: From Crisis to Development', Department of Planning and Regional Development, School of Engineering, University of Thessaly, Volos.

Philippopoulos, A. 2014. The Eurozone Crisis: Phoenix Miracle or Lost Decade?: Comment. *Journal of Macroeconomics* 39: 309–312.

Rogers, C., and S. Vasilopoulou. 2012. Making Sense of Greek Austerity. *The Political Quarterly* 83 (4): 777–785.

Saurugger, S. 2014. Europeanisation in Times of Crisis. *Political Studies Review* 12 (2): 181–192.

Streeck, W. 2011. The Crises of Democratic Capitalism. *New Left Review* 71: 5–29.

———. 2014. How Will Capitalism End? *New Left Review* 87: 35–64.

Transparency International. 2010. *Corruption Perceptions Index 2009*. Available at http://www.transparency.org/policy_research/surveys_indices/cpi/2009/cpi_2009_table. Accessed 23 Mar 2017.

Tsoukalis, L. 2012. The Political Economy of the Crisis: The End of an Era? *Global Policy* 3 (1): 42–50.

PART II

The Political Dynamics of the Crisis

CHAPTER 6

Narrating Crisis in Ireland's Great Recession

Nicholas Kiersey

Abstract The demise of Ireland's 'Celtic Tiger' is said not to have been the fault of any one group or class, but rather the result of something akin to a national weakness of character. Nevertheless, debate over solutions to the crisis has been organized around a distinction between those who accept and those who reject austerity. Reviewing the origins of this discourse, this chapter identifies two phases in Ireland's crisis. The first, from 2008 to 2013, is exemplified in the debates surrounding Ireland's public sector pay reforms. The second begins with the departure of the Troika and concerns Ireland's recovery. It is often remarked that 'the Irish don't protest', but recent mobilization and the results of the 2016 election suggest the need to reconsider this argument.

Keywords Irish politics • Austerity • Social partnership • Political resistance • European integration

While numerous technical causes can be listed for Ireland's recent financial woes, including lax oversight, poor fiscal strategy and the structural asym-

N. Kiersey (✉)
Department of Political Science, Ohio University, Athens, OH, USA

O. Parker, D. Tsarouhas (eds.), *Crisis in the Eurozone Periphery*,
Building a Sustainable Political Economy: SPERI Research & Policy,
https://doi.org/10.1007/978-3-319-69721-5_6

metries of the eurozone itself, the consensus among indigenous commentators appears to be that the permissive causes of the crisis were of a primarily cultural nature. Indeed, as Minister of Finance Brian Lenihan framed it in a primetime news interview, on 24 November 2010, just as the nation had effectively been put into receivership by the so-called Troika, the fall of the 'Celtic Tiger' was the fault not of any specific group or class but was rather the result of something akin to a generalized weakness of national character. 'We all partied', he noted, referring to the heady consumerism of the preceding decade, and this was the hangover.

Critically, this 'everyone partied' framing carried with it an implicit critique of the moral fibre of the Irish people. Thus, even as calls went out, from the Taoiseach (Prime Minister) on down, for all sectors of the workforce in Ireland to 'share the burden' of returning the nation to prosperity, there was also a sense that the coming austerity would be an act of penance. 'Good citizens' would be those who could confess they were part of this weak, inherently corruptible cultural formation, and accept thereby the necessity of a certain grappling with their own conscience, or identity, as part of the recovery process. Indeed, this point becomes especially clear in the case of Ireland's efforts to reform public sector pay during this period. Characterized as sharing neither the desire to be responsible nor the capacities of critical self-reflection demanded by the task of refloating the nation's economy, public sector workers were roundly vilified in the national press (Allen 2009; Arqueros-Fernandez 2015).

The dominance of this consensus is puzzling, however, for at least three reasons. First, it marks a notable shift in tone from the common-sense account of the Irish economy which circulated during the boom. Indeed, even today, critics cite the economy's pre-2001 performance as evidence of the nation finally having overcome its long-running developmental impasse as a peripheral-island economy, a testament to the maturity of a people determined to escape their traditional place on the margins of Western prosperity (McWilliams 2008a; Kay 2011). Second, the roots of Ireland's 'home grown' crisis cannot be so easily disentangled from the structural realities of global finance or, as Parker and Tsarouhas note in Chap. 1 of this volume, the core–periphery dynamic inherent to the eurozone itself. Crucially, the country's reputation for 'light touch' financial regulation was earned only subsequently to the implementation of the liberalizing reforms demanded by the 1992 Single European Act (Dooley 2015).

Third, and importantly, the discourse of generalized irresponsibility neglects some fundamental facts of the Republic's economic and political history. As scholars have argued, Ireland has, since its founding, been a *fiscally liberal, low-tax economy*, with a comparatively low rate of investment in social services (Adshead 2017). Moreover, this long history of austere economic governance is rooted in a conservative-leaning political party structure, largely the inheritance of its civil war origins (Lee 1989; Drudy and Collins 2011). The primary cleavage in Irish politics has revolved around two dominant, socially conservative political parties, Fianna Fáil (FF) and Fine Gael (FG). Labour as a smaller, third party, has traditionally enjoyed a nominal identification with the Left. Yet it has also suffered from what Purseill (2007) terms an inverse relationship with the fortunes of FF, which has traditionally appealed to poorer, agricultural and less anglicized segments of the population—famously, Labour decided to sit out the first national election, in 1918, a moment which some historians identify as 'the real foundation of contemporary Irish politics' (Adshead 2015, p.8).

Breaking with the Continental traditions common to most European regimes then, the social democratic model has not been a feature of the Irish Republic. Furthermore, as Adshead (2015) contends, two decades of 'social partnership', or state-led wage bargaining, from 1987 to 2008, have also played a major role in defanging what was already an anemic organizational basis for class-based politics. Moreover, while Sinn Féin (SF), the country's oldest political movement, can claim some legitimacy for its 'Left Republican' credentials, its association with terrorism and armed struggle in Northern Ireland has traditionally played a suppressing role concerning its electoral fortunes in the Republic (Finn 2016). Contradicting the mantra of a general cultural failure then, and contrary to the scornful accounts of the nation's conservative commentariat (Mercille 2014), Irish economic planning has been largely an elite affair, unchecked by any meaningful leftist force.

With these three puzzling aspects of Ireland's austerity discourse in mind, then, this chapter identifies two pivotal phases in the political development of the country's 'Great Recession'. It starts with a timeline of the key economic decisions taken by the government between 2008 and 2014. It notes how, notwithstanding the Troika's refusal to allow the burning of subordinated bondholders, the government's early moves were motivated by a desire to protect indigenous property developers and political donors. Next, it outlines some of the principal components of Irish austerity discourse, noting its historical roots, its role during the recession of the 1980s and, finally, its rapid ascent to power during the crisis. It looks in particular at the economist and public intellectual David McWilliams's bestselling book, *All the Pope's Children* (2008a). McWilliams is something of a 'rock star economist', by Irish standards (Morris 2016). Known not only for having predicted the crisis, but also as a seminal critic of the morally corrosive effects of *easy credit* on Irish culture, McWilliams's pre-crisis work exemplifies many of the 'common-sense' themes that we will see invoked later in key government documents and high-profile commentaries, contemporary to the crisis.

Finally, turning to the post-Troika phase, the chapter addresses the question of Ireland's recovery and the mobilization of social movements over government plans for the privatization of the public water system. It is often remarked that 'the Irish don't protest' (Cox 2013; Mercille 2013; O'Connor 2017), and it is indeed the case that austerity has proceeded in Ireland without much fuss; in the 2008–2014 period, social movements in Ireland failed to achieve anything like the same degree of influence as their Greek and Spanish counterparts. Moreover, the 2011 Irish election returned a FG-Labour coalition, which pursued austerity in an almost seamless continuity with the preceding FF-Progressive Democrats coalition, even though Labour had campaigned on an anti-austerity platform. By contrast, the results of the 2016 election suggested that the discourse of generalized responsibility was beginning to lose its sway. Occurring in the centenary year of the 1916 Rising, an event commonly regarded as a major inflection point in the struggle for national independence, the election radically transformed the distribution of power in the national parliament. While Labour collapsed, historical gains were achieved by a number of leftist parties, including SF, and a host of independent candidates opposed to austerity—an outcome which opened the possibility of a fundamental rearticulation of the Republic's post-Civil War consensus.

Austerity Begins

In 2000, Ireland's long record as an economic underperformer seemed a thing of the past (O'Sullivan 2010). The nation was in a remarkable macroeconomic situation. According to popular accounts, the state had rescued the country from a bitter financial crisis in the late 1980s, through a programme of expansionary fiscal contraction, involving reduced taxes and painful cuts to public spending (Considine and Duffy 2010). This austerity, it was thought, had positioned the Republic for a period of significant expansion in the mid-1990s, when the economy would post growth rates as high as 10 per cent (Phillips 2016). As Ó Riain (Chap. 2) recounts in this volume, Ireland's growth was largely export led, driven by US investment capital and high-tech manufacturing. The country's unemployment rate more than halved during this period, and the government enjoyed the unprecedented luxury of a budget surplus, along with a low debt-to-GDP ratio. Emigration, a phenomenon endemic to Irish history, had not only dried up, but a significant number of immigrants were now arriving from Eastern Europe (both figures from Donovan and Murphy 2013: 1).

By November 2010, however, the Irish economy was in a free fall: output had collapsed to an extent unprecedented among its post-war industrial peers; the budget deficit was out of control (32 per cent); and the debt-to-GDP ratio had soared to around 110 per cent (Donovan and Murphy 2013: 2). Shockwaves from the collapse of Lehmann Brothers in the USA had been felt globally, of course, exposing catastrophic weaknesses in the banking systems of Iceland and Spain, and shuttering major British banks like Northern Rock and Royal Bank of Scotland. Irish banks were in trouble, too. Flush with cash from international sources, obtained at low interest rates, and subject only to 'light touch' regulation (see below), Irish banks had concentrated their portfolios into the property and construction sectors, fuelling an asset bubble. Construction began to slow down in 2007 however, with completions reaching only half the record-breaking rate established in 2006 (Bowman 2008). With share prices of Anglo Irish Bank, the nation's largest indigenous commercial lender, under pressure throughout 2008, the global credit crunch that September would precipitate a major collapse in property values. Thereafter, with the national purse dependent on revenue from property-related taxes, including a stamp duty levied specifically on residential and non-residential property sectors, the exchequer found itself caught between an abrupt fall in revenue on the one side and a steep increase in support costs for the newly unemployed on the other.

Events taking place in the weeks leading up to 'Meltdown Monday' (Irish Independent 2008), 29 September 2008, remain some of the most controversial and contested in Irish history. On this day, the Irish stock market entered into a sharp decline, leaving Anglo and Irish Nationwide

Building Society (INBS) particularly affected. Not long before the crisis, Irish banks had all received 'clean bills of health' from the regulator (Nyberg 2011: 83). By that night, however, key government figures were meeting in a closed-door session and pondering how to prevent the collapse of Anglo. The next morning, Dáil Éireann (the Irish parliament) convened to pass the Credit Institutions (Financial Support) Bill, committing a nation-state for the first time in history to cover the liabilities of its entire banking system. The country was now responsible for €400 billion in asset-backed *loans*, almost ten times the national debt and almost 2.5 times the gross national product (GNP) (McCabe 2011, p.170). At the time, the prevailing view in government had been that Irish banks were dealing with a liquidity problem, and that 'the fundamentals were sound' (thejournal.ie 2014). The Minister of Finance was thus sanguine: the guarantees were unlikely to be called; it would be 'the cheapest bailout in the world so far' (Carswell 2008). Subsequent events would prove this assessment to be wildly off the mark, however. The Irish banking sector was effectively a 'zombie' (McCabe 2011, p.173). By spring 2011, the bill had already reached €70 billion, leading the Governor of the Central Bank of Ireland (CBI), Patrick Honohan, to dub it 'one of the costliest crises in history' (Elliott and Treanor 2011).

For many commentators, the decision to guarantee the banks was probably the most controversial taken by any government in Irish history (Farrell et al. 2011: 37). One way to grasp its significance is through the public disagreement that played out between Finance Minister Lenihan and economist David McWilliams (introduced above) at the time. On the night of 17 September, Lenihan had paid a visit to McWilliams's home. Accounts vary as to who initiated the meeting or what exactly was said. Government spokesmen would later claim that Lenihan was in fact consulting with a number of experts around the time (Byrne 2009). What is clear, however, is that McWilliams was an advocate of the so-called Swedish model, named after the strategy adopted by the Swedish government in response to what was effectively a banking insolvency crisis in 1992 (Dougherty 2008). Given the scale of the problem in Ireland, and the weakness of the available data, McWilliams argued that the typical options for dealing with these kinds of situations, like nationalization of the failing banks or forced merger with healthier banks, were off the table. The Swedish model was unique, he suggested, insofar as it would 'guarantee everything for a limited period to make sure that an illiquid dilemma didn't lead to an insolvency catastrophe' (thejournal.ie 2014).

According to the many observers, the Swedish option had not been discussed publicly until McWilliams raised it, and was 'the only blueprint' for how the guarantee would work (McWilliams 2010; thejournal.ie 2014). The bank guarantee plan was known among some in the government at the time as 'the McWilliams option' (thejournal.ie 2014). Critically, the article had suggested a limited timeframe of about two years (McWilliams 2008b). Moreover, as he would himself later insist before a government 'Banking Inquiry', at no time had McWilliams suggested that subordinated creditors should not be forced to compromise on what they were owed or that senior bank management should not be fired (Sheehy 2015). In the coming days, however, it would become clear that the government had a somewhat different plan in mind. On 30 September, under pressure from the European Central Bank (ECB), the Dáil passed a bill that was effectively a blanket guarantee. It was a turning point; that which had started as a banking crisis was now a crisis of sovereign debt, and 'the entire state' had been put up 'as collateral' (McCabe 2011: 169).

Even with the debts of all Irish banks now guaranteed, it became apparent that the loan books of Anglo and INBS were beyond repair (McCabe 2011: 177). The government was now facing three urgent tasks: to intervene to *recapitalize* the retail banks, to roll up the non-performing *assets* of the system in general and to address the inability of the commercial banks to service their *liabilities*. In terms of capitalization, the government's course would not be uncontroversial. On 14 December, a €10 billion plan to shore up the banks' ability to extend credit was announced, drawing on the National Pension Reserve Fund (Beesley 2008). Soon after, it was revealed that Anglo had issued loans worth €84–100 million to its chairman, Sean Fitzpatrick. To avoid discovery during the bank's annual audit, the loans had been temporarily transferred to INBS. Combined with what O'Toole describes as an 'insipid' response from the regulator (2009: 194), the credit plan sent confusing signals to the public as to the government's intentions. Even though Anglo's market was largely made up of developers, and it played no role in providing credit to the everyday retail market, it received €1.5 billion under the deal. This decision thus suggested a 'political logic' (Kelly 2008), prioritizing the needs of developers, FF's primary donor base, over the credit access to the wider population.

On the asset side, the government established the National Asset Management Agency (NAMA) on 21 December 2009. The purpose of NAMA was to roll up the non-performing loans from Irish banks into a so-called bad bank. The government intended to buy up to €77 billion of bad property loans from Irish banks. Controversially, the government was willing to pay €7 billion over the market price for a large portion of the properties, because of their 'long-term economic value' (Fahy and Meier 2009). Critical of this move, a number of Irish economists published a letter in the *Irish Times* arguing that the government was being too optimistic in its appraisal of the economy, and that the new bank would be a zombie, sustained at the taxpayer's expense. Worse, the plan effectively amounted to a reward for banks who had lost bets on speculative loans, doing nothing to pass losses on to the bondholders who would likely still be owed money after the equity had been sold (Lucey 2009).

While capitalization and NAMA would tackle some concerns in the retail market, they would not address the solvency of the commercial lenders. In January 2009, the Dáil passed the Anglo Irish Bank Corporation Bill, effectively nationalizing the bank. INBS would follow in August 2010. The state was effectively becoming a major shareholder in other institutions, too, in a kind of 'nationalization by drift' (Ó Riain 2014: 247). Worse, through 2010, a string of re-estimates appeared, indicating uncertainty as to the extent of the debts of the sector as a whole. These factors, combined with a worsening fiscal crisis for Greece in 2010, would conspire effectively to 'destroy' the country's credit rating (Forster 2016). Critically, the banks did not have collateral to back what they owed. The CBI thus sought approval from the ECB to cover the troubled loan books with Emergency Liquidity Assistance (ELA). This way, it was hoped, Anglo and INBS bondholders would be satisfied, and the banks could in theory repay the government later. Effectively a form of printing money, however, ELA is prohibited by the ECB unless it is to assist a solvent financial institution with only temporary liquidity issues (Whelan 2012). In November 2010, Honohan met with the 'Troika' institutions, namely the ECB, International Monetary Fund (IMF) and the European Commission (EC), to discuss options. It would subsequently be leaked, however, that Jean-Claude Trichet (ECB president at the time) had threatened Lenihan that permission would be withheld unless the government first applied for a conditional bailout (Hirst 2014).

The arrival of the Troika left many in an understandable state of shock. As an *Irish Times* editorial lamented, 'there is the shame of it all. Having obtained our political independence from Britain to be the masters of our own affairs, we have now surrendered our sovereignty' (Irish Times 2010). There was also a sense of awe at the scale of the problem. In July 2011, the country's credit rating would be cut to junk status (Brandimarte and Bases 2011). The government had issued €30.6 billion of so-called promissory notes, as a commitment to repay the CBI on behalf of Anglo. But a number of smaller institutions needed help, too, and so by July 2012, the total cost of bailing out the Irish banking system would double to €69.7 billion, or 45 per cent of 2011 GDP (NAMA Wine Lake 2012), not including a sum of €21 billion which would be paid out of the National Pension Reserve Fund. For the IMF, the Irish banking crisis was now 'the costliest ... in advanced economies since at least the Great Depression' (Molloy 2012). Critically, moreover, even these numbers understated the full bill, taking no account of the opportunity cost of forgone state investment in the economy (Ó Riain 2014, p.240).

It is important, however, not to overstate the extent to which foreign actors *pushed* austerity on Ireland. On the contrary, the government was in 2010 already pursuing a strategy of 'auto-austerity' (Roche et al. 2016). In McCabe's terms, the two years prior to the arrival of the Troika was a time when class forces 'revealed themselves in a way that had not been seen for decades' (McCabe 2011: 154). In October 2008, the government withdrew the automatic entitlement to medical care for the over-70s. The result was a significant mobilization of elderly people, protesting and blocking traffic in downtown Dublin, the sight of which caused the government promptly to yield (Irish Examiner 2008). Nevertheless, such early moves made it clear that the government was keen on fiscal consolidation. International economists like Paul Krugman and Joseph Stiglitz expressed strong criticisms, along with domestic voices like the National Economic and Social Council (NESC) and the Irish Congress of Trade Unions (ICTU), which articulated more Keynesian, and 'integrated' solutions (Roche et al. 2016). Whatever influence Irish unions might have had up to that point was not to last however for, as we revisit below, in December 2009, the country's 22-year-old system of social partnership would effectively fall apart.

From that point on, austerity programmes targeted the public sector directly. Immediately, the government imposed a wage cut on over 250,000 public servants. This came on top of a 7 per cent pension levy on public servants earlier in the year (Sheehan 2010). The government's 'Special Group on Public Service Numbers and Expenditure Programmes', also known as *An Bord Snip Nua*, chaired by economist Colm McCarthy, published a report on 16 July 2009 that proposed €5.3 billion of savings, including 17,300 public service job cuts and a 5 per cent cut in social welfare. There was a sense that the government's ultimate goal was simply to revert to the 'failed low-tax, low-spend model' that had created the conditions of the crisis in the first place (McDonough 2010). In the end, between 2008 and 2015, the government would seek to shrink the budget deficit from 12 per cent to just under 3 per cent, in 2008 terms. This scheme would comprise €20.5 billion in cuts to fiscal expenditure, principally in the form of wage cuts for workers in the public sector and a reduction of state services, together with €11.5 billion in tax increases, for a total of €32 billion (Roche et al. 2016). In practice, this translated into a cut of 30,000 public sector jobs, with pay reductions of 20 per cent (Coulter 2015: 9). Fully half of the €32 billion adjustment would have already been achieved by the time the Troika arrived.

Given that austerity was in this sense 'home grown', it is also fair to note the influence of external actors and forces in shaping both the context of the crisis and the government's response. To borrow from Parker and Tsarouhas' introduction (Chap. 1) to this volume, the Irish crisis can be understood as a case study of the uneven 'power relationship' between Europe's 'economically and politically dominant wealthy core' and its 'largely poor, dependent periphery'. To wit, Ireland's reputation as the 'Wild West' (Lavery and O'Brien 2005) of European financial governance was not to be developed until *after* the deregulation introduced with the 1992 European Single Market project. As Dooley puts it, already a decade before the crisis, 'European integration had … helped create an aggressive banking sector capable of driving debt-led growth' (Dooley 2015). Moreover, this asymmetry is also evident in terms of the handling of the crisis. On the one hand, as Honohan revealed in 2014, the decision not to 'burn' Anglo's subordinated bondholders was made under intense pressure from the Troika (Keenan 2014). Deficit hawks in Ireland tend to play down the significance of the debt, arguing that only one-third of the country's post-2008 debt can be blamed on the bank bailout. However, as Ó Riain (2014) argues, debt is a non-static phenomenon; had the government been allowed to share the costs with the bondholders, it would have enjoyed a disproportionately greater cushion in dealing with the fiscal imbalance of what would otherwise have been a much more ordinary recession. On the other hand, while the decision was made in order to create a firewall against further contagion, it postponed the need to address the structural weaknesses of the eurozone, raising questions specifically about its lack of any sort of tax and transfer system (Ryner and Cafruny 2016: 91).

Discourses of Partnership and Responsibility

The unevenness of Ireland's position within the eurozone has never been hidden from public view. Nevertheless, countervailing narratives about the crisis did not gain saliency during the Troika years. Indeed, it was not until after the departure of the Troika, and the beginning of the 2016 election season, that there would be any significant resistance to the austerity agenda. This absence is significant because, for its part, the government led a determined effort to legitimize its policies. As Coulter (2015: 10–15) details, there was a seamless continuity in discursive strategy between the FF-led government and the new, FG-led government, returned to parliament in 2011. This strategy had three principal threads. First, there was the 'we all partied' thread, which amounted to a retrospective reframing of the Celtic Tiger period, as one characterized by a universal irresponsibility. Second, was the 'we are where we are' trope. This was simply a localized iteration of the already well-known disciplinary Thatcherite refrain, 'there is no alternative' (TINA). Finally, evoking the burden-sharing spirit of the London Blitz was the 'we are all in this together' narrative; collective sacrifices would be necessary if the nation was ever to return to prosperity.

Yet the genealogy of pro-austerity sentiment in Ireland actually predates the events of 2008 by quite a margin. As Adshead (2017: 4–5) discusses, early governments of the Republic were dominated by a pro-market, 'fiscal liberal' mindset. While Ireland inherited a 'residual welfare regime' from Britain, the post-independence evolution of this system was shaped by an alliance between the country's agrarian elites and the Catholic Church. The upshot was an institutionalized ideological aversion to the left, combined with a preference for 'negotiated consensus' and 'gradual reform'. This attitude arguably also shaped fiscal policy. As Ferriter (2013a) describes, borrowing was deemed to run contrary to the prudential impulses of the revolutionary generation of 1916. Thus, CBI governor TK Whitaker warned in 1974 of the fate of 'profligate small countries' and their exposure to the vicissitudes of foreign lenders. Indeed, state involvement in the economy was thought to promote a *culture of dependency*. Subsequently, in 1981, Minister of Industry, Commerce and Tourism John Kelly gave what austerity champion Cormac Lucey (2014) has described more recently as the 'best political speech of the last half century'; addressed to the Claremorris Chamber of Commerce, the speech referred to the small-time Irish entrepreneur as 'in a way the quintessential human being' while also castigating the spirit of what he called 'demand democracy' as akin to a call for the state to be 'rent by a farrow of cannibal piglets' (Browne 1982).

David McWilliams's *All the Pope's Children* constitutes something of a bridge between this earlier fiscal liberalism and the austerity of today. As noted above, McWilliams is regarded as something of a celebrity economist in Ireland. His book was the bestselling Irish non-fiction book in 2006 and 2007, selling over 100,000 copies. It was also turned into a three-part documentary series (see http://www.rte.ie/tv/insearchofthepopeschildren/). Written for a general audience, using simple and often humorous prose, the book is interesting not so much for its prediction that the Irish property bubble would come asunder, but for its anecdote-driven account of the transformation of Irish identity in the consumerist mayhem of the Celtic Tiger.

McWilliams describes a nation that was once meekly Catholic, cautious towards outsiders, and governed by an 'old credit class system', where a rich 'economic respectocracy' lived in a cosy relationship with the domestic banks, and the limited credit they had to offer, while the 'nonrespectable' poor languished (McWilliams 2008a: 121–2). During the Tiger however, and thanks to an almost limitless influx of German savings (Parker and Tsarouhas, Chap. 1, this volume), all this was to change. For Irish society, the consequences were monumental. Starting in the 1990s, but occurring almost overnight, Ireland became a 'middle-class nation' (p.16). In an instance of what McWilliams terms 'Wonderbra economics', Ireland grew its middle class by 25 per cent, moving as many as 200,000 people out of the bottom rungs of the economy and leaving as many as 65 per cent of the population in the middle-income brackets (p.17).

Such growth was almost unheard of in developed countries. To explain it, McWilliams invokes the notion of the 'Pope's Children', a whole generation of Irish people born in the 1970s, during the country's decade-long baby boom. Curiously, this boom peaked in June 1980, 'nine months to the day' after the famous 1979 visit of Pope John Paul II (p.32). Uniquely, and in stark contrast with so many of its antecedents, this was a generation unthinned by emigration. It was coming of age in a country that had just emerged from recession, and which was finally beginning to relax its notorious protectionism. New, accessible sources of credit were starting to flow. Critically, it was also an Ireland where the ideological power of the Church had lost much of its influence. These constraints now gone, the Pope's children grew up not only to become 'the creative dynamo of Ireland' (p.32) but to indulge themselves in all manner of conspicuous and decadent consumption. They became 'the *expectocracy*', a generation of acquisitive, ambitious, oversexed, drug-snorting 30-somethings. They would be productive at work, to be sure, but they would enter adulthood as craven materialists, seeking only 'immediate personal gratification' (p.57).

Crucially, McWilliams offers no real explanation of why easy money had this effect on the Irish. Is it his belief that all nations recently freed from an overbearing church and paternalistic state succumb to easy credit in this way, or is it something specific to the Irish? Indeed, an interesting facet of the book in this regard is the *disjuncture* between its basic thesis, that economic forces were somehow the essential agency of socio-behavioural change in the boom years, and the descriptions it appends to the various tragi-comical archetypes it finds within the 'full-on nation': the Kell's Angel, the Breakfast Roll Man, the White Van Democrat, Low GI Jane and so on. For McWilliams, 'the role of economics has always been underplayed … in the traditional debate over what it means to be Irish' (p.240). What this actually means is unclear, however. 'White Van Democrat' for example is supposed to evoke a moneyed-yet-frustrated construction worker. Perpetually stuck in a traffic jam, he is the embodiment of Ireland's post-political moment, with its declining standards of political debate. Too lazy to vote, he sits nevertheless in his van, launching volleys of irate text messages at conniving radio talk show hosts, themselves only too happy to prey on his frustrations (p.63).

Such examples help McWilliams demonstrate his argument that consumerism has reduced the Irish to a passive, exploitable mass. The Pope's children are a post-political lot. Membership of the EU, notes McWilliams, signalled the beginnings of a death spiral in terms of Irish political participation. A whopping 76 per cent of registered voters turned out for the European Parliament elections in 1979, marking the nation's peak electoral moment (p.37). In the Celtic Tiger era, by contrast, voting was very weak. To wit, 'in Ireland, when you were born, rather than the letters after your name, is much more likely to determine whether you vote or not' (p.118). In this manner, McWilliams writes off the Pope's Children as a generation of political 'bimbos' (p.116). That is, idiots who allowed themselves to be seduced into massive debt, forgetting to safeguard those checks and balances on political power which might have secured their material interests into the future. They would have only themselves to blame for the fate that awaited them.

These generalizations seem to foreshadow what would come subsequently to constitute the *common-sense* interpretation of the causes of the crisis, as an indigenously produced affair. Reports commissioned by the Irish government, such as those of Honohan (2010) and former IMF officials Klaus Regling and Max Watson (2010), suggested that the roots of the crisis were indeed home grown and that, regardless of the shock waves roiling global markes in the wake of the collapse of Lehman Brothers, a catastrophe was inevitiable. While these reports address a broad range of causal variables, including loss of competitiveness through weak fiscal management, poor regulation of the banking sector and the hubris of managers, they also identify Irish culture as a specific factor. Regling and Watson, for example, write of 'underlying misjudgements about debt and property' that were 'so embedded in collective psychology that they could be imagined, perhaps, to mitigate institutional failures to some degree' (p.35). More explicitly, for Honohan, supervisors at the CBI were unwilling to swim 'against the tide of public opinion' and risk losing political capital by 'rocking the boat' and 'spoiling the party' (p.16).

As Blyth (2013) might put it then, Irish austerity discourse has followed all the stylistic conventions of the morality play; the crisis happened because of a weakness of character, and recovery would require a measure of tough, confessional work. In former Finance Minister Ruairi Quinn's terms, if the Irish would not accept the 'discipline' of the market, they would end up like the Greeks (Green 2010). Nowhere was this discourse more clearly on display than in relation to the question of public sector labour costs. As Allen notes, the idea that Irish workers are *overpaid* is one of the great myths of the post-Tiger era (2009: 126). It is a problematic myth, however, as pre-crisis statistics from the US Bureau of Labor, OECD and the EU suggest that Irish labour costs were in fact more or less in line with the average for the EU-15. Moreover, Irish workers in the Celtic Tiger years were more productive and took much less time off than their European peers, suggesting ultimately that wages were not a drag on competitiveness, all while Irish employers paid the lowest social security contributions in Europe (pp.126–8).

A second myth, however, is that Ireland has 'a bloated public sector where pay and job security are too high' (p.134). Allen details three reasons why this characterization should ring hollow. First, much of the public sector pay column in recent decades has been skewed towards 'CEO-style salary packages' for upper management, the introduction of which was supposed to promote efficiency (p.139). Second, such characterizations also take no account of the lack of equivalency between public and private sector workers in the contemporary Irish economy, there being no real equivalent in the private sector, for instance, to a policeman or prison officer (p.138). Third, OECD data covering the Celtic Tiger period suggests a decline in the number of public sector employees, as a percentage of GDP (p.136); while public sector expenses did increase in the 1995–2005 period, these increases were largely directed to frontline services like health and education and barely compensated for cuts made to those services in the 1980s (p.135).

The political power of this second myth comes into sharp relief when it is considered in the context of the 2010 Croke Park Agreement. As background, Ireland's Social Partnership model was formalized with the government, late in the recession of the 1980s. Union leadership at the time had come to believe that globalization was an inevitability, and that it was time to replace their traditional adversarial posture with a more cooperative approach (Arqueros-Fernandez 2015). Henceforth, unions would seek to soften the blow of cost-cutting measures rather than try to address the conditions promoting that logic in the first place. In this manner, following Ó Riain (Chap. 2), the partnership model has tended to channel redistributive claims into wage contestation as opposed to the provision of social services. Early in 2009, as the government began its attack on public sector pensions, the longer-term ramifications of this approach became apparent. With mainstream news media sources referring to a national strike planned for 30 March in terms of 'national sabotage', leadership called off the strike and agreed to talks with the Taoiseach (Arqueros-Fernandez 2015: 266). Ultimately, however, they got a 'seat under the table' (Allen 2010); in December 2009, the government unilaterally imposed a 15 per cent wage cut on public sector workers. All union leadership could do was to try to pressure government to return to the partnership model.

An agreement between the government and the ICTU, along with the Garda (the Irish national police force) and Defence Force Associations, Croke Park was intended as a replacement deal covering the 2010–2014 period. Despite the fact that it contained a no-strike clause, enforceable for the duration, it was approved by a slim majority of the unions party to the arrangement. Importantly, however, the negotiations were framed almost exclusively in terms of *pay and conditions*, and a host of politicians, business groups and well-known media pundits drew upon this framing as a metric of responsibility through which the public sector could be discounted as an avaricious and self-serving party (see McWilliams 2014).

Given the far greater job losses and pay cuts suffered in the private sector, these responses were understandable to a degree. After all, the 'morality play' account suggested that the causes of the crisis were universal, and that the solution should therefore involve an equally universal sharing of the burden. Such thinking, however, is an example of what Blyth (2013) terms the 'fallacy of composition'; just because one sector is facing cutbacks does not mean that cutbacks are necessarily a good thing across all sectors. In the Irish context, such reasoning served to pit the private sector against the public sector, as if both were locked in a zero-sum game, and placed a considerable constraint on debate over how best to sustain domestic demand. Thus, despite the government's victory, many would argue the pay cuts were too modest, and interpret the negotiations as an abject lesson in how, without the threat of any corrective sanctions on their behaviour, public sector workers would necessarily remain the sort of selfish and unruly subjects portrayed in *The Pope's Children*.

A Risen People?

One remarked-upon aspect of Ireland's Great Recession has been the relative lack of social unrest (Lewis 2011), a point which has not been lost on the government. Indeed, early on, Lenihan felt compelled to note, 'the steps taken have impressed our partners in Europe, who are amazed at our capacity to take pain. In France, you would have riots if you tried to do this' (Finn 2011: 34). In 2012, as the Greek crisis was worsening, key Irish and European policymakers began to speak of Ireland as a 'poster child' model for recovery (Coulter et al., 2017). Indeed, for their part, it is reported that Greek anti-austerity protestors chanted, 'We are not Ireland, we will resist' (p.34). However, as Adshead explains, if 'conservatives' captured 'the narrative of the crisis' at the outset, things began to change as the economy entered into recovery (2017: 7). Citing Doris et al. (2014), she notes that public sector workers had suffered real wage cuts upwards of 27 per cent. In this sense, as awareness grew that austerity really had 'hit everyone', there came a point where 'large-scale antipathy' was reserved solely for bankers and property developers (p.8).

Critically, some observers of Irish social movements have been keen to point out that resistance to government narratives was present pretty much from the beginning. These scholars point to a variety of microresistances in everyday scenes of Irish political life, such as the Ballyhea protests (Cox 2016) and squatting campaigns associated with Occupy Dame Street (Szolucha 2013, 2014), as evidence of an effervescent anti-austerity movement. Yet, while it would be hard to deny the significance of these examples, not least as incubators of potential future resistance, it can hardly be said that they constituted a counter—power capable of compelling a major shift in government policy.

A variety of theories have been offered to explain the history of Irish complacency when it comes to the pursuit of economic justice. Some of the factors cited are bound up with the idiosyncratic political history of the country, while others appear to be of more recent provenance, connected to the vicissitudes of life in austerity capitalism itself. First, while the Irish have no affinity for extreme right ideologies, it cannot be said that they are an especially left-wing people (Mair 1992); as noted above, the primary cleavage in Irish politics has revolved around the country's civil war origins, and its two dominant, socially conservative political parties, FF and FG. A second reason, as Ferriter (2013b) posits, is that emigration has long served as a kind of a safety valve for the country's social ills. Third, as noted by Allen and O'Boyle (2013), is widespread disaffection with union leadership, with union density in the private sector dropping from 55 per cent to 20 per cent in the space of just a few decades. A fourth reason, in the contemporary context, and as cultural psychologists Power and Nussbaum contend, is that the Irish seem to have internalized the narrative that they are 'partly responsible for their own misfortune and are prepared to reap what they sowed' (Power and Nussbaum 2014). Fifth and finally, it could be that, particularly in the conjuncture of the Great Recession, economic circumstances have had a material-disciplinary effect on Irish daily life, constraining 'political entrepreneurs' who might otherwise be inclined to organize and lead protest (Adshead 2017).

These factors are all plausible in explaining why the Irish response to austerity was so unimpressive, especially when contrasted with the scenes of resistance that occurred in Spain, Portugal and Greece (see chapters by Clua-Losada, David, and Prodromidou, in this volume). With the recovery, however, all this was to change. In 2013, with the agreement of the ECB, the Dáil voted to restructure the Irish Bank Resolution Corporation's (IBRC) debt from the front-loaded Promissory Notes to new, 40-year government bonds (Münchau 2013). Then, in December of that year, the Troika made its last visit. The country's perseverance throughout its painful ordeal was remarked upon by IMF mission chief for Ireland, Craig Beaumont, who described it as 'an example to other debt-hit nations' (RTE 2013). The so-called recovery was unevenly distributed, however. A report from the Thinktank for Action on Social Change (TASC) in 2015 pointed to the profound human impact of the austerity, which had burdened many with hunger, homelessness and addiction. Indeed, Ireland was now the most unequal country in the EU in terms of income distribution (O'Brien 2015), with the bottom 90 per cent of all those at work earning an average taxable income of €27,400 (O'Connor and Staunton 2015: 29).

Even though the election was still quite far off, it became clear throughout 2014 and 2015 that the political mainstream was starting to fear for its left flank. Assisted by well-known voices in the media, the coalition parties attempted to stoke fears of 'hard-left Trotskyite' factions (Collins 2015). As O'Toole noted, this frame was somewhat predictable—with the worst of the financial woes now in the past, it made sense for the government to present the election as a choice between 'stability or chaos' (O'Toole 2015). For Irish political blogger Richard McAleavey (2015), the new turn was driven by a fear of anti-austerity politics, encouraged both by the recent success of Syriza in Greece and by the unexpected explosion at home of a social movement opposing the imposition of water charges. What had triggered this sudden awakening? In 2014, the Irish government had announced plans to institute a new tax on water, ranging from €176 to as much as €500, depending on the size of the household (Fleming 2014). These plans were accompanied by a number of troubling revelations about the management of the new semi-state water company, Irish Water, suggesting not only that the firm had allocated €86 million of its total setup costs to consultancy fees but also that it had been established in order to facilitate privatization of the national water system (thejournal.ie 2015).

Media figures tried to spin the Right2Water movement as led somehow by a 'small group' of 'elite' and 'fascist' pied pipers (see Howlin 2016). Missed in such characterizations however was the spontaneous, neighbourhood-level nature of the movement itself, which was of a scale beyond anything that could have been contrived by the organized Left. At the community level, people were working together to obstruct the independent contractors sent to install metres near their homes (Lee-Murphy 2015). Moreover, a mysterious 'water fairy' phenomenon was taking place, likely motivated by an instructional video on YouTube (https://youtu.be/2PTIV2GNF-g) that demonstrated an easy method for sabotaging the meters. Moreover, as many as 70 per cent of households were refusing to pay the charge at all (Tierney 2015). It was not without cause then that some would suggest a new mode of active Irish citizenship was 'kicking off' (Hearne 2014; Maleney 2014).

Understandably enough, the government responded with an election campaign based on the slogan that Irish voters needed to 'keep the recovery going'; the swingeing cutbacks had been hard, no doubt, but it was important to see the job through. The government would make only stumbling progress on this goal, however, with some notable gaffes along the way. In one speech, the Taoiseach referred to the anti-austerity movement as 'whingers' (thejournal.ie 2016). Moreover, declarations of support for the government's tax regime from well-known public figures like U2's Bono (Neate 2014) notwithstanding, the government was put in the awkward position of having to defend Apple Inc. against a record $14.5 billion ruling by the European Commission concerning tax avoidance practices in the country (Scott 2016).

These developments loomed large over the election. In 2011, FF had been nearly eliminated, and FG and Labour installed in their place. After four years of austerity, however, the 2016 election dealt major blows to these parties in turn. FG support decreased, with a loss of more than 20 seats, while the Labour party suffered the worst election performance of its history, returning just 7 seats. FF, while regaining some of the ground lost in 2011, did nothing to reverse its longer-term decline. Among the big winners were SF, which gained nine seats, though not enough to pursue its ambition to lead a coalition, and non-party affiliated Independent candidates, who won a shocking 23 seats. As a result, the 32nd Dáil is something of a *zombie parliament*. For most Irish voters, the idea of any sort of coalition between FF and FG would be completely unthinkable—nevertheless, FF agreed to a 'confidence and supply' (Kelly 2016) arrangement, the job of which was effectively to maintain FG's parliamentary majority (which includes a fluctuating number of Independents) until such time as the parties are ready for another election.

For some commentators, the almost total defeat of Labour, and the slightly increased vote for FF, meant that the electorate had 'swung to the centre'; a survey at the time showed that 60 per cent of Independent voters classified themselves as 'centrist' (O'Malley 2016). This conclusion is problematic, however. In terms of actual votes cast, the increase in support for candidates with positions to the left of Labour (i.e. the combined increase in votes for SF, the Anti-Austerity Alliance / People Before Profit and the self-identifying left 'Independents 4 Change' group) was approximately 111,000, not far off the 24.3 per cent 'swing' (126,200 votes) towards FF (all figures from https://en.wikipedia.org/wiki/Irish_general_election,_2016). It is clear in this sense that Labour was outflanked on the left by a coalition of anti-austerity parties, all of whom had mobilized against the water charges.

Yet it might also be said that the election was something of a missed opportunity for the Irish left. While left-wing parties have never performed well in Ireland, the large spike in support for Independents in the 2016 election indicates something of the potential for a major rearticulation of the Irish political horizon. In 2015, however, as the Right2Water movement was gathering pace, SF unilaterally announced a vote-transfer pact with the other Right2Water-affiliated parties, for the upcoming election. Problematically, however, two of the parties were not at the time in a position to reciprocate, because SF would not rule out a coalition with FF, FG or Labour as a junior partner. Moreover, the Anti-Austerity Alliance also argued that the now-rebranded Right2Change campaign had become a 'prop' for SF (Kelly 2015), refusing to form a government with SF full stop, on account of the cutbacks it had implemented in Northern Ireland. With SF putting power before principle then, and AAA-PBP putting principle before power, it might be argued that the Irish parliamentary left failed to present the electorate with a convincing united front.

Early in 2017, the issue of homelessness emerged on the Irish recovery landscape. This was partly driven by an increase in repossessions (Holland 2015), and partly by the difficulty homeowners still faced in obtaining credit. The latter factor had relegated many families to the rental market, driving rental prices in Dublin to unprecedented heights (Dunçan 2014). Moreover, as O'Byrne (2016) notes, NAMA's 2014 decision to start selling off its commercial assets had attracted the attention of international vulture funds, tightening the availability of land for residential development in large urban centres. In this context, over Christmas 2016, a number of activists and homeless people entered Apollo House, a disused NAMA building, beginning what would be a month-long occupation. Operating under the title Home Sweet Home, the group sought to draw attention to the plight of Ireland's record-breaking 6000 homeless people, and the poor quality of available emergency accommodation (Steward 2017). The group received the support of a number of well-known Irish media personalities (Cullen 2016).

In Taoiseach Enda Kenny's terms, Ireland had 'taken its medicine', and the country was emerging now as the fastest-growing economy in the EU (Dooley 2015). Yet the oft-cited 'poster child' appellation might have hidden more than it revealed. While government strategy remained predicated on a 'wait and see' approach, deflating wages in anticipation of global recovery, evidence began to accumulate that austerity had been self-defeating, with little or no impact on the deficit because of reduced growth and increased unemployment costs (Taft 2015). Meanwhile, a major spike in the national tax take in 2016 was revealed to be of a fleeting nature (Phillips 2016). The upshot was that the Republic still lacked any kind of meaningful industrial strategy, and welfare cuts for those under 25 meant the emigration safety valve remained in effect (McNeice 2013). Adding to the uncertainty, the 2016 Brexit referendum in Britain raised the possibility of a potentially devastating departure from the EU of 'Ireland's largest export partner' (O'Carroll and Collins 2016).

Thus, in 2017 the fate of Ireland's economic recovery remained unclear (see also Ó Riain, Chap. 2, this volume). Austerity had ratified a massive transfer of wealth from the taxpayers of an advanced Western nation to foreign bondholders and inflicted massive human costs. Yet, despite the evident need for a debate on the subject, the government's recovery strategy remained predicated on the same crude 'morality play' common-sense exemplified in McWilliams's *Pope's Children*, pitting the private sector against the 'protected' public sector (Irish Times 2017). Meanwhile, as the results of the 2016 election suggested, the country's patience with this approach was running thin.

References

Adshead, M. 2015. *Irish Responses to Austerity*. Presented at the International Conference of Europeanists, 1–26, Paris.

———. 2017. Who's Left in the Wake of Irish Austerity? [online first]. Capital & Class. https://doi.org/10.1177/0309816817692128.

Allen, K. 2009. *Ireland's Economic Crash: A Radical Agenda for Change*. Dublin: The Liffey Press.

———. 2010. The Cause of Ireland's Crisis [online]. *Socialist Worker*. Available: https://socialistworker.org/2010/12/03/cause-of-the-ireland-crisis. Accessed 7 Apr 2017.

Allen, K., and B. O' Boyle. 2013. *Austerity Ireland*. London: Pluto Press.

Arqueros-Fernandez, F. 2015. Lessons from the Era of Social Partnership for the Irish Labour Movement. In *Ireland Under Austerity*, ed. C. Coulter, and A. Nagle, 219–240. Manchester: Manchester University Press.

Beesley, A. 2008. Government to Underpin Banks with €10bn Plan [online]. *Irish Times*. Available: http://www.irishtimes.com/news/government-to-underpin-banks-with-10bn-plan-1.923794. Accessed 7 Apr 2017.

Blyth, M. 2013. *Austerity: The History of a Dangerous Idea*. Oxford: Oxford University Press.

Bowman, P. 2008. Ireland: Housing Crash, Credit Crunch, Poses Need to Nationalise Banks [online]. *In Defence of Marxism*. Available: https://www.marxist.com/ireland-housing-crash-credit-crunch.htm. Accessed 6 Apr 2017.

Brandimarte, W., and D. Bases. 2011. Ireland's Credit Rating Downgraded to Junk by Moody's [online]. *Huffington Post*. Available: http://www.huffingtonpost.com/2011/07/12/irish-bonds-downgraded_n_896305.html. Accessed 7 Apr 2017.

Browne, V. 1982. John Kelly—Why I Went to the Backbenches [online]. *politico.ie*. Available: http://politico.ie/archive/john-kelly-why-i-went-backbenches. Accessed 7 Apr 2017.

Byrne, C. 2009. Lenihan and McWilliams Lock Horns Over Book's "Late Night Meeting" Claim [online]. *Irish Independent*. Available: http://www.independent.ie/irish-news/lenihan-and-mcwilliams-lock-horns-over-books-late-night-meeting-claim-26577660.html. Accessed 7 Apr 2017.

Carswell, S. 2008. Irish Bailout Cheapest in World, Says Lenihan [online]. *Irish Times*. Available: http://www.irishtimes.com/business/irish-bailout-cheapest-in-world-says-lenihan-1.900393. Accessed 7 Apr 2017.

Collins, S. 2015. Labour Party Must Now Fight for Its Survival [online]. *Irish Times*. Available: http://www.irishtimes.com/opinion/stephen-collins-labour-party-must-now-fight-for-its-survival-1.2120517. Accessed 8 Apr 2017.

Considine, J., and D. Duffy. 2010. Tales of Expansionary Fiscal Contractions in Two European Countries: Hindsight and Foresight. *Journal of Public Finance and Public Choice* 27: 147–167.

Coulter, C. 2015. Ireland Under Austerity: An Introduction to the Book. In *Ireland Under Austerity*. Manchester: Manchester University Press.

Coulter, C., F. Arqueros-Fernandez, and A. Nagle. 2017. Austerity's Model Pupil: The Ideological Uses of Ireland During the Eurozone Crisis. *Critical Sociology* 48 (95). https://doi.org/10.1177/0896920517718038.

Cox, L. 2013. Why Are the Irish Not Resisting Austerity? [online]. *openDemocracy*. Available: http://www.opendemocracy.net/can-europe-make-it/laurence-cox/why-are-irish-not-resisting-austerity. Accessed 6 Apr 2017.

———. 2016. The Irish Water Charges Movement: Theorising 'the Social Movement in General' [online]. *academia.edu*. Available: https://www.academia.edu/31075937/The_Irish_water_charges_movement_theorising_the_social_movement_in_general. Accessed 28 Jan 2017.

Cullen, P. 2016. Apollo House Protesters to Meet Owners Over Occupation [online]. *Irish Times*. Available: http://www.irishtimes.com/news/ireland/irish-news/apollo-house-protesters-to-meet-owners-over-occupation-1.2910660?mode=sample&auth-failed=1&pw-origin=http%3A%2F%2Fwww.irishtimes.com%2Fnews%2Fireland%2Firish-news%2Fapollo-house-protesters-to-meet-owners-over-occupation-1.2910660. Accessed 8 Apr 2017.

Donovan, D., and A.E. Murphy. 2013. *The Fall of the Celtic Tiger: Ireland and the Euro Debt Crisis*. Oxford: Oxford University Press.

Dooley, N. 2015. The Real Political Economy of Ireland [online]. *speri.comment: The Political Economy Blog*. Available: http://speri.dept.shef.ac.uk/2015/09/02/real-political-economy-ireland/. Accessed 5 Apr 2017.

Doris, A., D. O'Neill, and O. Sweetman. 2014. *Wage Flexibility and the Great Recession: The Response of the Irish Labour Market* [online]. National University of Ireland Maynooth. Available: https://www.tcd.ie/Economics/assets/pdf/Aedin%20Doris%20 et%20al%20Wage%20Flexibility.pdf. Accessed 25 May 2016.

Dougherty, C. 2008. How Sweden Solved Its Bank Crisis. *New York Times*, September 22.

Drudy, P.J., and M.L. Collins. 2011. Ireland: From Boom to Austerity. *Cambridge Journal of Regions, Economy and Society* 4 (3): 339–354.

Duncan, P. 2014. Dublin Property Prices 24% Higher in a Year [online]. *Irish Times*. Available: http://www.irishtimes.com/news/ireland/irish-news/dublin-property-prices-24-higher-in-a-year-1.2015668. Accessed 8 Apr 2017.

Elliott, L., and J. Treanor. 2011. Ireland Forced into New £21bn Bailout by Debt Crisis [online]. *The Guardian*. Available: http://www.theguardian.com/world/2011/mar/31/ireland-new-bailout-euro-crisis. Accessed 7 Apr 2017.

Fahy, L., and S. Meier. 2009. Government 'Squandering' Money in Bank Bailout Plan [online]. *Irish Independent*. Available: http://www.independent.ie/business/irish/government-squandering-money-in-bank-bailout-plan-26571958.html. Accessed 7 Apr 2017.

Farrell, S., C. Meehan, G. Murphy, and K. Rafter. 2011. Assessing the Irish General Election of 2011: A Roundtable. *New Hibernia Review* 15 (3): 36–53.

Ferriter, D. 2013a. The State We Are and the State We Can Become [online]. *Irish Times*. Available: http://www.irishtimes.com/news/ireland/irish-news/the-state-we-are-and-the-state-we-can-become-1.1624455. Accessed 7 Apr 2017a.

———. 2013b. A Questionable Republic. *Sunday Business Post*, July 28.

Finn, D. 2011. Ireland on the Turn? Political and Economic Consequences of the Crash. *New Left Review* 67: 5–39.

———. 2016. The Adaptable Sinn Féin [online]. *Jacobin*. Available: https://www.jacobinmag.com/2016/02/sinn-fein-gerry-adams-irish-republican-army/. Accessed 21 Apr 2017.

Fleming, D. 2014. Anger at Irish Water Charges Reaches Boiling Point [online]. *BBC News*. Available: http://www.bbc.com/news/business-29426733. Accessed 8 Apr 2017.

Forster, K. 2016. Ireland Jails Three Top Bankers Over Financial Crisis [online]. *The Independent*. Available: http://www.independent.co.uk/news/world/europe/ireland-bankers-jailed-financial-crisis-2008-anglo-irish-bank-a7163711.html. Accessed 7 Apr 2017.

Green, H. 2010. Ruairi Quinn: International Asshole [online]. *The Punishment of Sloth*. Available: https://hughgreen.wordpress.com/2010/05/05/ruairi-quinn-international-asshole/. Accessed 7 Apr 2017.

Hearne, R. 2014. Protests Are a New Type of Active Citizenship Politics Here [online]. *Irish Examiner*. Available: http://www.irishexaminer.com/analysis/protests-are-a-new-type-of-active-citizenship-politics-here-298452.html. Accessed 8 Apr 2017.

Hirst, T. 2014. Here's the Secret Letter that Shows the ECB Forced Ireland to Ask for a Bailout [online]. *Business Insider*. Available: http://www.businessinsider.com/heres-the-secret-letter-that-shows-the-ecb-forced-ireland-to-ask-for-a-bailout-2014-11. Accessed 7 Apr 2017.

Holland, K. 2015. Home Repossessions Accelerate to 60 Each Week [online]. *Irish Times*. Available: http://www.irishtimes.com/news/social-affairs/home-repossessions-accelerate-to-60-each-week-1.2308040. Accessed 8 Apr 2017.

Honahan, P. 2010. *The Irish Banking Crisis Regulatory and Financial Stability Policy 2003–2008: A Report to the Minister for Finance by the Governor of the Central Bank*. Dublin: Central Bank of Ireland.

Howlin, G. 2016. Elitist Far-Left Has Gained Traction but Its Fascism Is Affront to Democracy [online]. *Irish Examiner*. Available: http://www.irishexaminer.com/viewpoints/columnists/gerard-howlin/elitist-far-left-has-gained-traction-but-its-fascism-is-affront-to-democracy-427474.html. Accessed 8 Apr 2017.

Irish Examiner. 2008. O'Keeffe: Medical Card Fiasco Was Collective Cabinet Error [online]. *Irish Examiner*. Available: http://www.irishexaminer.com/ireland/okeeffe-medical-card-fiasco-was-collective-cabinet-error-75358.html. Accessed 7 Apr 2017.

Irish Independent. 2008. Meltdown Monday [online]. *Irish Independent*. Available: http://www.independent.ie/business/world/meltdown-monday-26480973.html. Accessed 6 Apr 2017.

Irish Times. 2010. Was It for This? [online]. *Irish Times*. Available: http://www.irishtimes.com/opinion/was-it-for-this-1.678424. Accessed 20 Apr 2017.

———. 2017. Michael O'Leary Praises Shane Ross Over Bus Éireann Dispute [online]. *Irish Times*. Available: http://www.irishtimes.com/news/politics/michael-o-leary-praises-shane-ross-over-bus-%C3%A9ireann-dispute-1.3033998. Accessed 22 Apr 2017.

Kay, S. 2011. *Celtic Revival?* Lanham: Rowman & Littlefield Publishers.

Keenan, B. 2014. Revealed—The Troika Threats to Bankrupt Ireland [online]. *Irish Independent*. Available: http://www.independent.ie/irish-news/politics/revealed-the-troika-threats-to-bankrupt-ireland-30621197.html. Accessed 20 Apr 2017.

Kelly, M. 2008. Better to Incinerate €1.5bn than Squander It on Anglo Irish Bank [online]. *Irish Times*. Available: http://www.irishtimes.com/opinion/better-to-incinerate-1-5bn-than-squander-it-on-anglo-irish-bank-1.1275609. Accessed 7 Apr 2017.

Kelly, F. 2015. Anti-Austerity Alliance Out of Left-Wing Transfer Pact [online]. *Irish Times*. Available: http://www.irishtimes.com/news/politics/anti-austerity-alliance-out-of-left-wing-transfer-pact-1.2412037. Accessed 8 Apr 2017.

———. 2016. The Full Document: Fine Gael-Fianna Fáil Deal for Government [online]. *Irish Times*. Available: http://www.irishtimes.com/news/politics/the-full-document-fine-gael-fianna-f%C3%A1il-deal-for-government-1.2633572. Accessed 8 Apr 2017.

Lavery, B., and T.L. O'Brien. 2005. For Insurance Regulators, Trails Lead to Dublin [online]. *New York Times*. Available: https://www.nytimes.com/2005/04/01/business/worldbusiness/for-insurance-regulators-trails-lead-to-dublin.html. Accessed 7 Apr 2017.

Lee, J. 1989. *Ireland, 1912–1985*. Cambridge: Cambridge University Press.

Lee-Murphy, M. 2015. Ireland's Resurgent Left [online]. *Jacobin*. Available: https://www.jacobinmag.com/2015/01/ireland-water-charges-sinn-fein/. Accessed 8 Apr 2017.

Lewis, M. 2011. When Irish Eyes Are Crying [online]. *Vanity Fair*. Available: http://www.vanityfair.com/business/features/2011/03/michael-lewis-ireland-201103?printable=true. Accessed 10 Dec 2011.

Lucey, B. 2009. Nama Set to Shift Wealth to Lenders and Developers [online]. *Irish Times*. Available: http://www.irishtimes.com/opinion/nama-set-to-shift-wealth-to-lenders-and-developers-1.725976. Accessed 7 Apr 2017.

Lucey, C. 2014. IBEC and Unions Fooling Themselves Over Austerity. *Sunday Business Post*, July 13.

Mair, P. 1992. Explaining the Absence of Class Politics in Ireland. In *The Development of Industrial Society in Ireland*, ed. J.H. Goldthorpe and C.T. Whelan. Oxford: Oxford University Press.

Maleney, I. 2014. An 'Unmitigated Disaster': 8 Reasons It's Kicking Off in Ireland [online]. *Novara Media*. Available: http://novara.media/2ditmFn. Accessed 8 Apr 2017.

McAleavey, R. 2015. The Hard Left, Redux [online]. *Medium*. Available: https://medium.com/@hiredknave/the-hard-left-redux-33c59de7202c. Accessed 8 Apr 2017.

McCabe, C. 2011. *Sins of the Father*. Stroud: Nonsuch Publishing Limited.

McDonough, T. 2010. All the Wrong Options Have Been Pursued [online]. *Irish Times*. Available: http://www.irishtimes.com/opinion/all-the-wrong-options-have-been-pursued-1.634597. Accessed 7 Apr 2017.

McNeice, S. 2013. POLL: The Cut to Social Welfare for Under-25s Will… [online]. *newstalk.com*. Available: http://www.newstalk.com/POLL:-The-cut-to-social-welfare-for-under25s-will. Accessed 8 Apr 2017.

McWilliams, D. 2008a. *The Pope's Children*. Hoboken: John Wiley & Sons.

———. 2008b. State Must Act as a Safeguard. *Sunday Business Post*, September 21.

———. 2010. *Follow the Money*. Dublin: Gill & Macmillan.

———. 2014. Public Sector: The Insider Story. *Sunday Business Post*, September 1.

Mercille, J. 2013. Why Don't the Irish Protest Against Austerity? [online]. *thejournal.ie*. Available: http://www.thejournal.ie/readme/why-dont-we-protest-in-ireland-1177504-Nov2013/. Accessed 6 Apr 2017.

———. 2014. The Role of the Media in Fiscal Consolidation Programmes: The Case of Ireland. *Cambridge Journal of Economics* 38 (2): 281–300.

Molloy, T. 2012. Irish Meltdown Was World's Worst Since 1930s—IMF Report [online]. *Irish Independent*. Available: http://www.independent.ie/business/irish/irish-meltdown-was-worlds-worst-since-1930s-imf-report-26869930.html. Accessed 20 Apr 2017.

Morris, J. 2016. The UK's 100 Most Powerful Economists [online]. *City A.M.* Available: http://www.cityam.com/221308/uk-economists-top-100-george-magnus-stephen-king-these-are-most-influential-economic-experts. Accessed 7 Apr 2017.

Münchau, W. 2013. Ireland Shows the Way with Its Debt Deal [online]. *FT.com*. Available: http://www.ft.com/intl/cms/s/0/a4564eae-713a-11e2-9d5c-00144feab49a.html#axzz2KXKnfWTD. Accessed 8 Apr 2017.

NAMA Wine Lake. 2012. €69.7bn, the Gross Cost of Bailing Out Ireland's Banks (So Far) [online]. *namawinelake*. Available: https://namawinelake.wordpress.com/2012/07/08/e69-7bn-the-gross-cost-of-bailing-out-irelands-banks-so-far/. Accessed 7 Apr 2017.

Neate, R. 2014. Bono: Controversial Tax Laws Have Brought Ireland the Only Prosperity It Has Ever Known [online]. *The Guardian*. Available: http://www.theguardian.com/world/2014/oct/12/bono-tax-laws-bring-ireland-prosperity-apple-google-u2. Accessed 8 Apr 2017.

Nyberg, P. 2011. *Misjudging Risk: Causes of the Systemic Banking Crisis in Ireland*. Dublin: Ministry of Finance.

O'Brien, C. 2015. Ireland at Risk of Reaching US Levels of Income Inequality, Says Study [online]. *Irish Times*. Available: http://www.irishtimes.com/news/social-affairs/ireland-at-risk-of-reaching-us-levels-of-income-inequality-says-study-1.2105125. Accessed 8 Apr 2017.

O'Byrne, M. 2016. How Finance Is Shaping Dublin's Ongoing Housing Crisis [online]. *Dublin Inquirer*. Available: http://www.dublininquirer.com/2016/02/17/mick-how-finance-shaping-dublin-housing-crisis/. Accessed 8 Apr 2017.

O'Carroll, L., and S. Collins 2016. Irish Leaders Fear Brexit Will Bring Economic Disaster. *The Guardian*, October 16.

O'Connor, F. 2017. The Presence and Absence of Protest in Austerity Ireland. In *Late Neoliberalism and Its Discontents in the Economic Crisis Comparing Social Movements in the European Periphery*, 65–98. Cham: Springer International Publishing.

O'Connor, N., and C. Staunton. 2015. *Cherishing All Equally: Economic Inequality in Ireland*. Dublin: Think-tank for Action on Social Change (TASC).

O'Malley, E. 2016. The Centre Still Holds—So FF Should Make Hay [online]. *Irish Independent.* Available: http://www.independent.ie/opinion/comment/the-centre-still-holds-so-ff-should-make-hay-34534981.html. Accessed 8 Apr 2017.

Ó Riain, S. 2014. *The Rise and Fall of Ireland's Celtic Tiger.* Cambridge: Cambridge University Press.

O'Sullivan, M. 2010. Ireland's Bubble: The Great Transformation. In *Understanding Ireland's Economic Crisis*, ed. A.J. Leddin. Dublin: Blackhall Publishing Limited.

O'Toole, F. 2009. *Ship of Fools: How Corruption and Stupidity Sank the Celtic Tiger.* London: Faber and Faber Ltd.

———. 2015. Radical Change the Only Way to Achieve Stability [online]. *Irish Times.* Available: http://www.irishtimes.com/opinion/fintan-o-toole-radical-change-the-only-way-to-achieve-stability-1.2466369. Accessed 8 Apr 2017.

Phillips, M. 2016. Ireland's 26% Growth Is More Paper Tiger than Celtic Tiger [online]. *Quartz.* Available: https://qz.com/730030/irelands-26-growth-is-more-paper-tiger-than-celtic-tiger/. Accessed 6 Apr 2017.

Power, S.A., and D. Nussbaum. 2014. The Fightin' Irish? Not When It Comes to Recession and Austerity [online]. *The Guardian.* Available: http://www.theguardian.com/science/head-quarters/2014/jul/24/the-fightin-irish-not-when-it-comes-to-recession-and-austerity. Accessed 7 Apr 2017.

Puirséil, N. 2007. *The Irish Labour Party, 1922–73.* Dublin: University College Dublin Press.

Regling, K., and M. Watson. 2010. *A Preliminary Report on The Sources of Ireland's Banking Crisis* [online]. Available: http://www.bankinginquiry.gov.ie/Preliminary%20Report%20into%20Ireland%27s%20Banking%20Crisis%2031%20May%202010.pdf. Accessed 5 Nov 2017.

Roche, W.K., P.J. O'Connell, and A. Prothero. 2016. *Austerity and Recovery in Ireland* [online]. Oxford: Oxford University Press. Available: http://www.oxfordscholarship.com/view/10.1093/acprof:oso/9780198792376.001.0001/acprof-9780198792376-chapter-1.

RTE. 2013. 'Historic Day' as Troika Concludes Visit [online]. *RTE.ie.* Available: https://www.rte.ie/news/2013/1107/485113-troika-final-visit/. Accessed 8 Apr 2017.

Ryner, M., and A. Cafruny. 2016. *The European Union and Global Capitalism.* London: Palgrave.

Scott, M. 2016. Ireland to Appeal Tax Ruling in Apple Case [online]. *New York Times.* Available: https://www.nytimes.com/2016/09/03/technology/apple-ireland-tax-ruling-appeal.html. Accessed 8 Apr 2017.

Sheehan, B. 2010. End of Social Partnership as Public Sector Talks Collapse [online]. *Eurofound.* Available: https://www.eurofound.europa.eu/observatories/eurwork/articles/industrial-relations/end-of-social-partnership-as-public-sector-talks-collapse. Accessed 7 Apr 2017.

Sheehy, C. 2015. Bank Guarantee Was 'the Only Decision' Says David McWilliams [online]. *Irish Independent*. Available: http://www.independent.ie/business/irish/banking-inquiry/bank-guarantee-was-the-only-decision-says-david-mcwilliams-31026335.html. Accessed 7 Apr 2017.

Steward, A. 2017. 'We Are Staying Here,' Says Home Sweet Home Movement [online]. *Hotpress*. Available: http://www.hotpress.com/We-are-staying-here-says-Home-Sweet-Home-movement/19484572.html. Accessed 8 Apr 2017.

Szolucha, A. 2013. No Stable Ground: Living Real Democracy in Occupy. *Interface*: 5 (2): 18–38.

———. 2014. Real Politics in Occupy: Transcending the Rules of the Day. *Globalizations*: 12 (1): 1–17.

Taft, M. 2015. Begruding the Recovery [online]. *Notes on the Front*. Available: http://notesonthefront.typepad.com/politicaleconomy/2015/11/begruding-the-recovery.html. Accessed 8 Apr 2017.

thejournal.ie. 2014. 30 Days in September: An Oral History of the Bank Guarantee [online]. *thejournal.ie*. Available: http://www.thejournal.ie/bank-guarantee-oral-history-30-september-2008-1103254-Dec2014/. Accessed 7 Apr 2017.

———. 2015. The Story of 'NO' … 15 Moments that Have Defined the Irish Water Protest Movement [online]. *thejournal.ie*. Available: http://www.thejournal.ie/irish-water-protests-timeline-1963363-Aug2015/. Accessed 8 Apr 2017.

———. 2016. 'Mea Culpa and I'm Sorry About that': Enda Finally Apologises for THAT "Whingers" Remark [online]. *thejournal.ie*. Available: http://www.thejournal.ie/enda-kenny-whingers-fianna-fail-2616864-Feb2016/. Accessed 8 Apr 2017.

Tierney, R. 2015. Read Em and Weep [online]. *Rabble*. Available: http://www.rabble.ie/2015/10/20/read-em-and-weep/. Accessed 8 Apr 2017.

Whelan, K. 2012. Briefing Paper on the IBRC, ELA and Promissory Notes [online]. *www.karlwhelan.com*. Available: http://www.socialjustice.ie/sites/default/files/attach/policy-issue-article/3086/2012-02-15-karlwhelanbriefingtooireachtascommonibrcelaandpromissorynotes.pdf. Accessed 7 Apr 2017.

CHAPTER 7

The Unfolding of Spain's Political Crisis: From the Squares to the Ballot Box

Mònica Clua-Losada

Abstract Spain's economic crisis became a political crisis from 2011, when protest movements erupted in response to the direct effects of the former and the austerity regime that followed. However, this chapter suggests that the particularities of developments from 2011 are explicable not simply with reference to the proximate economic crisis but require an examination of Spain's broader transition from dictatorship from the 1970s and its Europeanisation thereafter. Prioritising stability, that transition was built upon the marginalisation or incorporation of non-mainstream groups and the formation of a narrow two-party system. It is against this backdrop that this chapter traces post-2011 events: the emergence of the 'indignados' movement, the growth of separatism in Catalonia and the institutional challenges to the status quo at both local and national levels.

Keywords Spanish politics • Political crisis • Transition • Social movements • Catalonia

M. Clua-Losada (✉)
Department of Political Science, University of Texas – Rio Grande Valley, Edinburg, TX, USA

O. Parker, D. Tsarouhas (eds.), *Crisis in the Eurozone Periphery*, Building a Sustainable Political Economy: SPERI Research & Policy, https://doi.org/10.1007/978-3-319-69721-5_7

This chapter focuses on the changes to the political landscape that have unfolded in Spain during the 2011–16 political crisis. It does so by tracing the events and movements from the 15-M protests in 2011 to the situation of political impasse that characterised Spanish politics in 2016. In June 2016, Spaniards were called to the polls for the second time in six months, with the media wondering if we were witnessing an imminent collapse of the two-party system that had characterised Spanish politics for the previous 30 years. The previous months and years had seen the emergence of two national political parties—*Podemos* and *Ciudadanos*—as electoral forces seriously competing with the mainstream social democratic *Partido Socialista Obrero Espanol* (PSOE) and conservative *Partido Popular* (PP). The election results signalled their enduring importance on the Spanish political landscape, even as the status quo endured.

The emergence of this new politics can be traced to the 2008 global financial crisis, which affected the Spanish economy particularly badly (see Buendia, Chap. 3, this volume). This crisis and the responses to it—in a word, austerity—had huge social consequences, with significant increases in unemployment, poverty rates and housing repossessions, as well as decreasing wages and job security. It was not, however, until 15 May 2011, when a popular outcry brought hundreds of thousands of people onto the streets, that this translated into a political crisis. This outcry did not lead to immediate change to the political status quo; indeed, the popular outcry in the squares was followed by an unprecedented landslide victory for the conservative *Partido Popular* (PP) at the municipal level (and in the case of Catalonia, by the Christian-Democrat/Liberal coalition, *Convergència i Unió*). This was initially understood by many on the political Left, as indicating that popular protest should be limited when the Left is in power because it can weaken the electoral chances of left-wing parties already in office. However, as the chapter will show, the 15-M protests were the starting point for the more substantive change that would become apparent in national politics in 2015–16.

More generally, those protests can be read as the first moments of a regime exhaustion, which, at the time of writing, remained incomplete. To understand the enduring resilience of the system and the particularities of the opposition that has emerged to it in the Spanish context, it is important to consider the historical lineages of what is currently happening and the associated institutional limits to change. Thus, while the main focus is

2011–16, this period is explored and explained in relation to the broader context of democratisation in Spain that has been under way since the 1970s.

The chapter is divided into two principal parts: the first explores the key political processes that led to the institutional status quo in the Spanish state and in particular, the historical context of a transition to democracy based around an elite pact during the 1970s and the subsequent process of Europeanisation during the 1980s. The second part focuses on the period between 2011 and 2016, emphasising two interdependent processes. On the one hand, the appearance of breaks or ruptures with the pre-existing institutional order described in the first part and, on the other, the (from certain perspectives, surprising) resilience of such an order.

The Historical Context

In order to understand the institutional setup in contemporary Spain, it is useful to go back to the 1970s and the transition to democracy that was heralded across the world as the perfect model of the third wave of democratisation (Huntington 1991). The Spanish road to democracy can be delineated in relation to three key factors. First, the terms of the democratic transition, in particular, the type of political system it gave rise to and the ways in which trade unions and left movements were accommodated within that system. Second, the Europeanisation that took place in the process of democratic transition (and consolidation) in Spain. Third and finally, the accommodation of the historic nations of Catalonia, the Basque Country and Galicia in the new configuration of the state. This final factor will be considered separately in the second substantive part of the chapter as it signals a key challenge to the continuity of the Spanish state as we know it. In this first part, I will explore the first two factors in order to contextualise the current political crisis in Spain.

The Spanish Transition

The current political settlement in Spain followed the death of Franco in 1975. After nearly 40 years of military dictatorship, Spain developed what would become a model for democratic transitions around the world (see e.g. Grugel 2002; Gunther 1992; Huntington 1991; Tarrow 1995). This model was based around an elite pact, which was initiated and designed by the dictatorial regime that preceded it. The Spanish elite pact united key actors in the state in order to maintain stability. It incorporated the Left (both parties and trade unions) and the bourgeoisie sections of Catalan and Basque nationalism into state structures. It neutralised the church and the military by allowing them to maintain a strong influence on certain aspects of society (such as education, for the church). Therefore, while a two-party system emerged, it depended on the incorporation into the major parties and state apparatus of a plurality of social forces. Spain's elite pact was able to succeed due to patterns of 'pact making and demobilization from above' (Tarrow 1995: 229). In particular, the incorporation of left-wing organisations into the state and other state and substate political institutions had an important demobilising effect. While the Francoist dictatorship had encountered resistance from a vibrant clandestine pro-democracy movement, the transition to democracy was characterised by the incorporation of these movements into the institutions and the *removal* of politics from the streets. This led to a mutation of already existing authoritarian tendencies (Clua-Losada and Ribera-Almandoz 2017) and the depoliticisation of key civil society organisations, such as neighbourhood associations.

A tension between incorporation and marginalisation was clear in the processes that saw the main trade union confederations, *Union General de Trabajadores* (UGT) and *Comisiones Obreras* (CCOO), being incorporated into corporatist structures, while neighbourhood associations (which had been crucial in maintaining pro-democracy mobilisations during the final years of the dictatorship) were depoliticised and marginalised through different settlements at the local level. Consequently, this led to the destruction of a societal counter-power, and opposing groups either withered away or were integrated into the state apparatus. The politics of compromise was particularly harmful to workers' interests, as unions and leftist parties were required 'to persuade workers to accept limitations – or even sacrifices – in the pursuit of immediate economic interests by virtue of broad political conceptions and commitments' (Fishman 1982: 288). The development of corporatist structures in Spain and their role in demobilising the working class has been widely reported. Bermeo, for instance, affirms that, 'corporatism is supposed to institutionalize labor power but in Spain, pact-making accompanied the disintegration of organized labor instead' (1994: 609).

The imperative of stability provided a platform for the development of a type of democratic culture based around 'presidentialism'—the notion that a majority government has the legitimacy to rule as it wishes—as we have seen develop in some Latin American contexts (Mainwaring and Shugart 1997). This means that, for example in 2011, the PP interpreted its absolute majority as a green light to rule with a free rein. Paradoxically though, this happened at a time when social protest was reaching its peak in contemporary Spain. The development of these two parallel processes—a dominant one-party government plus social unrest—characterised both the 1970s and the period between 2011 and 2016.

Colomer (1998) has argued that the establishment of a system in which the ruling party (and, in particular, the executive branch) has a large amount of leeway should be understood in relation to the inherent contradictions created by Spain's particular transition to democracy. Rather than a pluralist system, a bipolar model emerged, which, to this day, primarily addresses a deeply ingrained fear of instability (1998: 177). This model reflects some continuities from the authoritarian Francoist Fundamental Laws; for instance, it includes a constitutional framework that provides primacy to 'executive dominance over parliament' (Hopkin 2005: 8). This, of course, begs the question as to whether the Spanish transition to democracy has been a complete triumph after all (Heywood 2005: 39).

Indeed, the period since 2011 can be read as the weakening—if not failure—of both the incorporation and marginalisation strategies. The state appears unable to further incorporate different interests or secure their depoliticisation. On the contrary, we have seen a myriad of processes of repoliticisation of civil society. However, this has not led to any shift in the 'presidentialism' mentioned above; rather it has accentuated its authoritarian traits. To highlight but one example, the PP's rejection of a large public petition initiated by the *Plataforma de Afectados de la Hipoteca* (Platform of those affected by mortgages), PAH, in favour of reforming mortgage law in 2013 showed the unwillingness of the government to make concessions.

This can be understood as part of a broader shift in the way in which hegemony is maintained via an authoritarian turn. Such a turn relies upon 'the explicit exclusion and marginalization of subordinate social groups through the constitutionally and legally engineered self-disempowerment of nominally democratic institutions, governments and parliaments' (Bruff 2014: 116). In Spain, the democratic process has been emptied of even the most basic formal procedures. Since 2011, the country has been ruled by executive royal decrees rather than by parliamentary debate or social dialogue, therefore not allowing opposition parties or groups to contribute to new legislation, and thereby eliminating processes of political negotiation (Clua-Losada and Ribera-Almandoz 2017). In its first year, the PP government passed 28 acts by royal decree and 16 laws (El Diario.es 20/12/2012).

Europeanisation

The second key contextualising factor in the Spanish case is European integration. The process of European integration has been used as a validation mechanism for Spanish democracy. Indeed, the 'European' excuse has been a useful currency 'to legitimate or de-legitimate certain policies or political proposals' (Moreno 2013: 218). More often than not, 'Europe' has been seen as a positive force by the Left, and while historically Euroscepticism has also been of a leftist nature, it has never been a particularly strong force in a country where the Left has been preoccupied with leaving behind the Fascist connotations of recent (and past) Spanish nationalism.

As Spourdalakis (2014) highlights, unlike in Greece, where there has long been a strong anti-EU leftist discourse, in Spain, the narratives surrounding resistance and protest movements have focused primarily on 'internal' issues. For instance, there has been a focus on democratic and constitutional rights, the electoral system, the relationship between the banking industry and the different layers of state institutions and the specificities of Spain's political system and how it has managed the crisis. In other words, what is strikingly different is the perception of Europe in the political narratives of both countries. The Left in Spain has often been unequivocally European (Clua-Losada 2015), a willing victim of the European single currency and the economic straitjacket it offers (see Parker and Tsarouhas, Chap. 1, this volume). Unlike in Greece there has been almost no debate on the Left regarding membership of the EU. As a senior economic adviser, and former MP in the Catalan Parliament, to *Iniciativa per Catalunya–Els Verds* (ICV) explained, 'if we initiate such a debate, it will mean that we are accepting we got it wrong in the 1980s and 1990s when we argued in favour of the single currency. We are not ready to admit we were wrong' (interview with senior economic adviser to ICV, June 2012).

In summary, current debates around the authoritarian turn of the state (Tansel 2017) are best understood in the Spanish context against the historical backdrop of both the transition to democracy and Europeanisation.

The former was in many ways incomplete and the latter in certain respects served to rhetorically legitimate that incompleteness even in the context of the Eurozone crisis. As Jean Grugel reminds us, dictatorships are totalising regimes that impregnate all areas of social and political life. They do not have a clear end point, but rather '[the price of dictatorships] continues to be paid for a long time after the regime actually falls' (Grugel 2002: 87).

Spain's Political Crisis and Regime Resilience

The second part of this chapter focuses on the period between 2011 and 2016. This period, which has certainly been tumultuous and dramatic, has brought about the possibility of systemic and institutional change. However, at the time of writing, this change had not materialised. Instead, what we witnessed was an impasse, characterised by push and pull, between a resilient regime and various forms of resistance to it. In what follows, I first consider the appearance of large-scale protest movements since May 2011, which shook up existing political parties and civil society organisations. Second, I explore the challenge presented by the rise and mass appeal of the Catalan pro-independence movement. Finally, I highlight the appearance of new political actors, on both the Left and the Right, and show how these new actors were pushing for new forms of engagement with the institutions while simultaneously finding themselves restrained by what remains of the 1978 regime.

The Rise of New Protest Movements

The political, financial and social crisis that engulfed Spain after 2008 saw the appearance of non-political (yet, highly politicised) grassroots movements with mass appeal. Most notably it led to the advent of the 15-M movement, whose participants are often referred to as the *Indignados* (the indignant). Given the impact of the crisis on housing and public services, movements focused on highlighting those issues also arose: among many others, the abovementioned *PAH* and the so-called *Mareas* ('tides') focused particularly on healthcare services and education (for a detailed analysis of the different protest movements that have appeared in Spain since 2008, see Bailey et al. 2017).

In a context of acute economic crisis (and a crisis of economic crisis management—see Buendia, Chap. 3, this volume) millions took to the streets in 2011, chanting the slogans 'they do not represent us' and 'we are not commodities in the hands of bankers and politicians'. It was the year that signalled the start of a possible rupture within the existing order. The failure of traditional left-wing parties and trade unions to pose a challenge, or even offer a reactive defence, to the management of the crisis was one of the reasons why so many people found no alternative but to occupy the squares. But the 15-M moment was primarily a critique of attempts by Spain's mainstream parties (PSOE and PP) and the EU to manage the crisis; a critique that it shared with the Left. Indeed, while the 15-M represented a break with existing structures, it had been simultaneously fed and watered from existing left-wing traditions. For instance, on 29 September 2010, the main trade union confederations issued a call for a general strike in response to the initial austerity package imposed by the socialist Zapatero administration, which included a 5–10 per cent pay cut for public sector employees, as well as a highly regressive labour reform, which removed barriers to dismissals. It has been noted that this was a rather lukewarm call (López and Rodríguez 2011: 24), probably due to the fact that the socialist PSOE—a traditional union ally—was in government. What was most noteworthy about the strike for current purposes was the way in which it provided the space for different social movements to interact and in that respect laid the foundation for what would follow. Notably, many participants in that strike were later organisers of the 15-M demonstrations and square occupations.

Concurrent with the development of the 15-M, the PAH was also growing in importance. Created in 2009 by a group of housing activists, who had been protesting during the 2000s against the consequences of the housing bubble (such as astronomically high house prices), the PAH both fed into the 15-M and benefited hugely from it. When protesters left the squares, the PAH offered homes to those activists who had experienced a life-changing involvement in a resistance movement, and were not ready to go back to non-political activity. The PAH had four principal aims. First, the prevention of repossessions and evictions through direct protest outside the evictees' homes on the day of the eviction. Second, the development of collective negotiation strategies with repossessing banks, which also included activities of more direct civil disobedience at times. Third, the lobbying of political parties and the government to change mortgage contract legislation. Finally, the rehousing of people in need in squatted homes owned by banks.

While the 15-M, the PAH and, to a lesser extent, the various *Mareas* have been widely researched and held up as key examples of the high level of mobilisation within Spanish society during the crisis, there have been other examples in the creation of alternative structures. For instance, Wigger (2016) shows how the revived solidarity economy—defined as 'cooperatives and other horizontally organized and democratically run self-management practices' (Ibid.)—in Spain (and particularly in Catalonia) has strong historical connections to previous movements of struggle while simultaneously being strongly connected to the rise of mass grassroots movements after 2011. The appearance and organisational characteristics of these movements matter, particularly in terms of understanding what has happened in more formal political contexts during the crisis.

The Breaking Up of the State: The Catalan Challenge

The transition to democracy in Spain was based on important compromises, as the first part of the chapter has shown. On the one hand, this consisted of the incorporation or marginalisation of the political Left. On the other hand, and this is where the focus turns in this section, it consisted of the cooptation of the 'historic nationalities' into the state. Spain's recognition of its historic nationalities in the Spanish constitution of 1978 has often been heralded as an example of accommodation. Yet the question has remained far from resolved, as the current movement for Catalan self-determination demonstrates. While the movement for self-determination is certainly connected to the economic crisis that began in 2008 (and the broader political crisis that followed), it is far more closely connected to the political crisis that was postponed in 1978.

If we consider the elite pact of 1978 as a key configurative moment of modern Spanish democracy, then a crucial aspect of the pact was the relationship between Catalonia and Spain. This had never been an easy relationship and after 40 years of political, cultural and linguistic repression, it was clear that Spain needed to find a way to secure consent from one of its most industrialised and productive regions. In addition, and just as important, was the concern of the Catalan bourgeoisie to placate rising working-class organisations in workplaces and communities, which were threatening the stability of capitalist accumulation. This led to the 1978 Spanish Constitution being co-written by some of the leaders of the Catalan bourgeois parties (*Convergència i Unió*). In securing a good seat at the table, they also secured what they perceived to be a good settlement for their interests in Catalonia (Elias 2015). The development of the Catalan self-determination movement, particularly from around 2010, represented the deepest erosion of the elite pact of 1978.

The 2012 Catalan election called by the then president, Artur Mas, earlier than required, signalled the acute tension in relations between Catalonia and the Spanish central government. The election was called after it became clear that negotiations for further devolution had stalled, and the promise of delivering a referendum on self-determination had been made. For some, this raised the question of whether this was 'the first step towards independence' (Martí 2013). This was linked to an enormous demonstration in Catalonia, which saw 1.5 million people take to the streets in Barcelona on Catalonia's national day (11 September).

A key factor in the erosion of the Spanish elite pact was the self-destruction of the Catalan coalition led by Mas. *CiU* was the most successful electoral coalition in Catalan political history, composed of *Convergència Democràtica de Catalunya* (CDC), a centre-right liberal party and *Unió Democràtica de Catalunya* (UDC), a right-wing Christian-Democratic party. Between 1979 and 2014, the CiU coalition stood in every election (EU, state, regional and municipal) and between 1980 and 2003 they were the governing coalition in Catalonia. However, party differences began to publicly emerge around 2010–11, primarily because of their different visions of Catalonia's relationship with Spain, with CDC adopting a more pro-independence stand. These differences were born out of the distinct roles performed by the two parties. While a majority of CDC MPs were located in the Catalan parliament, UDC's role in the coalition's division of labour was primarily to serve in the Spanish Congress. So, for example, the leader of UDC was also the spokesperson of the coalition in Madrid. When, in 2014, the coalition split, it had devastating electoral consequences particularly for UDC, which was wiped off the political map. CDC had to rebrand itself and suffered a legitimacy crisis following several corruption scandals (an issue it shared with the other partners of the broader elite pact, the PP and PSOE).

The underlying motivation for the increasing Catalan pro-independence sentiment was presented by many in the mass media as a self-interested desire to secure economic resources for an already relatively prosperous Spanish region in a time of recession. But this is at best a partial assessment. Key to the rise of the movement was the broader inability of Spain to accommodate difference and plurality, rooted in the historical context of transition described above. The Spanish state's increasingly authoritarian neoliberalism since 2011 is a manifestation of the inherent weakness of the state institutions that were forged in the 1970s (see also, Clua-Losada and Ribera-Almandoz 2017). It is a state that has become increasingly unable to deal with the internal contradictions and tensions between executive 'presidentialism' and social protest articulated above. As noted, Spain's moments of crisis have been characterised by governing through imposition and an unwillingness to enter into dialogue. In short, then, Catalan pro-independence is about more than economic or even cultural self-interest (Crameri 2015; Gillespie 2015); it is part of the broader popular response to an increasingly authoritarian neoliberalism described in the previous section. In accordance with such a conclusion, Serrano (2013) highlights that support for Catalan independence is complex, with many of those in Catalonia self-identifying with a Spanish identity, supporting a possible secessionist move.

What is perhaps most striking about the crisis is the break-up of the longstanding coalition in Spanish politics between one of the two parties in power and the Catalan nationalists. Since the mid-1980s, whether it was the PSOE or the PP in power, they could govern confidently even if they did not attain an absolute majority. Catalan nationalists had been reliable partners in exchange for further devolution. In fact, the impasse that characterised the results of the general elections of 2015 and 2016 would probably not have happened had *CiU* still been a powerful and willing force of the 1978 elite pact. This erosion, together with the appearance of large protest movements has given rise to two new national-level political movements in Spain. On the one hand, *Ciudadanos* ('Citizens'), a right-wing anti-Catalan-independence party, and on the other, *Podemos* ('We Can') and the different municipal candidatures that appeared in 2015.

New Local Politics

Following their success in the municipal elections in May 2011, the PP went on to secure an absolute majority in the Spanish general election in November of the same year. This created a new environment for the movements that developed through and from the 15-M square occupations and prompted the formulation of new strategies. A combination of direct action, civil disobedience and large mass movements marked the following few years. The movements that developed during this period soon realised, however, that despite these protests the PP government was not willing to negotiate or engage in concessions. This, together with increasing popular sympathy to the claims of the PAH, led key people within the newly emerging social movements to think that the time had come to enter the electoral arena.

This 'institutional assault' was initially most evident at the local level, with the emergence of the so-called new municipalities (Zechner 2015). The May 2015 regional and municipal elections saw support for the PP fall from the close to the 11 million votes they had received in the 2011 municipal election (that occurred a week after the 15-M occupation of the squares) to just under 6 million. A large part of the explanation for this electoral turnaround was the emergence of hundreds of so-called citizen candidatures or municipal movements throughout Spain. Perhaps the most well-known of these was *Barcelona en Comú* (Barcelona in Common) led by Ada Colau, who had previously been the PAH spokesperson. Following these elections, she became the mayor of Barcelona. Similarly, in Madrid, under the banner of *Ahora Madrid* (Now Madrid), the former judge and labour lawyer, Manuela Carmena, was elected as mayor. Other places such as La Coruña, València and Cádiz, to name just the larger cities, saw similar results, with new citizen candidatures removing both the PP and PSOE from some of their traditional strongholds.

The municipal level has always been an important arena of struggle in Spain. It was perhaps in the minds of many in mid-2014, that the achievement of the Second Spanish Republic in 1931—which overthrew the military dictatorship of General Miguel Primo de Rivera—owed much to local mobilisation. At the time, the pro-democracy republican forces met clandestinely and decided that the overthrow of the dictatorship would be possible by organising from below. Many candidatures stood at the municipal election with locally decided names and no evident common national strategy. Many of these candidatures won and proceeded to successfully proclaim the Spanish Republic from the municipalities. This unique process offered an example of a relatively peaceful regime change from below.

The municipal level had already been identified as key by the leaders of the transition. In particular, in the 1990s, national and regional parties recognised the municipal level as a key space for party presence, partly because it was seen as a site where many material and institutional resources could be obtained. For example, key decision-making positions in the *Diputaciones* (which distribute financial resources to parties), are determined by the number of votes a party has received in the province during the municipal elections. Furthermore, the linkage between the saving banks system in Spain (*cajas de ahorros*) and regional and local governments, gave political parties direct access to the banking system. This created many possibilities for connecting local and regional governments with property developers and the banking system (Buendia, Chap. 3, this volume; López and Rodríguez 2011: 17–18).

Moreover, since the 1990s, the local level has become a sphere of experimentation in coalition building for the Left, and those coalitions have proved successful in obtaining local majorities (Ubasart-González 2012). This included the development of political 'white brands' which were created depending on local conditions by national and regional parties. These 'white brands' were locally organised coalitions by national and/or regional parties with local names. It was particularly successful in Catalonia, where many coalitions between Leftist parties obtained majorities at the local level throughout the 1990s and the 2000s.

The focus on municipalities is therefore not entirely new when considered in historical context, and even in recent decades it has been strong in places such as Catalonia (where, for instance, the *Candidatures per la Unitat Popular* (CUP) has been successfully standing in municipal elections). However, it is a recent novelty in the broader Spanish national context that can be traced to the publication in March 2014 of a book entitled *La apuesta municipalista* (The Municipal Bet) by the Madrid-based *Observatorio Metropolitano*. This explicitly aims to transform the spirit of the 15-M into an institutionalisation from below. It understands the local or municipal level as key to untangling and exposing the unhealthy relationship between business, finance and political parties. It is argued that it is precisely at this local level that such relationships are most evident, and therefore, where they have the most detrimental impact on the public interest. Indeed, the local level has been the arena within which parties of the 1978 elite pact have frequently found an enabling location to engage in corrupt practices, thanks to the institutional set up between *cajas de ahorros*, access to money in the *diputaciones* and the ability of local governments to requalify land use.

New National Politics

The local level is not the only one to have been significantly shaken up during this period. Indeed, the 'institutional assault' has also taken place at the national level. Internationally, most of the focus of that 'assault' has been on the rapid and remarkable emergence of *Podemos* (for instance, Tremlett 2015). With its outspoken, media savvy and non-conforming leader, Pablo Iglesias, *Podemos* successfully captured much of the anger and indignation that had been brewing since 2011. It was created by a small group of young, activist political science professors at the *Universidad Complutense* in Madrid, as well as an established group of Trotskyists (*Anticapitalistas*). *Podemos*' key strategy was to obtain political power through the electoral process, and it has pursued a purposefully popular (some would say popul*ist*) rhetorical media and publicity strategy to that end. It does not have a traditional party membership base but rather sympathisers who have registered on its website and are able to vote for key decisions. In line with its stated goal of returning power to the people, some grassroots organising did appear initially, around what they called *círculos* (circles). However, it proved very difficult to manage such a model given Podemos' rapid and unexpected growth and its principal aim of electoral success. Indeed, there was a tension between a centrist approach geared towards such success and the idea of handing power to the people; a tension that led to some dispute within the party and among its supporters, particularly from around 2014–15.

However, the party was highly successful in terms of its central strategy: electoral success. The party's first major success arrived at the 2014 European Parliament elections, when five MEPs were elected, and this certainly was a shock (even to themselves!). Yet, clearly, it showed that the Spanish electorate was ready for a new actor to enter the political arena. The next electoral challenge was the 2015 municipal elections. As discussed above, by that point many of the social movements connected to the PAH and the *Mareas* had started organising citizen candidatures from below. While the citizen candidatures appeared alongside and independent from *Podemos*, eventually *Podemos* opted to support them, rather than to compete electorally with them. These two surprising results gave *Podemos* the belief that they could be successful at the general election in December 2015. However, it was not just *Podemos* that saw an opportunity.

The Spanish establishment was certain that they did not want to scare the financial credit markets and become another Greece. They already had a project in place, led by a young generation of ex-bankers, that contained a good mix of socially liberal policies and neoliberal economics (Campabadal and Miralles 2015). One vehicle for this project was another new, but far more conservative, national political party, *Ciudadanos*, headed by another youthful leader, Albert Rivera. The party gained some notoriety internationally as an emergent moderate centre-liberal force—a 'Podemos of the right' (Kassam 2015)—and for many within Spain, *Ciudadanos* represented the new anti-corruption politics that was appearing across the country. However, the party was not an entirely new phenomenon; it first appeared in Catalonia in 2006, with a strong populist anti-Catalan-nationalism platform. The party won sympathy across Spain and gained votes within Spanish-speaking communities in Catalonia which felt increasingly alienated by the *Catalanism* espoused by the Catalan branch of the PSOE (the PSC, Socialist Party of Catalonia).

Systemic Resilience

The national elections in 2015 and 2016 certainly revealed a system in flux (Parker 2016) and under strain (see Fig. 7.1). On 15 December 2015, the PP and PSOE received the largest vote shares—28 per cent and 22 per cent—of the vote respectively, but with significant reductions as compared with 2011. Indeed, the result marked a break with the two-party system, with *Podemos* receiving 21 per cent and *Ciudadanos* 14 per cent of the vote. The Spanish 'presidential' system described above does not lend itself to a multiparty reality and despite various attempts to form a governing coalition, these ultimately proved unsuccessful. Thus, an unprecedented repeat election was triggered, and it took place on 26 June 2016. As Fig. 7.1 shows, the vote was, once again, very close and similarly split, albeit on a lower turnout. However, in 2016, following a change in leadership, the PSOE controversially reversed its previous position and chose not to oppose the formation of a government by the PP, meaning that Mariano Rajoy became prime minister for a second term in October 2016.

Thus, while these elections clearly marked an important break with the past, they did not lead to a change in the status quo. Indeed, the aftermath of the 2016 election illustrated the resilience of the Spanish party system. The PP, even with large corruption scandals looming and the continued imposition of harsh austerity measures, managed to maintain itself as the party with the largest number of votes. Although the PSOE suffered a large defeat—and lost a significant number of votes in 2016—it was not wiped off the electoral map as a consequence of *Podemos'* rise (a fate which other European socialist parties are facing). Moreover, while *Podemos'* success is unquestionable, the considerable haemorrhaging of votes from 2015 to 2016—even after creating an electoral coalition with *Izquierda*

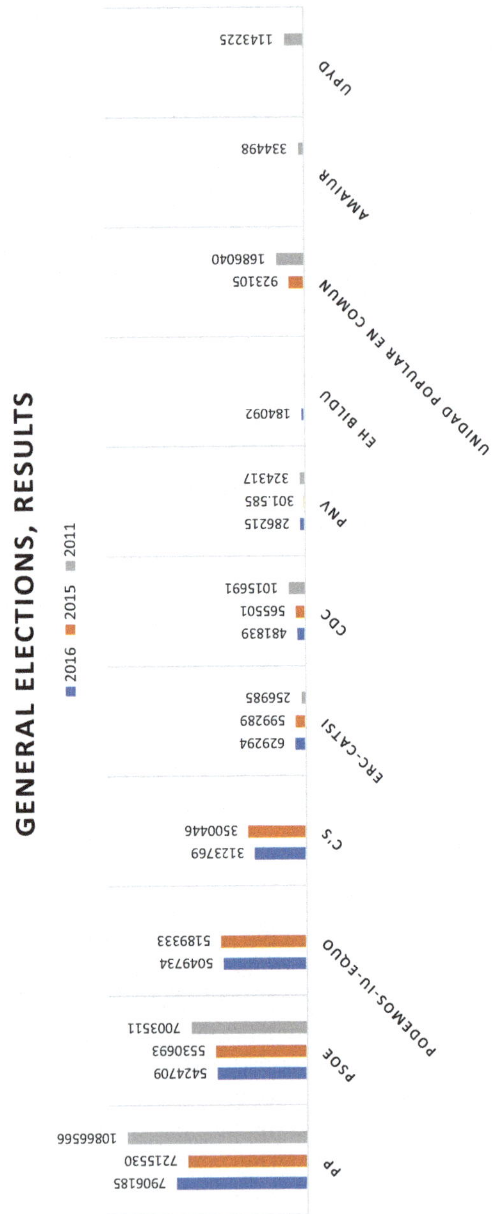

Fig. 7.1 Data from El Pais (http://resultados.elpais.com/elecciones/generales.html)

Unida (IU)—has created strategic debates within the party. Those favouring a clearer left-wing stance—signalled by the coalition with IU—have been criticised by those favouring the more populist outlook and cross-cutting appeal that arguably brought the party its initial successes. Finally, while *Ciudadanos* is now a strong presence in the Spanish electoral and political arena, it has not been the success story that many were hoping, despite striking a popular chord in terms of its anti-corruption and anti-Catalan stance. *Ciudadanos* should have been the centrist mainstream party that either the PP or the PSOE could negotiate with to obtain a workable majority, but it (together with either the PP or the PSOE) failed to obtain enough votes and MPs to avoid the stalemate that characterised Spanish politics from late 2015.

Conclusion

The economic crisis that began to unfold in 2008 became a political crisis in Spain that shook the political establishment. This chapter has focused on three key aspects of that crisis: the rise of new social movements, the strengthening of a powerful Catalan pro-independence movement and the political 'institutional assault' at local, regional and national levels. The appearance of new political parties, both on the left and the right, has had a powerful impact on the further fragmentation of the Spanish political system. The stalemate during the first half of 2016, where neither of the two main parties (PP and PSOE) was able to form a government, was unprecedented. However, while each of these aspects of the political crisis has posed a threat to the status quo, it has proved remarkably resilient. Both the political crisis and the resilience of the system can be understood with reference to the broader historical context described in the opening section of the chapter.

On the one hand, the novelty of the social and political forces that appeared following the onset of the economic crisis and initial governmental responses to it, can be best understood in the context of a broad suppression of plurality within the mainstream that dates back to the 1978 elite pact. This pact maintained a level of political stability in Spain following the transition from dictatorship but the price was the demobilisation of various forms of institutionalised opposition via their incorporation into the state. As the historical contextualisation of the chapter has explored, this stability was maintained thanks to a purposefully designed strategy of depoliticisation. The key ingredients in the mix were the demobilisation of trade unions and neighbourhood organisations via their incorporation into the state, together with the coopting of the Catalan bourgeoisie into the state project developed in 1978, which was and remains a key pillar of the Spanish state. The appearance from 2011 onwards of each of the forms of resistance to the status quo described in this chapter can, therefore, be understood as an important moment of exhaustion of this 1978 elite pact.

On the other hand, the 1978 elite pact has shown its resilience in the face of political opposition. Stability remains a valued ideal for the Spanish establishment and for many voters it means the preservation of a system that has not only showed itself to be corrupt but also unable to deal effectively and equitably with the crisis. Perhaps for similar reasons, there has been no crystallisation of a clear anti-European or anti-EU sentiment in the crisis context, notwithstanding the culpability of the single currency regime and a broader neoliberal orientation promoted at the EU level (Parker and Tsarouhas, Chap. 1, this volume). As noted in the foregoing, in the Spanish case, the stability offered by Europeanisation and democratic consolidation were seen as part of the same package and this explains the muted critique of the EU and single currency project in the Spanish context.

In short, change is certainly ongoing, but at the time of writing, Spanish politics provided a perfect example of Gramsci's famous quote: 'the old is dying but the new cannot be born' (1971: 275–6).

Bibliography

Bailey, D., M. Clua-Losada, N. Huke, and O. Ribera-Almandoz. 2017. *Beyond Defeat and Austerity: Disrupting (the Critical Political Economy) of Neoliberal Europe*. London: Routledge.

Bermeo, N. 1994. Sacrifice, Sequence, and Strength in Successful Dual Transitions: Lessons from Spain. *The Journal of Politics* 56 (3): 601–627.

Bruff, I. 2014. The Rise of Authoritarian Neoliberalism. *Rethinking Marxism: A Journal of Economics, Culture & Society* 26 (1): 113–129.

Campabadal, P., and F. Miralles. 2015. *De Ciutadans a Ciudadanos. La otra cara del neoliberalismo.* Madrid: Ediciones Foca.

Charnock, G., T. Purcell, and R. Ribera-Fumaz. 2014. *The Limits to Capital in Spain. Crisis and Revolt in the European South.* Basingstoke: Palgrave.

Clua-Losada, M. 2015. Tracing the Competitiveness Discourse in Spain: Social Dumping in Disguise? In *Social Dumping: Political Catchphrase or Threat to Labour Standards?* ed. M. Bernaciak. London: Routledge, Routledge Advances in European Politics.

Clua-Losada, M., and O. Ribera-Almandoz. 2017. Authoritarian Neoliberalism and the Disciplining of Labour. In *States of Discipline. Authoritarian Neoliberalism and the Crises of Capitalism*, ed. C.B. Tansel. Lanham: Rowman & Littlefield International.

Colomer, J.M. 1998. *La transición a la democracia: el modelo español*. Barcelona: Anagrama.

Crameri, K. 2015. Political Power and Civil Counterpower: The Complex Dynamics of the Catalan Independence Movement. *Nationalism and Ethnic Politics* 21 (1): 104–120.

Day, R.J.F. 2005. *Gramsci Is Dead. Anarchist Currents in the Newest Social Movements*. London: Pluto Press.

Diario.es. 2012. *Un año de gobierno: 28 decretos y 16 leyes*. Weblink: http://www.eldiario.es/politica/decreto-decretazo-Rajoy-aniversario-gobierno-ley_0_81542266.html. Last accessed 15 Dec 2016.

Dowling, A. 2005. Convergència i Unió, Catalonia and the new Catalanism. In *The Politics of Contemporary Spain*, ed. S. Balfour. London: Routledge.

Elias, A. 2015. Catalan Independence and the Challenge of Credibility: The Causes and Consequences of Catalan Nationalist Parties' Strategic Behavior. *Nationalism and Ethnic Politics* 21 (1): 83–103.

Fishman, R. 1982. The Labor Movement in Spain: From Authoritarianism to Democracy. *Comparative Politics* 14 (3): 281–305.

Flesher Fominaya, C. 2014. Debunking Spontaneity: Spain's 15-M/Indignados as Autonomous Movement. *Social Movement Studies: Journal of Social, Cultural and Political Protest* 14: 142–163.

Gillespie, R. 2015. Between Accommodation and Contestation: The Political Evolution of Basque and Catalan Nationalism. *Nationalism and Ethnic Politics* 21 (1): 3–23.

Gramsci, A. 1971. *Selections from the Prison Notebooks*. London: Lawrence and Wishart.

Grugel, J. 2002. *Democratization. A Critical Introduction*. Basingstoke: Palgrave Macmillan.

Gunther, R. 1992. Spain: The Very Model of Modern Elite Settlement. In *Elites and Democratic Consolidation in Latin America and Southern Europe*, ed. J. Highley and R. Gunther. Cambridge: Cambridge University Press.

Heywood, P. 2005. Corruption, Democracy and Governance in Contemporary Spain. In *The Politics of Contemporary Spain*, ed. S. Balfour. London: Routledge.

Hipsher, P. 1996. Democratization and the Decline of Urban Social Movements in Chile and Spain. *Comparative Politics* 28 (3): 273–297.

Hopkin, J. 2005. From Consensus to Competition. The Changing Nature of Democracy in the Spanish Transition. In *The Politics of Contemporary Spain*, ed. S. Balfour. London: Routledge.

Huke, N., M. Clua-Losada, and D. Bailey. 2015. Disrupting the European Crisis: A Critical Political Economy of Contestation, Subversion and Escape. *New Political Economy* 20: 725–751.

Huntington, S.P. 1991. *The Third Wave. Democratization in the Late Twentieth Century*. London: University of Oklahoma Press.

Jordana, J. 1996. Reconsidering Union Membership in Spain, 1977–1994: Halting Decline in a Context of Democratic Consolidation. *Industrial Relations Journal* 27 (3): 211–224.

Kassam, A. 2015. Ciudadanos, the 'Podemos of the Right' Emerges as a Political Force in Spain. *The Guardian*, March 13. Available at: https://www.theguardian.com/world/2015/mar/13/ciudadanos-podemos-of-right-political-force-spain-albert-rivera. Last accessed 15 Dec 2016.

López, I., and E. Rodríguez. 2011. The Spanish Model. *New Left Review* 69: 5–28.

Mainwaring, S., and M.S. Shugart, eds. 1997. *Presidentialism and Democracy in Latin America*. Cambridge: Cambridge University Press.

Martí, D. 2013. The 2012 Catalan Election: The First Step Towards Independence? *Regional & Federal Studies* 23 (4): 507–516.

Moreno, L. 2013. Spain's Catch Up with the EU Core: The Implausible Quest of a 'Flying Pig'? *South European Society and Politics* 18 (2): 217–236.

Observatorio Metropolitano. 2014. *La apuesta municipalista. La democracia empieza por lo cercano*. Madrid: Traficantes de Sueños.

Parker, O. 2016. *Spanish Politics in Major Flux*. SPERI Blog. Available from: http://speri.dept.shef.ac.uk/2016/01/20/spanish-politics-in-major-flux/.

Rodríguez, E. 2013. *Hipótesis Democracia. Quince tesis para la revolución anunciada*. Madrid: Traficantes de sueños.

Serrano, I. 2013. Just a Matter of Identity? Support for Independence in Catalonia. *Regional & Federal Studies* 23 (5): 523–545.

Spourdalakis, M. 2014. The Miraculous Rise of the "Phenomenon SYRIZA". *Critical Thought* 4: 354–366.

Tansel, C.B. 2017. *States of Discipline: Authoritarian Neoliberalism and the Contested Reproduction of Capitalist Order*. Lanham: Rowman & Littlefield International.

Tarrow, S. 1995. Mass Mobilization and Regime Change: Pacts, Reform and Popular Power in Italy (1918–1922) and Spain (1975–1978). In *The Politics of Democratic Consolidation. Southern Europe in Comparative Perspective*, ed. R. Gunther, P. Diamandouros, and H.J. Puhle. London: The Johns Hopkins University Press.

Tremlett, G. 2015. The Podemos Revolution: How a Small Group of Radical Academics Changed European Politics. *The Guardian*, March 31. Available at: https://www.theguardian.com/world/2015/mar/31/podemos-revolution-radical-academics-changed-european-politics.

Ubasart-González, G. 2012. Municipalizo Alternativo y Popular. ¿Hacia una consolidación de las tesis del nuevo localismo y la politización del mundo local? *Revista de Estudios Políticos* 157: 135–162.

Wigger, A. 2016. From Dissent to Resistance: Locating Patterns if Horizontalist Self-Management Crisis Responses in Spain. *Comparative European Politics*. OnlineFirst. https://doi.org/10.1057/s41295-016-0076-4.

Zechner, M. 2015. Barcelona en Comú: The City as Horizon for Radical Democracy. *RoarMagazine*. Availablefrom: https://roarmag.org/essays/barcelona-en-comu-guanyem/.

CHAPTER 8

Portuguese Democracy Under Austerity: Politics in Exceptional Times

Isabel David

Abstract This chapter addresses the changes produced in the Portuguese political system in the wake of the sovereign debt crisis. While in many European countries traditional political parties have lost a large share of the votes to anti-systemic parties, Portugal has bucked the trend. However, the crisis has produced a major political change, otherwise impossible, given past antagonisms. A Socialist minority government is now supported in Parliament by the other two left-wing political parties (the Portuguese Communist Party and the Left Bloc). The alliance, in its second year at the time of writing, has been gradually reversing austerity measures, offering an interesting example of anti-austerity politics in (governmental) practice.

Keywords Portugal • Crisis • Political economy • Protest • Party politics

The implementation of neoliberal reforms in the Eurozone in response to the sovereign debt and subsequent economic crisis has been accompanied by declining living standards and, frequently, the demise of the welfare

I. David (✉)
Centre for Administration and Public Policies, Institute of Social and Political Sciences, Universidade de Lisboa, Lisbon, Portugal

O. Parker, D. Tsarouhas (eds.), *Crisis in the Eurozone Periphery*, Building a Sustainable Political Economy: SPERI Research & Policy, https://doi.org/10.1007/978-3-319-69721-5_8

state (International Federation of Red Cross and Red Crescent Societies 2013; Oxfam 2015). As a consequence, the political system has been severely shaken. Many European citizens, disillusioned with austerity policies enacted by mainstream parties, have come to distrust conventional politics. Trust levels towards national institutions for the EU-28 (governments and Parliaments) have consistently declined. According to 2015 Eurobarometer data from 2007 to 2015, trust towards national governments and Parliaments has declined from 41 and 43 to 31 and 31 per cent respectively (European Commission 2015: 6). Meanwhile, the share of votes for traditional parties diminished sharply, as did voter turnouts (see *Guardian* 2014; Belortaja 2015). The centre-left/social-democratic parties in particular have to date been unable to present alternatives to neoliberal policies (Bailey et al. 2014), a failure for which they have been penalized in most recent elections. Populist parties, in turn, have soared, both to the left and to the right.

In Portugal, despite the devastating effects of austerity (see Dooley, Chap. 4, this volume) these upheavals are absent. The far right is insignificant and its main exponent, the National Renovator Party (PNR), did not get more than 0.50 per cent of the votes in the 2015 legislative elections (Ministério da Administração Interna 2011, 2015). While the biggest political parties, the centre-right Social Democrat Party [PSD] and the centre-left Socialist Party [PS] have maintained their dominant position in Portuguese politics, there has been a major shift in the latest legislative elections. A PS minority government is supported in Parliament by the Portuguese Communist Party (PCP) and the Left Bloc (BE). This alliance, dubbed *geringonça* (contraption) by the former leader of the Democratic Social Centre-People's Party (CDS, a Christian Democratic party) Paulo Portas, would have been unthinkable were it not for the crisis. It is still early to fully assess the implications of this change. At the time of writing, the alliance is in its second year. The PS government is slowly reversing the neoliberal policies of the previous centre-right government, while at the same time enhancing the state's fiscal position and gaining Brussels' favour as a result.

This chapter addresses the impact of austerity politics on the Portuguese political system. In so doing, it tries to answer the following questions: What is the impact of austerity on the political system? How does austerity affect democracy and citizens' perception of it? The Portuguese case is instructive for three reasons: (a) austerity developed an ideological frame and *praxis* that tries to downplay and render illegitimate different visions aiming at solving the crisis, trying to conceal the 'moral economy' of neoliberal policies; (b) the party system has remained relatively stable; (c) an improbable alliance among leftist parties has now materialized.

The rest of this chapter proceeds as follows. The first section addresses the political system that emerged after the 1974 revolution. The subsequent section refers to the effects of the bailout on the political system and explores how the neoliberal right established its ideological hegemony. The third section examines the emergence and influence of social movements as a response to austerity and the reconfiguration of the Portuguese left. The final section concludes by providing insights on the implications of political events in Portugal.

A Young Democracy: The Portuguese Political System

Portugal's current democratic system dates from 1974. On 25 April, the Movement of the Armed Forces (MFA) composed mostly of captains and other officers dissatisfied with the continued colonial war (1961–74) and opposed to the dictatorship (1926–74), carried out an almost bloodless coup (five dead). Post-coup stabilization included the military, which had dictated the terms of power since the early nineteenth century. After the 1974 revolution, the military supervised political life until 1982, when a constitutional revision eliminated the military-led Council of the Revolution and replaced it with the Constitutional Court. The military decided on the main parties by associating them with the power structures (government, civil service, municipalities and trade unions). These parties were to be the PS, the Popular Democratic Party (the first designation of PSD), the Portuguese Communist Party (PCP) and the Portuguese Democratic Movement (MDP, which would subsequently disappear). The military provided them with the resources and legitimacy that allowed for their existence and thriving (Ramos 2010: 724–5).

Except for the PCP (founded in 1921 and whose fight against dictatorship was waged as a clandestine, cell-based party, thus allowing it to root itself in the urban proletariat in the Lisbon region and rural wage labourers in the south [Magalhães 2003: 193–4]), the approximately 50 parties that emerged following the revolution (Rebelo de Sousa 1984) had no societal, political or historical roots. This also explains the low levels of party membership and affiliation. For that reason, and to guarantee the stability of the democratic regime, Portuguese parties tend to be highly centralized and disciplined, with low levels of autonomy enjoyed by parliamentary groups (Medeiros Ferreira 1994: 275). These constraints explain the choice for a semi-presidential system (Ramos 2010: 754), although the president does not hold any executive powers.

The PCP's historical leader, Álvaro Cunhal, led the party from 1940, establishing it as a strongly Marxist-Leninist party (*O Militante* 2013), loyal to Moscow, with a 'democratic centralist' organization. Between 1974 and 1976, the PCP was the only Communist Party in power (in the provisional governments) in Western Europe (Medeiros Ferreira 1994: 246), mainly due to its strong connections to a large segment of MFA. The party took control of many municipalities and dominated the trade union movement through the General Confederation of Portuguese Workers (CGTP).

PCP's growing stance would lead to a period known as PREC (Processo Revolucionário Em Curso, or Ongoing Revolutionary Process) aiming to guide the country towards socialism. Starting from 1975, the Council of the Revolution nationalized basic economic sectors (banks, transportation, energy, insurance companies) and proceeded with agrarian reform through the expropriation and occupation of large estates in Southern Portugal. Those believed to be 'fascists' and 'uncommitted to the revolutionary process', in total 20,000 people, were purged from several economic and social sectors (Ramos 2010: 732). It was during this period that the left split. The PS and PCP disagreed on major issues, such as whether they should pursue the electoral or the revolutionary way, on the role of the MFA (arbiter or motor of the revolution), on trade union unity or pluralism, as well as on parliamentary democracy or opposition to it (Medeiros Ferreira 1994: 206). The failed 25 November 1975 coup, effected by the radical left (a number of forces to the left of the PCP), put an end to PREC and established the victory of the democratic forces. While the Communists contended that they refrained from mobilizing their militants in support of the coup, others accused them of orchestrating it. Progressively, the PCP lost momentum and power, particularly within the military. The PCP's monopoly over trade unionism ended in 1976 with the founding of General Union of Workers (UGT), sponsored by the PS and PSD (Medeiros Ferreira 1994: 155).

The PS was created in exile in Germany in 1973 by Mário Soares, with a democratic Socialist ideology, establishing itself as a centre-left party. The CDS was founded in 1974 by conservatives Diogo Freitas do Amaral,

Adelino Amaro da Costa and Xavier Pintado. Highly critical of the MFA, the party did not participate in the provisional governments and thus its implantation was harder since it did not benefit from institutional support (Medeiros Ferreira 1994: 252). It voted against the approval of the Constitution in 1976, due to to the Constitution's Socialist penchant. The PPD (later renamed PSD) was founded in 1974 by members of the liberal opposition from the erstwhile dictatorship Francisco Sá Carneiro, Joaquim Magalhães Mota and Francisco Pinto Balsemão. The PPD encompassed three distinct lines (social Catholicism, social liberalism and a technocratic line) and has traditionally represented a centre-right constituency. Finally, only one new political party has been able to establish itself in Parliament in recent years, the Left Bloc (BE). BE is a far-left party, considering itself akin to Syriza, founded in 1999. It defines itself as a 'political movement' of citizens committed to the defence of freedom and seeking alternatives to capitalism through the promotion of a civic culture of participation (BE 2014a).

On 28 March 1977, the Socialist government applied for membership to the then European Economic Community (EEC), with only the PCP opposing the process and presenting itself as a staunch defender of Portuguese sovereignty, arguing that accession would destroy the country's welfare state and the economy. Accession was accomplished in 1986 and was fundamental in stabilizing the economy and democracy, contributing also to ending the fragmentation of the party system. Until 1987, governments were short-lived. Since then, the PS and PSD, the dominant parties, have stayed in power throughout the four-year term. In 1975, both parties combined circa 78 per cent of the seats and 69 per cent of the votes, while in 2002, those percentages were 87 per cent and 80 per cent (Magalhães 2003: 191). Both parties have also controlled the composition of the Constitutional Court throughout the years (10 of the 13 judges are elected by Parliament). Araújo and Magalhães (2000) argue that the 'judicial activism' of the court has been low, interspersed only with a 'counter-majoritarian' period during PSD governments (1985–95) during which it blocked several structural reforms. Only two coalition governments have been formed since 1985, both between the PSD and CDS, in 2002–04 and 2011–15. The PCP stabilized around 7 per cent of the vote after the fall of the Union of Soviet Socialist Republics (USSR), at times becoming the third most voted party, alternating with CDS and BE (Left Bloc). Since 1987, the PCP runs for elections in coalition with the Greens, under the name CDU (Unitary Democratic Coalition) (Table 8.1).

Table 8.1 Selected legislative election results since 1975 (percentages of votes)

Years	1975	1979	1985	1987	1995	2002	2005	2009	2011	2015
Parties										
PS	37.9	27.3	20.8	22.2	43.8	37.8	45.0	36.6	28.0	32.3
PSD	26.4	-	29.9	50.2	34.1	40.2	28.8	29.1	38.6	-
PCP	12.5	-	-	-	-	-	-	-	-	-
CDS	7.6	-	9.9	4.4	9.0	8.7	7.2	10.4	11.7	-
BE	-	-	-	-	-	2.7	6.3	9.8	5.2	10.2
CDU	-	-	-	12.1	8.6	6.9	7.5	7.9	7.9	8.2
PSD-CDS	-	-	-	-	-	-	-	-	-	36.9

Source: Author's own compilation with data derived from www.portaldoeleitor.pt/paginas/historicoderesultados.aspx

Enter the Crisis: Neoliberal Politics and Ideological Hegemony

The first austerity measures in response to the debt crisis were enacted in 2010 by the minority Socialist government: three 'programmes of stability and growth' introduced cuts to public spending, increases in value-added tax (VAT) and cuts in civil servants' wages. On the three occasions, the measures were only approved in Parliament thanks to PSD support. In March 2011, the government introduced a new austerity package, but this was rejected by all opposition parties, prompting Prime Minister Sócrates to resign and call for early elections. These took place in June, shortly after the signing of the Memorandum of Understanding with the Troika.

Although party representation in Parliament did not change as a result of the elections, the electorate penalized the PS and BE: the Socialists lost 23 seats in comparison to the 2009 elections (from 97 to 74) and with 28 per cent of the votes recorded their worst result since 1987. The BE lost half of its MPs (from 16 to 8) (Ministério da Administração Interna 2009, 2011). The PSD won 108 seats with 38.6 per cent of the votes, while the CDS gained 24 seats with 11.7 per cent of the votes. The ideological proximity between the two parties allowed the establishment of a coalition government enjoying an absolute majority in Parliament.

The first outcome of the electoral defeat was the resignation of the PS leader Sócrates, succeeded by António José Seguro. Seguro, who was always an opponent of the rightist turn of his predecessor (during his two terms as prime minister, Sócrates pushed for labour market deregulation and privatizations), set out to defend free National Healthcare Service and education, rejecting any type of constitutional revision (*Diário Económico* 2011a, b).

Once in power, PSD and CDS applied a neoliberal reform agenda shielded in the Memorandum of Understanding (MoU) with the Troika, but which, in fact, corresponded to the parties' ideology, particularly PSD's under its leader since 2010, Pedro Passos Coelho.[1] Some PSD members (including a former finance minister, Eduardo Catroga, and Carlos Moedas) actively tried to influence the course of negotiations with the Troika, so that the MoU would correspond to PSD's vision (*Observador* 2015a).

Throughout its four-year term, the coalition government bet on a strategy anchored on discrediting and delegitimizing alternative views on neoliberal austerity. The first component of this strategy was blaming the former Socialist government for the bailout. Whitewashing the impact of the international financial crisis on sovereign debts, the coalition systematically cited fully domestic causes, namely the mismanagement of the country's finances through overspending (see, e.g., *Jornal da Madeira* 2012; *Correio da Manhã* 2015), stating that the country had been 'living above its means'. PSD and CDS members and pundits alike kept on repeating that it was under previous Socialist governments that the country became bankrupt and had to ask for bailouts in 1978 and 1983[2] (*Expresso* 2013).

The second component of the strategy was to present austerity as indispensable (or else the country would face a new bailout) and merely technical, trying to conceal the 'moral economy' behind it. According to Prime Minister Coelho, European countries in crisis needed to correct budget imbalances (*Público* 2015). The TINA (There is No Alternative) narrative was systematically used to create a climate of fear among the population, by presenting alternative proposals (namely variations of Keynesian approaches) as dangerous and unrealistic. The government tried to disassociate the Portuguese crisis from the Greek crisis, insisting that 'we are not Greece', and that Syriza's plans were 'stories for children' with catastrophic results (*Público* 2015). Instead, Coelho was intent on justifying cuts in the welfare state with the will to create a modern country while gluing PS's criticism of austerity to Syriza's debacle in the summer of 2015 (Ibid.).

The project was completed by portraying as 'radicalism' the Keynesian consensus that stabilized and brought prosperity to Europe in the post–World War II period. An analysis of the alternatives proposed by the Portuguese left in their programmes allows us to conclude they are, in the main, anchored on the traditional components of social democracy, including public investment, social protection, free health care and education, and workers' rights (see BE 2014b, pp. 63–6, 2015; PCP n.d.; PS 2015). These elements are in fact enshrined in the EU Charter of Fundamental Rights.[3]

At the same time, the government normalized the consequences and impact of the austerity measures. Claiming to refuse demagoguery, the prime minister stated that 'we can only get out of this situation by becoming poorer' (*Expresso* 2011). Hence, the Portuguese had two options, in his view: either emigrate (*Jornal de Negócios* 2013) or stop being 'mushy', establish a culture of work (*Expresso* 2012) and see unemployment as 'an opportunity' (*Observador* 2015b).

The three years of the 'adjustment programme' were marked by confrontations between the government's proposed cuts and the rulings of the Constitutional Court, which became a key anti-austerity player. Several of the austerity measures were ruled 'unconstitutional', namely, the elimination of two extra months paid in the summer and at Christmas (2012 and 2013), cuts in sickness and unemployment benefits (2013 and 2014), the possibility of firing civil servants (2013), changes to the Labour Code (2013), the convergence of the public and private pension systems (2013) and cuts in salaries and survival pensions (2014) (*Rádio Renascença* 2014).

As a response, the government talked about changing the Constitution, considering it outdated and an obstacle to reform. The government intended to adapt it to market demands by constitutionalizing the 3 per cent budget deficit, reducing the number of civil servants and municipalities, enacting privatizations, changing the pension scheme, flexibilizing civil servants' working contracts, introducing tax cuts and creating 'freedom of choice' for citizens in terms of education and health care (*Jornal de Negócios* 2011; Governo de Portugal 2013). The government's rhetoric cunningly associated constitutional reform to sovereignty: by harmonizing the Constitution with EU economic rules, reforms would be a matter of national choice and not a foreign diktat (Governo de Portugal 2013: 23). Thus, the rulings of the Constitutional Court only contributed, in the government's view, to forcing the executive to raise taxes and hinder growth (Ibid.: 14–5). The changes to the Constitution never materialized, as the government could not find any support from the opposition parties (changes to the Constitution need a two thirds majority in Parliament).

From Dissent to New Political Configurations

Portuguese civil society has been traditionally portrayed as apathetic, with declining levels of satisfaction with democracy since its institutionalization in 1974. As Freire and Magalhães (2002: 47–50) observe, in the late 1970s, Portugal was one of the Western countries without compulsory voting where turnout was higher while in the late 1990s and early 2000s turnout was below the average for West European democracies (the sharpest decline among Organisation for Economic Co-operation and Development [OECD] nations). Table 8.2 shows the abstention rate in general elections between 1976 and 2015. The results are even more staggering when looking at presidential elections (Table 8.3).

As Magalhães (2005) demonstrated, there has been no correlation between weak support for the political class/political parties and greater adherence to alternative forms of political participation (other than representative democracy mechanisms, such as voting). In the Portuguese case, dissatisfaction has been traditionally shown in the loss of votes for the incumbent party. In fact, civil society organizations and social movements have been traditionally weak and strongly dependent on political parties and institutional resources for the transformation of their demands into concrete policies.[4] At the same time, partisan conflicts spill over to civic associations, thus triggering their fragmentation (Lisi 2013). On the other hand, political parties have been extremely effective in diffusing any competition coming from civil society organizations by taking over their structures.

According to Eurobarometer figures (European Commission 2015), the Portuguese rank lowest in the EU regarding interest in politics: only 10 per cent reveal a strong interest while 28 per cent have no interest whatsoever. In a 2013 Flash Eurobarometer survey on Europeans' engagement in participatory democracy, 49 per cent of the Portuguese stated that citizens do not need non-governmental organizations (NGOs) in order to influence decision-making processes (European Commission 2013a). Only 27 per cent said they signed a petition in the two previous years, while 67 per cent declared they have no NGO or association affiliation, including trade unions and professional associations. According to yet another Eurobarometer survey devoted to the political participation of young people, only 48 per cent of the Portuguese youth voted in an election in the three years prior to 2013, and 56 per cent stated they have no interest in European politics or elections, the eighth highest percentage of the member-states (European Commission 2013b).

Table 8.2 Abstention rate, in percentages and in general elections between 1976 and 2015

Years	1975	1976	1980	1983	1985	1987	1991	1995	1999	2002	2005	2009	2011	2015
Abstention	8.34	16.47	16.06	22.21	25.84	28.43	32.22	33.70	38.91	38.52	35.74	40.32	41.97	44.14

Source: http://www.portaldoeleitor.pt/paginas/historicoderesultados.aspx

Table 8.3 Abstention rate, in percentages, in presidential elections

Years	1976	1980	1986	1991	1996	2001	2006	2011	2016
Abstention	24.53	15.61	24.62	37.84	33.71	50.29	38.47	53.48	51.34

Source: http://www.portaldoeleitor.pt/paginas/historicoderesultados.aspx

In that context, when social movements emerged during the crisis, few could have anticipated their ability to mobilize Portuguese citizens. In early 2011, four young precarious workers naming themselves *Geração à Rasca*[5] (Generation in Trouble) called for a demonstration against precariousness and bleak future prospects. The demonstration gathered over 280,000 people in Lisbon and Oporto (*Jornal de Notícias* 2011a) and included members of some left-wing political parties and the leader of CGTP. It provided the inspiration for the *Democracia Real Ya*-organized demonstration in Spain on 15 May 2011 (*Jornal de Notícias* 2011b; see also Clua Losada: Chap. 7, this volume). The activists of *Geração à Rasca* created the 12 March Movement, which called for participatory democracy, involving synergies and cooperation among various movements and citizens, while announcing a series of actions (legislative citizen initiatives, public debates, questioning of political parties and a citizen audit on public debt).[6] They joined other social movements and politicians (including BE members, the Secretary-General of CGTP, Carvalho da Silva, and a former secretary of state of a Socialist government, Ana Benavente) to engage in a citizen audit on public debt.[7] Together with BE and CGTP, *Geração à Rasca* founded the Democratic Congress for Alternatives, their goals being an end to austerity, defending the welfare state and building forms of participatory democracy.[8]

In June 2012, a group of journalists, professors, musicians, actors and students formed another social movement, *Que se Lixe a Troika* (QSLT, Screw the Troika),[9] calling for a demonstration against austerity which gathered about a million people across the country (*Correio da Manhã* 2012). QSLT started to cooperate with BE, PCP and CGTP. CGTP supported a QSLT-organized demonstration on 2 March 2013, which put over one million people on the streets, probably the largest demonstration since the post-revolution period (TSF 2013).

Cooperation with autonomous social movements and other political parties constituted a notable change in PCP's strategy. The Communists had always considered themselves the vanguard of the masses and looked at social movements as 'a temporary, unstable and inorganic form of mobilization lacking any real ability to achieve policy change' (Lisi 2013: 30). As Accornero and Ramos Pinto (2014: 498) show, between 2010 and 2013 there were five general strikes, three of which were jointly organized by trade unions CGTP and UGT, another new development motivated by austerity.

Social movement activism faded after 2013, but the synergies it created are at the origin of the biggest change in Portuguese politics since the revolution: a minority PS government supported by CDU (the Communist-Green electoral coalition) and BE in Parliament. Capitalizing on the momentum, in May 2013 Mário Soares promoted a meeting between PS, PCP, Greens, BE, the military that carried out the 1974 coup, trade unions, representatives of the Catholic Church and social movements. The gathering envisioned an alliance and a potential future coalition government comprising the PS, PCP, Greens and BE, in an effort to refound the Left (*Público* 2013). The initiative continued in November 2013 and in January 2014 (Esquerda.net 2013, 2014).

The October 2015 legislative elections provided the opportunity to put the Soares plan in practice. The PSD-CDS coalition got 36.86 per cent of the votes, falling short of an absolute majority. The combined votes of the left, on the other hand, totalled 50.75 per cent (Ministério da Administração Interna 2015). PS was under a new leadership since November 2014, when António Costa successfully challenged Seguro, after the party's lukewarm performance in the 2014 European elections.

The alliance owes a great deal to BE's leader, Catarina Martins. During a TV debate between Martins and the PS leader Costa during the election campaign, Martins challenged Costa to form an alliance provided he agreed to abandon cuts in pensions and in the single social tax (a social security tax paid by workers and employers) and abandon the conciliatory dismissal of workers on fixed contracts (*Jornal de Negócios* 2015). Costa is known as a pragmatic leader, with an unusual ability to forge alliances and compromises with unlikely partners, a reputation he earned during his terms as mayor of Lisbon. In October, PCP's leader, Jerónimo de Sousa, in an historical declaration, admitted the party's support for a PS government (PCP 2015a). The agreement included salary rises, measures against labour precariousness, the reversal of 'hire and fire' changes in labour law, an end to cuts in salaries and pensions, a fair fiscal policy, an increase of social benefits, an end to the cuts in the national healthcare service, an end to privatizations and revoking the changes made to the law on abortion by the centre-right coalition (PCP 2015b). BE and PCP decided to leave aside their hostility to Portuguese membership of North Atlantic Treaty Organization (NATO) and, in the case of the Communists, membership of the EU and particularly the Eurozone.[10] Further, the agreement between PS and the Greens, in November, follows essentially the same lines as the other two agreements, while adding environmental concerns, namely a refusal to privatize water services, development of public transportation networks (especially rail), protection of water resources and expansion of forest areas.[11] The pact allows for the approval of the budget in Parliament by PS, PCP, Greens and BE while maintaining the parties' autonomy and initiative in all matters that do not jeopardize the content of the agreements.

Following the initial refusal of the then President of the Republic, Aníbal Cavaco Silva, a former PSD leader, to appoint a PS government (under the justification that Portuguese governments had never depended on 'anti-EU' forces and that the country could not transmit 'wrong signs' to the markets [TSF 2015]), Silva decided to appoint Costa as Prime Minister after the rejection of the PSD-CDS programme in Parliament. The agreement with the left is not without its critics within PS, who fear the party is committing suicide by tilting to the left and whether the alliance would last for the whole term (four years) (*Sol* 2015).

The first budget of the new government sought to put an end to austerity, by increasing social benefits for the unemployed, the elderly and the poor, reducing VAT in restaurants, progressively eliminating cuts in civil servants' wages and increasing the minimum wage (*Jornal de Negócios* 2016). The final version was the product of a long struggle against interference from the European Commission, the Eurogroup, the European Peoples' Party (EPP), the Troika, rating agencies (DBRS,[12] Fitch, Moody's), the markets and the Portuguese right (TSF 2016; *Expresso* 2016a; *Diário Económico* 2016c). The European institutions repeatedly manifested their worries concerning the initial document presented by the Portuguese government (see *Diário Económico* 2016a, b; *Observador* 2016a). The European Commission is keeping Portugal under tight scrutiny (*Diário de Notícias* 2016a). The Troika returned to the country in late January 2016 for an evaluation of the progress made after the end of the adjustment programme only to renew demands of austerity and disapprove of the initial sketch of the budget (*Expresso* 2016b). Commerzbank (2016) called Portugal 'the new problem-child in the Eurozone' in a four-page report. Moreover, Jean-Claude Juncker expressed his doubts about the stability of the alliance (*Diário de Notícias* 2016b) while the EPP's parliamentary group president, Manfred Weber, stated that 'we don't want extremists influencing legislation' (*Expresso* 2015a). EPP's president, Joseph Daul, argued that the alliance could destroy the 'efforts' of the Portuguese people and offered Syriza as a negative example (*Expresso* 2015b).

The improbable left alliance has caused shifts in the Portuguese right. Despite his re-election as PSD leader in March 2016, Coelho faces increasing pressure from the so-called notables of the party to return to a more Social Democratic ideological vision (*Observador* 2016b; *Diário de Notícias* 2016c). Coelho's opposition to PS is considered feeble (see *Diário de Notícias* 2016d). Paulo Portas, the longest-serving leader of a party in Portugal, anchoring CDS' constituency on pensioners and farmers, resigned from the leadership but prepared a successor, Assunção Cristas, former agriculture minister. Cristas is tilting the CDS to liberalism: a practising Catholic, she is a feminist and in favour of adoption by homosexual couples and gay marriage.

Conclusion

Portugal provides an intriguing example of the impact of austerity on national politics. Unlike most EU states, political parties pre-dating the crisis continue to dominate the political system. This can be attributed to the political apathy that has traditionally characterized the Portuguese and the declining levels of satisfaction with democracy. Despite increased citizen activism visible in the emergence of social movements and the huge demonstrations against austerity policies between 2011 and 2013, the traditional way of demonstrating dissatisfaction has been the protest vote against the incumbent party. This was clearly seen in the 2011 and 2015 legislative elections. However, the protest vote against the PSD-CDS coalition had not fully materialized in the latest elections, and this can be attributed to the ideological hegemony created by the rhetoric of the neoliberal right, which successfully created a climate of fear of political, social and economic alternatives to austerity. This hegemony was fully internalized not only by large swathes of the population but also by many within the political class.

Given this context, the alliance of the left that followed the 2015 elections constituted a major novelty in Portuguese politics brought about by austerity and the lack of alternatives to the hardening position of the political antagonists. At the time of writing, the responsibility on these parties to successfully navigate internal and external pressures could hardly have been greater.

Notes

1. The neoliberal turn has not been immune to internal criticism (see *TSF* 2012; *Rádio Renascença* 2013; *Sol* 2014).
2. The first bailout, a one-year agreement with the International Monetary Fund (IMF), was motivated by the imbalance in the balance of payments, as a result of expansionary monetary policy and the loss of competitiveness in internal and external markets. The 1983 bailout, a two-year plan, took place due to similar reasons but was aggravated by rampant foreign debt (two-thirds of GDP) and a very high current account deficit (13.5 per cent of GDP).
3. Available from http://eur-lex.europa.eu/legal-content/EN/TXT/?uri=uriserv%3Al33501. [accessed: 23 October 2016].
4. This relationship is particularly evident in the cases of PCP and BE. While the Communists are strongly tied to the trade unions, BE has, from the outset, been intimately connected with social movements.
5. The manifesto is available at https://geracaoenrascada.wordpress.com/manifesto/.
6. https://geracaoenrascada.wordpress.com/2011/04/21/apresentacao-do-m12m-movimento-12-de-marco-2/.
7. http://auditoriacidada.info/.
8. http://www.congressoalternativas.org/.
9. http://queselixeatroika15setembro.blogspot.pt/.
10. The full list of measures agreed by the three parties is available at: http://www.esquerda.net/dossier/medidas-acordadas-entre-ps-bloco-pcp-e-pev/39520.
11. The agreement is available at: http://www.osverdes.pt/media/Parlamento/PosicaoConjuntaPS_PEV.pdf.
12. The Canadian DBRS (originally Dominion Bond Rating Service) is the only major rating agency that maintains Portugal's debt above the 'trash' level. It is, therefore, fundamental in securing Portugal's financing by the European Central Bank.

References

Accornero, G., and P. Ramos Pinto. 2014. "Mild Mannered"? Protest and Mobilization in Portugal Under Austerity, 2010–2013. *West European Politics* 38 (3): 491–515.

Araújo, A., and P.C. Magalhães. 2000. A justiça constitucional: uma instituição contra as maiorias? *Análise Social* XXXV: 207–246.

Bailey, D.J., J. de Waele, F. Escalona, and M. Vieira. 2014. *European Social Democracy During the Global Economic Crisis. Renovation or Resignation?* Manchester: Manchester University Press.

BE. 2014a. Estatutos. IX Convenção Nacional de 22 e 23 de Novembro de 2014. http://www.bloco.org/index.php?option=com_content&task=blogsection&id=18&Itemid=40.

———. 2014b. Moção unitária em construção. http://www.bloco.org/media/mocao_IXconvbloco.pdf. Date accessed 3 July 2016.

———. 2015. Manifesto Eleitoral. Legislativas 2015. http://www.bloco.org/media/manifestolegislativas2015.pdf. Date accessed 10 July 2016.

Belortaja, M. 2015. *The End of the Two-Party System?* Voxeurop. http://www.voxeurop.eu/en/content/news-brief/4914619-end-two-party-system. 3 Apr.

Commerzbank. 2016. Economic Insight. *Portugal: The New Old Problem Child.* https://research.commerzbank.com/delegate/publication?params=rgRBmflA42mirvet0QBzTrF9l3Hf2b6yTTLDsi%2BvIrG9dLM6sGJ1smz5YSY6etBo. 19 Jan.

Correio da Manhã. 2012. Quem mandou lixar a troika. http://www.cmjornal.xl.pt/domingo/detalhe/quem-mandou-lixar-a-troika.html. 23 Sept.

———. 2015. Passos culpa PS pela austeridade. http://www.cmjornal.xl.pt/cm_ao_minuto/detalhe/eleicoes_lider_psd_culpa_ps_pela_austeridade_costa_acusa_passos_de_ser_passa_culpas.html. 17 Sept.

Diário de Notícias. 2016a. Comissão Europeia vai "dar conselhos" a Portugal mas não quer intervir politicamente. http://www.dn.pt/dinheiro/interior/comissao-europeia-vai-dar-conselhos-a-portugal-mas-nao-quer-interferir-politicamente-5070671.html. 10 Mar.

———. 2016b. Governo português é estável? "Isso ainda está para se ver", diz Juncker. http://www.dn.pt/mundo/interior/governo-portugues-e-estavel-isso-ainda-esta-para-se-ver-diz-juncker-4968824.html. 7 Jan.

———. 2016c. Ex-governantes querem ver para crer na social-democracia de Passos. http://www.dn.pt/portugal/interior/ex-governantes-querem-ver-para-crer-na-social-democracia-de-passos-5020028.html. 8 Feb.

———. 2016d. Fim das tréguas pós-congresso: críticas a Passos sobem de tom. http://www.dn.pt/portugal/interior/fim-das-treguas-pos-congresso-criticas-a-passos-sobem-de-tom-5173824.html. 14 May.

Diário Económico. 2011a. Seguro, um político de carreira com Guterres como referência. http://economico.sapo.pt/noticias/seguro-um-politico-de-carreira-com-guterres-como-referencia_123233.html. 23 July.

———. 2011b. António José Seguro eleito líder do PS. http://economico.sapo.pt/noticias/antonio-jose-seguro-eleito-lider-do-ps_123232.html. 23 July.

———. 2016a. Juncker "muito preocupado" com o Orçamento português. http://economico.sapo.pt/noticias/juncker-muito-preocupado-com-o-orcamento-portugues_241483.html. 2 Feb.

———. 2016b. Comissão não aceita argumentos do Governo e vai pedir revisão do OE. http://economico.sapo.pt/noticias/comissao-nao-aceita-argumentos-do-governo-e-vai-pedir-revisao-do-oe_241447.html. 2 Feb.

———. 2016c. Moody's diz que esboço do OE/2016 é optimista e repete erros do passado. http://economico.sapo.pt/noticias/moodys-diz-que-esboco-do-oe2016-e-optimista-e-repete-erros-do-passado_240768.html. 26 Jan.

Esquerda.net. 2013. Demissão do governo e críticas a Cavaco marcam iniciativa em defesa da Constituição. http://www.esquerda.net/artigo/demiss%C3%A3o-do-governo-e-cr%C3%ADticas-cavaco-marcam-iniciativa-em-defesa-da-constitui%C3%A7%C3%A3o/30325. 22 Nov.

———. 2014. Sessão cívica em Coimbra prossegue iniciativa da Aula Magna. http://www.esquerda.net/artigo/sess%C3%A3o-c%C3%ADvica-em-coimbra-prossegue-iniciativa-da-aula-magna/31025. 21 Jan.

European Commission. 2013a. *European's Engagement in Participatory Democracy. Flash Eurobarometer 373.* ec.europa.eu/public_opinion/flash/fl_373_en.pdf. Date accessed 6 June 2016.

———. 2013b. *European Youth: Participation in Democratic Life. Flash Eurobarometer 375.* ec.europa.eu/youth/library/reports/flash375_en.pdf. Date accessed 6 June 2016.

———. 2015. *Public Opinion in the European Union. Standard Eurobarometer 83.* http://ec.europa.eu/public_opinion/archives/eb/eb83/eb83_en.htm. Date accessed 6 June 2016.

Expresso. 2011. Passos Coelho: só vamos sair da crise empobrecendo (vídeo). http://expresso.sapo.pt/dossies/dossiest_economia/OramentodoEstado2012/passos-coelho-so-vamos-sair-da-crise-empobrecendo-video=f683176. 25 Oct.

———. 2012. Passos pede aos portugueses para serem "menos piegas". http://expresso.sapo.pt/actualidade/passos-pede-aos-portugueses-para-serem-menos-piegas=f703170. 6 Feb.

———. 2013. Não foi Mário Soares quem trouxe a troika para Portugal? http://expresso.sapo.pt/blogues/blogue_paulo_gaiao/nao-foi-mario-soares-quem-trouxe-a-troika-para-portugal=f793111. 13 Mar.

———. 2015a. PCP e Bloco reagem a acusações sobre "extremistas de esquerda". http://expresso.sapo.pt/politica/2015-10-27--PCP-e-Bloco-reagem-a-acusacoes-sobre-extremistas-de-esquerda-. 27 Oct.

———. 2015b. Centro-direita europeu sai em defesa de Passos e aponta o dedo ao PCP. http://expresso.sapo.pt/politica/2015-10-21-Centro-direita-europeu-sai-em-defesa-de-Passos-e-aponta-o-dedo-ao-PCP. 21 Oct.

———. 2016a. Fitch faz novos alertas a Portugal. http://expresso.sapo.pt/dossies/diario/2016-01-28-Fitch-faz-novos-alertas-a-Portugal. 28 Jan.

———. 2016b. Troika teme regresso ao passado. http://expresso.sapo.pt/economia/2016-01-30-Troika-teme-regresso-ao-passado. 30 Jan.

Freire, A., and P. Magalhães. 2002. A abstenção portuguesa em perspectiva comparativa. *Eleições* 7: 7–36.

Governo de Portugal. 2013. Um Estado melhor. www.portugal.gov.pt/media/1228115/20131030%20guiao%20reforma%20estado.pdf. Date accessed 23 July 2016.

Guardian. 2014. *A Crisis of Trust—and the Rise of New Political Parties*. http://www.theguardian.com/news/datablog/2014/nov/06/podemos-a-crisis-of-trust-and-the-rise-of-new-political-parties. 6 Nov.

International Federation of Red Cross and Red Crescent Societies. 2013. *Think Differently. Humanitarian Impacts of the Economic Crisis in Europe*. http://www.ifrc.org/PageFiles/134339/1260300-conomic%20crisis%20Report_EN_LR.pdf. Date accessed 4 Apr 2016.

Jornal da Madeira. 2012. PSD culpa "herança Sócrates", PS promete separar águas face ao governo. http://www.jm-madeira.pt/artigos/psd-culpa-heran%C3%A7-s%C3%B3crates-ps-promete-separar-%C3%A1guas-face-ao-governo. 12 Sept.

Jornal de Negócios. 2011. Passos Coelho quer alterar Constituição para impor limite ao défice. http://www.jornaldenegocios.pt/economia/detalhe/passos_coelho_quer_alterar_constituiccedilatildeo_para_impor_limite_ao_deacutefice.html. 9 Dec.

———. 2013. As várias declarações de apelo à imigração. http://www.jornaldenegocios.pt/economia/detalhe/as_varias_declaracoes_de_apelo_a_emigracao.html. 17 Jan.

———. 2015. Catarina Martins coloca a Costa condições para um diálogo de Governo PS/BE. http://www.jornaldenegocios.pt/economia/politica/eleicoes/legislativas/detalhe/catarina_martins_coloca_a_costa_condicoes_para_um_dialogo_de_governo_psbe.html. 15 Sept.

———. 2016. As principais medidas do Orçamento do estado para 2016. http://www.jornaldenegocios.pt/economia/financas_publicas//detalhe/as_principais_medidas_do_orcamento_do_estado_para_2016.html. 16 Março.

Jornal de Notícias. 2011a. Milhares saíram à rua em nome da "Geração à Rasca". http://www.jn.pt/PaginaInicial/Nacional/Interior.aspx?content_id=1804830&page=-1. 12 Mar.

———. 2011b. Geração à Rasca é referência para Espanha. http://www.jn.pt/PaginaInicial/Mundo/Interior.aspx?content_id=1857358&page=-1. 20 May.

Lisi, M. 2013. Rediscovering Civil Society? Renewal and Continuity in the Portuguese Radical Left. *South European Society and Politics* 18 (1): 21–39.

Magalhães, P.C. 2003. Elections, Parties, and Policy-Making Institutions in Democratic Portugal. In *Contemporary Portugal. Politics, Society and Culture*, ed. A.C. Pinto. New York: Columbia University Press.

———. 2005. Disaffected Democrats: Political Attitudes and Political Action in Portugal. *West European Politics* 28 (5): 973–991.

Medeiros Ferreira, J. 1994. *História de Portugal. Portugal em transe (1974–1985)*. Lisboa: Círculo de Leitores.

Ministério da Administração Interna. 2009. Eleições legislativas 27 Setembro 2009. http://www.eleicoes.mai.gov.pt/legislativas2009/.

———. 2011. Eleições legislativas 5 Junho 2011. http://www.eleicoes.mai.gov.pt/legislativas2011/.

———. 2015. Eleições legislativas 4 outubro 2015. http://www.eleicoes.mai.gov.pt/legislativas2015/.

O Militante. 2013. Álvaro Cunhal e a construção do Partido. http://www.omilitante.pcp.pt/pt/323/alvaro_cunhal_centenario/782/%C3%81lvaro-Cunhal-e-a-constru%C3%A7%C3%A3o-do-Partido.htm. No. 323. Mar/Abr.

Observador. 2015a. Fact Check. Quem trouxe a troika? Quem negociou com ela? http://observador.pt/2015/09/14/fact-check-quem-trouxe-a-troika-quem-negociou-com-ela/. 14 Sept.

———. 2015b. Pedro e os mitos. O que Passos disse e não disse—em oito frases polémicas. http://observador.pt/2015/06/19/7-frases-polemicas-passos-coelho-disse-mesmo-isto/. 19 June.

———. 2016a. Bruxelas pressiona. Pede "mais medidas" e "bom senso" a Portugal. http://observador.pt/2016/02/02/bruxelas-pressiona-pede-medidas-bom-senso-portugal/. 2 Feb.

———. 2016b. Rui Rio: "Gostaria de ver o PSD flectir um bocadinho mais à esquerda". http://observador.pt/2016/02/11/rui-rio-gostaria-ver-psd-flectir-um-bocadinho-esquerda/. 11 Feb.

Oxfam. 2015. *A Europe for the Many, Not the Few*, Oxfam Briefing Paper 206. https://www.oxfam.org/sites/www.oxfam.org/files/file_attachments/bp206-europe-for-many-not-few-090915-summ-en.pdf. 9 Sept.

PCP. 2015a. Comunicado do Comité Central do PCP, de 6 de Outubro de 2015. http://www.pcp.pt/comunicado-do-comite-central-do-pcp-de-6-de-outubro-de-2015.

———. 2015b. Posição conjunta do PS e do PCP sobre solução política. http://www.pcp.pt/sites/default/files/documentos/posicao_conjunta_pcp_ps_sobre_situacao_politica.pdf. 10 Nov.

———. n.d. Programa do PCP. Uma democracia avançada—os valores de abril no futuro de Portugal. http://www.pcp.pt/programa-do-pcp. Date accessed 29 July 2016.

PS. 2015. Programa eleitoral do Partido Socialista. Eleições Legislativas 2015. http://www.ps.pt/wp-content/uploads/2016/06/programa_eleitoral-PS-legislativas2015.pdf. Date accessed 4 Aug 2016.

Público. 2013. Uma conferência para derrubar a direita e amarrar o PS à esquerda. http://www.publico.pt/portugal/jornal/uma-conferencia-para-derrubar-a-direita-e-amarrar-o-ps-a-esquerda-26608792. 30 May.

———. 2015. Ideias do Syriza do Syriza são "conto de crianças", diz Passos Coelho. https://www.publico.pt/politica/noticia/ideias-do-syriza-sao-conto-de-crianca-diz-passos-1683419. 26 Jan.

Rádio Renascença. 2013. Portugal não quer um PSD liberal. http://rr.sapo.pt/bolabranca_detalhe.aspx?fid=27&did=106525. 7 May.

———. 2014. Um governo, um TC, oito chumbos. http://rr.sapo.pt/bolabranca_detalhe.aspx?fid=27&did=158870. 14 Aug.

Ramos, R. 2010. *História de Portugal*. Lisboa: A Esfera dos Livros.
Rebelo de Sousa, M. 1984. *Os partidos politicos no direito constitucional português*. Lisboa: Livraria Cruz.
Sol. 2014. Passos inquieta PSD com agenda liberal para 2015. http://www.sol.pt/noticia/120743/passos-inquieta-psd-com-agenda--liberal-para-2015. 20 Dec.
———. 2015. PS: veja quem é contra ou a favor de um governo de esquerda. http://www.sol.pt/noticia/416500/ps-veja-quem-%C3%A9-contra-ou-a-favor-de-um-governo-de-esquerda. 12 Oct.
TSF. 2012. PSD: Miguel Veiga alerta para "deriva liberal". http://www.tsf.pt/portugal/politica/interior/psd-miguel-veiga-alerta-para-deriva-liberal-2778734.html. 19 Sept.
———. 2013. Mais de um milhão e meio de portugueses saíram à rua. http://www.tsf.pt/portugal/interior/mais-de-um-milhao-e-meio-de-portugueses-sairam-a-rua-video-3084756.html. 3 Mar.
———. 2015. Comunicação de Cavaco Silva na íntegra. http://www.tvi24.iol.pt/politica/presidente-da-republica/comunicacao-de-cavaco-silva-na-integra. 22 Oct.
———. 2016. Dívida. DBRS admite cortar ranking. Financiamento do BCE em risco. http://www.tsf.pt/economia/interior/divida-dbrs-admite-cortar-rating-financiamento-do-bce-em-risco-5005863.html. 29 Jan.

CHAPTER 9

Continuity and Change in Greek Politics in an Age of Austerity

Alexandra Prodromidou

Abstract This chapter discusses the impact of austerity policies on Greek politics and attempts to identify patterns of continuity and change in the post-1974 era. The first part maps the evolution of politics in Greece, with a focus on the development of the clientelistic state, which shaped state policies largely based on political cost. The second part discusses the changes occurring post-2010, including the decline of the socialist PASOK in favour of the rise of fringe populist parties. It is argued that the political and social turmoil created by the austerity measures adopted have been conditioned by the already existing particular brand of populist and clientelistic governance, which stood at the core of the country's party political system at least since the 1980s.

Keywords Greek crisis • SYRIZA • Populism • Clientelism • Austerity

A. Prodromidou (✉)
Department of Business Administration and Economics,
The International Faculty of the University of Sheffield-CITY College,
Thessaloniki, Greece

O. Parker, D. Tsarouhas (eds.), *Crisis in the Eurozone Periphery*,
Building a Sustainable Political Economy: SPERI Research & Policy,
https://doi.org/10.1007/978-3-319-69721-5_9

Introduction

The Eurozone crisis has been evolving since 2009 into a multiyear debt crisis with severe consequences on the social and political equilibria of the countries in need of rescue packages. Asymmetrics in the Eurozone structure and the absence of a fiscal union restrained both the European Union (EU) and the individual governments in their response (see Parker and Tsarouhas, Chap. 1, this volume). At the same time, the local characteristics of each state's political economy conditioned the extent of its debt crisis as well as the state's ability to comply with the requested neoliberal measures adopted as a remedy to the crisis. The impact of the debt crisis had significant adverse economic effects causing a rise in unemployment and poverty levels in the countries affected. The political and social commotion that followed was linked to the growing levels of mistrust towards the political establishment in all countries affected and mistrust towards the neoliberal practices and model of democracy employed by the EU. Social unrest, political power shifts, growing abstention and the rise of populist anti-EU/anti-Memorandum fringe parties to power have become common phenomena.

Greece is an interesting case study as it combines the example of a country facing severe difficulties in successfully coping with the challenge of EMU participation, (see Gkasis, Chap. 5, this volume), with a political background immersed in clientelism and populism. The latter provide fertile ground for the rise of populist fringe parties, which on their way to the top sweep away mainstream parties. Crisis-infused political and social resistance in Greece has been evident since 2010 reflecting the opposition of Greek citizens to the neoliberal, austerity-driven measures accompanying the various Memoranda of Understanding (MoUs) that are administered by the 'Troika' of EU, ECB and IMF. That is mainly because austerity measures attacked the fundamental basis of the relationship between the Greek state and the Greek electorate, built on the two pillars of clientelism and populism, over and beyond the inadequacies and skewed distributional consequences of these Memoranda.

When Greece entered EMU, 'bureaucratic clientelism' (Lyrintzis 1984) was pushed to its limits. The crisis caused the malfunction of this relationship between the state and the Socialist Panhellenic Socialist Party (PASOK) as the party of power for most of the post-1974 period and its voters. The MoUs and subsequent austerity measures permanently damaged this clientelistic relationship and although it would be precarious to suggest that clientelistic practices and ties between the party/parties in power and voters no longer exist, it is evident that they do not exist at the mass level that could establish any party as a mass party/a party of power and guarantee to it stable support.

Citizens showed their discontent in their voting behaviour by following two trajectories. The first was expressed by supporting populist fringe parties, with the phenomenon of SYRIZA being one example and the rise of Golden Dawn as the third largest party in Parliament another. The second relates to a steady rise in abstention evident in the last years and also witnessed elsewhere in Southern Europe (see David, Chap. 8, this volume).

This chapter discusses the impact of the crisis and austerity measures on the Greek political scene. The first part of the chapter maps the evolution of politics in the post-1974 era, with a focus on the rise of PASOK and the development of the clientelistic state, which shaped state policies and state responses to EU/EMU policies based largely on political cost. The second part discusses the impact of austerity on the political landscape of Greece and the political and social turmoil it created in the form of annihilating the governmental influence of PASOK, giving rise to populist fringe parties and increasingly rejecting the political system through abstention from voting. Finally, the conclusion discusses whether it would be fair to talk about post-crisis in Greece or whether it would be more precise to talk about a continuous crisis instead.

Greek Politics Post-1974

The institutional deficiencies of the Greek state have existed since the inception of its modern form and include different types of corruptive mechanisms such as nepotism, favouritism and, most importantly, clientelism. Clientelism has been an essential part of Greek politics since the independence of the Greek state in the nineteenth century. Ever since, the inequities and dysfunctions created by clientelism have been a hurdle to every governmental policy linked to attempts towards economic modernization and civil service restructuring. Clientelism has not been a static mechanism but has rather evolved through time. The traditional concept of clientelism refers to interpersonal patron–client relations, based on a dyad linking two individuals, the voter and the patron. Irrespective of how widespread traditional clientelism can be, it is constrained to the relationship between two individuals or a patron and a group of people at the most. ‘Pyramids’ structured around the clientelistic relationship between different individuals or different groups of people with a politician at the top were created, dominating the relationship since the founding of the Greek state (Mavrogordatos 1997).

During this period and up until the military coup of 1967, Greek politics could be described roughly as a trichotomy among the traditional Right, Left and Centre, where the Right and the Centre dominated electoral preferences by operationalizing the tools of traditional clientelism and populism. This period came to a halt during the colonels' coup, which although short-lived (it lasted until 1974), caused a disruption major enough to demand a restart of the party political system (Lyrintzis 1984). In the immediate post-1974 period, also known as Metapolitefsi,[1] New Democracy (ND), the successor party to the right-wing National Radical Union, dominated the Greek political scene under the leadership of Konstantinos Karamanlis. ND won both parliamentary elections overwhelmingly in 1974 and in 1977.

Changes in the post-1974 political scene also included the rise to prominence of PASOK. PASOK capitalized on three parameters that had emerged after 1974; the gradual disintegration of the old centrist forces (Centre Union Party), the inability of ND to incorporate these voters and the inability of the Greek Communist Party (KKE) to represent the aversion that Greek civilians developed against the previous state and political establishment. In the 1970s and early 1980s, 'PASOK proved to be extremely successful in combining anti-capitalist discourse with the historically articulated symbols of the political Centre [...]. Andreas Papandreou, the leader and founder of PASOK, personified this combination in an exemplary fashion, unifying his centrist origin with Marxist analysis' (Moschonas 2001: 11). As a result, and as shown in Fig. 9.1, PASOK rose to prominence seven years after its first election, by absorbing the then powerful Centre Union Party while at the same time appealing sufficiently to the Left to confine KKE to 10 per cent (Couloumbis 1993).

Populism and clientelism evolved during the Metapolitefsi period, with PASOK as a core agent in that process. Populism was mainly based on criticizing the colonels' junta and the Greek Right as a whole and in so doing upholding PASOK's advantage over ND. The first defeat suffered by PASOK in the 1974 elections triggered a softening of its harsh anti-EEC and anti-NATO rhetoric as well as a toning down of its anti-market stance. PASOK began advocating a special relationship with the EEC and a selective nationalization of key industries. Successfully appealing to diverse constituents and special groups in combination with high inflation in 1980 and the change in the leadership of ND after the departure of Konstantinos Karamanlis, gave PASOK its first electoral victory (Lyrintzis 1982). From its second term (1985) onwards, PASOK moved from being

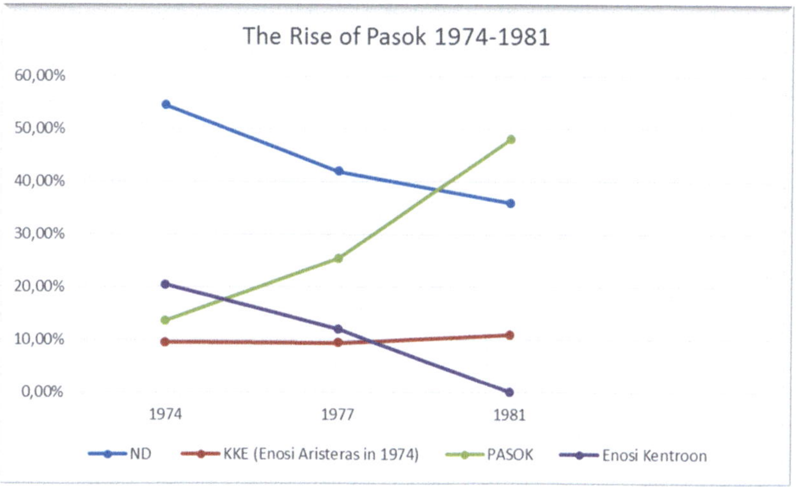

Fig. 9.1 Election results, 1974–1981, in percentage of votes gained (Source: Greek Ministry of the Interior, http://www.ypes.gr/en/Elections/)

an anti-EEC party to a full supporter of EEC and later EU integration. Although its rhetoric was at times anti-systemic, the actual policies that the PASOK governments followed were moderate (Kalyvas 1997). In essence, PASOK became a Euro-friendly party accepting the Maastricht Treaty and turning Greece's participation in Economic and Monetary Union (EMU) into a national goal, especially under Kostas Simitis, PASOK's leader from 1996 to 2004.

At the same time, clientelism was transformed from its traditional form into what Mavrogordatos (1997) refers to as 'machine politics' and Lyrintzis (1984) calls 'bureaucratic clientelism'. This is the idea that the role of either the client or the patron, or both, is not occupied by an individual but by a collective organization or a party. Here the crucial difference with traditional clientelism is that the party machine is fundamentally impersonal and its organizational core is a group, not an individual. Consequently, loyalty and identification of voters benefits the party as such (Mavrogordatos 1997). Clientelism worked on the nexus among trade unions, bureaucratic clientelism and populism. Clientelism and favouritism played an important role, not just in the economy but also for the purposes of sustaining the clientelistic structures of the state in order to guarantee the survival of the government (Featherstone et al. 2000).

Public finances were mostly targeted towards preserving an inefficient public sector where party voters would be accommodated (Philippopoulos 2013; Algan and Cahuc 2010).

Inside this context of the clientelistic relationship between any party in power and the electorate, any attempt to break the link came at great political cost in the years following EU accession, accomplished in 1981. The pattern of the clientelistic state continues until the present. Figure 9.2 depicts all election results for the three political parties around which governments have been formed throughout the Metapolitefsi era.

Clientelism has been a particularly important element in blocking the deep-seated reforms necessary for Greece to comply with its obligations either as EU or EMU member (Sotiropoulos 1993; Spanou 1996; Featherstone 2011). When it came to the implementation of EMU (Maastricht) accession criteria, consecutive Greek governments found it difficult to adhere to the adjustment programmes. The 1990–1993 period, under the ND government headed by the late Konstantinos Mitsotakis, offers an example of what Trantidis calls 'collective action against economic reforms that affect groups attached to political parties' (Trantidis 2014: 218). The economic policies followed by the Mitsotakis govern-

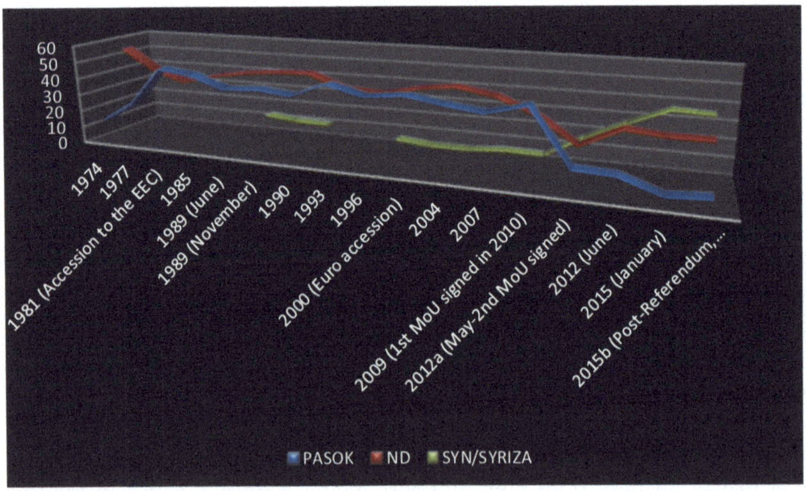

Fig. 9.2 Election results, 1974–2015 (Source: Greek Ministry of the Interior http://www.ypes.gr/en/Elections/)

ment were based on extensive structural reforms, including the privatization of state-owned companies in view of joining EMU.

The clientelistic relationship between public sector employees and trade unions with PASOK, in contrast to the weak links that ND had formed with the public sector, was disadvantageous to the ruling party. The reforms were somewhat different from the 'stabilization programme' followed by PASOK between 1985 and 1987, which had relied on 'taxation and incomes policy that diffused the cost of macroeconomic adjustment across the population (horizontal measures), leaving most of the privileges of the unionised employees of the public sector unscathed' (Trantidis 2014: 219). The proposed reforms soon led to a wave of protests, strikes and demonstrations, leading to their non-implementation. As a result, support for ND declined and by the time of the next election, held early in 1993, PASOK returned to office. Between 1993 and 1996, when Andreas Papandreou fell ill and the party leadership passed on to Kostas Simitis, the government was careful to avoid any reforms disruptive to public sector employees or to embark on large-scale privatization schemes. Greece moved from the alleged 'shock therapy' of the Mitsotakis government's attempts to impose debt control and market liberalization to the gradual adjustment and reform by consensus of the Simitis government.

In the wake of Andreas Papandreou's death in June 1996, Simitis had been elected as a 'modernizing' PASOK leader. His ascent to power and his consequent electoral win in September 1996 marked a turn to policies that were much more aligned with EMU accession requirements than any previous PASOK government. Simitis equated the term 'modernization' with 'Europeanization', whereby Greece's priority was to be part of the new EU core; that is, to become an EMU member (Featherstone 2005).

Greece was expected to join EMU later in the second phase of accession, but by 1999, it had achieved nominal convergence, and by 2000, it had satisfied the two-year Exchange Rate Mechanism (ERM) membership criterion. It thus entered EMU in 2001, only with a two-year delay compared to the first wave of members. However, high public debt levels and unemployment persisted (Featherstone 2003).

The structural reforms implemented in the run-up to EMU included the sale of shares in large companies under government management and the employment of a strict fiscal and incomes policy (Trantidis 2014). Changes in labour market regulation, pension provision and the privatization of state enterprises were part and parcel of the 'Lisbon Programme', and Greece was unable to effectively comply with it (Featherstone 2008).

Nearly every reform attempt created a series of protests by the groups mostly affected by the policies, especially as these took place at the expense of social policies (Spourdalakis and Tassis 2006). In the face of spiralling dissatisfaction, the popularity of the government decreased. Simitis stepped down and the foreign minister and son of Andreas Papandreou, George Papandreou, took over as PASOK leader in 2004 just before the next general election.

ND, under the leadership of Kostas Karamanlis, the nephew of the party's founder, capitalized on accusations against the previous government regarding data falsification on the nation's fiscal position to enter EMU. ND adopted policies that eventually led to higher inflation, such as the 1 per cent hike in value added tax. At the same time, student protests erupted at universities over proposed reforms in higher education (Gemenis 2008). In March 2007, there was speculation that government officials might have been involved in an allegedly shady deal of overpriced, structured bonds bought by four state pension funds, leading to calls from the opposition for early elections. The government asked for a renewed mandate and focused its campaign on the economy, while PASOK focused on corruption charges against the government (Gemenis 2008).

ND managed to get re-elected in the 2007 elections and lasted for another two years in power. The second term of the Karamanlis government was characterized by scandals involving members of his government, rising public debt and social unrest. The shooting of a 15-year-old boy by a police officer on 6 December 2008 in Athens prompted large protests and demonstrations, which spread to many cities and turned into rioting. While the trigger was the shooting incident, the rioting that followed was perceived to have its roots in the commonly shared feeling of frustration, especially among the youth and with regard to high youth unemployment, and the widespread corruption of the Greek state (Kalyvas 2010; Simiti 2014; for a discussion on the crisis and social justice, see Venieris 2013). Although no politically organized action came out of those undertakings, the nationwide protests had all the characteristics of an anti-statist movement including civil disobedience and public unruliness (Kalyvas 2010).

ND called for early elections in 2009 and based its electoral programme on introducing structural economic reforms to cut back on public spending and reduce public debt. PASOK put forward an agenda based on stimulating economic growth through a strategy based on the 'green economy' (Pappas 2010). PASOK secured a victory over ND and formed a government under George Papandreou. Just two weeks into its term, the government released dramatically increased figures over the country's public deficit, as it became apparent that the 'figure of 3.6 per cent of GDP reported by the previous government of Costas Karamanlis (New Democracy) was inaccurate: it was upgraded to 12.8 percent of GDP, then increased further to 13.6 percent when further calculations were made in 2010' (Featherstone 2011: 209). This was to trigger the crisis for Greece and for the Eurozone that followed (Gkasis; Parker and Tsarouhas, Chaps. 5 and 1, both this volume). Unable to borrow in international markets the Papandreou government was forced to request financial assistance and sign the first MoU.

On 5 March 2010 Parliament passed the cost-cutting Economy Protection Bill and on 23 April 2010 the Greek government requested a bailout package from the 'Troika' of EU, European Central Bank (ECB) and the International Monetary Fund (IMF). The Memorandum signed between Greece and the Troika became very unpopular, and the protests that followed were widespread and violent, escalating on 5 and 6 May 2010 and leading to the deaths of three people. Unemployment rates increased dramatically and speculation on the possibility of Greek exit (Grexit) from EMU began. Further cuts in public spending prompted more demonstrations and strikes between 2010 and 2012 (Simiti 2014), and similar protests started to take place in other periphery states during the same period.

The austerity measures profoundly affected Greek politics, as neoliberal policies characterized by punitive austerity and market protection were imposed. Cuts in public spending impacted heavily on pensions and health care. Unemployment and poverty levels rose significantly, and public outrage towards the government was expressed through mass demonstrations and crippling nationwide strikes as well as in the voting patterns of Greek citizens throughout the crisis. Figure 9.3 depicts the steep increase in unemployment during the crisis.

The consequences of punitive austerity, however, went deeper than rising unemployment. The dramatic increase in the percentage of households living below the poverty level is a perfect example, and is graphically depicted in Fig. 9.4.

Rüdig and Karyotis (2014) locate the Greek protests within a broader category of protest around the world in opposition to neoliberal austerity policies and focused on material issues such as public expenditure cuts, unemployment and inequality. Their research concludes that these were mass protests with the protesters coming from different social and educa-

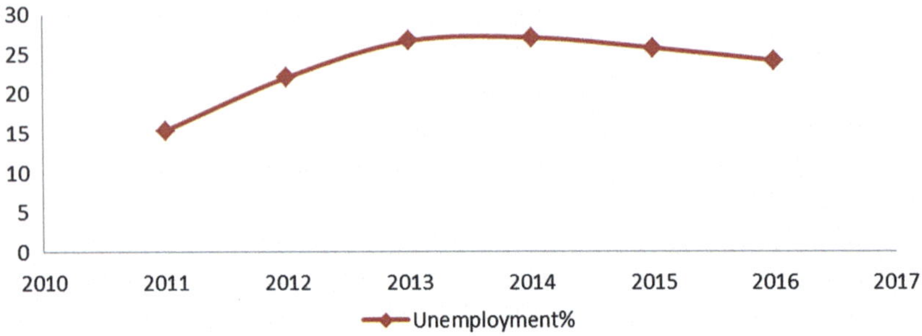

Fig. 9.3 Unemployment rate in percentage points, 2010–2017 (Source: ELSTAT 2016a)

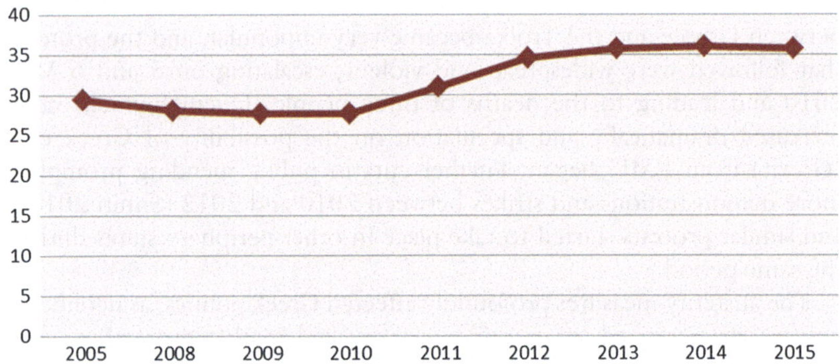

Fig. 9.4 Risk of poverty in Greece in percentage points, 2005–2015 (Source: ELSTAT 2016b)

tional backgrounds but with economic deprivation and feelings of injustice being a common denominator. Diversity in the groups protesting included socio-economic and ideological backgrounds, including a medley of Far Right and Far Left people, though the media painted a much more Left-led picture of the protests (Simiti 2014).

The tumultuous state of the Greek society has been reflected in voting behaviour and the results of elections since 2010. As mentioned before, one of the main factors hindering the adoption of the measures necessary for the restructuring of the Greek economy has been political cost and the backslash on the Greek political system, a risk no government was willing to take (Spanou 1996; Smaghi 2014).

The post-Memorandum political landscape has been characterized by three main developments: the serious blow to the Metapolitefsi system after the adoption of successive austerity measures, which saw the severe weakening of the dominant parties, PASOK and ND; the creation of several parties which attempted to fill the vacuum; and the rise of left-wing SYRIZA and the neo-Nazi party of Golden Dawn. The main driver of change has been the widespread sentiment that traditional parties no longer represented voters' interests.

The May 2012 general election was the first after the crisis erupted. The system of representative democracy in Greece was already in crisis. The PASOK government had resigned in autumn 2011 under pressure from public protest and an uncompromising refusal to cooperate with it expressed by all opposition parties. From November 2011 until the elections, a technocratic government headed by the former ECB Vice President Lucas Papademos ruled Greece. The move to install a non-elected prime minister to head the government shocked public opinion and created the necessity for fresh elections. Opinion polls conducted during April 2012 showed three tendencies: a strong preference towards a coalition government (59 per cent in favour); nearly one out of every two voters (48.6 per cent) felt that they were not being represented by the two dominant parties, while 45.2 per cent thought that no leader from the two dominant parties was fit to be the prime minister (To Vima 2012).

The 2012 elections were unique in the sense that 42.6 per cent of voters felt that they were deciding with their vote whether or not they would support the austerity measures imposed by the memorandum,[2] instead of supporting a political party ideology per se (see Vasilopoulou and Halkiopoulou 2013). About 34.4 per cent felt that in the 2012 elections they were deciding whether or not Greece should stay in the Eurozone. Finally, 77.1 per cent felt that they wanted the government to guarantee that Greece would remain in the Eurozone as opposed to 13 per cent seeking a return to the national currency.

The parliamentary elections of 6 May 2012 failed to produce a majority government as traditional political parties received historically low percentages. Table 9.1 compares the May 2012 results with those of 2009, illustrating the seismic shift in Greek party politics. The May 2012 elections demonstrated three tendencies: the growing gap between the traditional parties and their voters, the increase in voter abstention and the unusually high percentage of votes in favour of smaller parties. Both ND and PASOK saw popular support shrink dramatically. By contrast, newly

Table 9.1 Parliamentary elections results, 2009 and 2012

Political Party	Parliamentary Elections 2009 (May)	Parliamentary Elections 2012 (May)
New Democracy	33.47	18.85%
SYRIZA	4.60%	16.78%
PASOK	43.92%	13.18%
Independent Greeks (ANEL)	------------	10.61%
Communist Party (KKE)	7.54%	8.48%
Golden Dawn (*Hrisi Avgi*)	------------	6.97%
Democratic Left (DIMAR)	------------	6.11%

Source: Greek Ministry of the Interior. http://ekloges-prev.singularlogic.eu/v2012a/public/index.html#{"cls":"main","params":{}}

founded political parties like the centre-left DIMAR and 'anti-Memorandum' parties, like SYRIZA and Golden Dawn, recorded big gains. It is worth mentioning that SYRIZA became the second biggest party in Parliament by receiving 16.78 per cent of the vote in May 2012.

The rise of the extreme-right was also notable, with the normally fringe neo-Nazi party Golden Dawn acquiring 6.97 per cent of the votes, indicating voter dissatisfaction towards the traditional two-party system as well as their heightened anti-Memorandum sentiments.[3] Finally, an unusually high percentage of votes went to smaller parties that failed to pass the 3 per cent nationwide threshold necessary for representation in Parliament. This percentage accounted for 19.02 per cent of all votes cast and, when added to the unusually high number of abstentions, accounted for 35 per cent of all registered voters. The upshot was that an exceptionally high 54.02 per cent of all eligible voters were not represented in Parliament (see Table 9.2).

The ambiguous results of the May election gave both other EU member-states and global markets reason for concern as to whether there could be a strong Greek government able to implement tough austerity measures adhering with its bailout commitments. The failure to form a viable coalition led to fresh elections a month later. In this respect the June 2012 election campaign 'was framed along the lines of a pro- versus anti-euro division' (Vasilopoulou and Halkiopoulou 2013: 538).

Greek voters returned to the polls giving ND 29.66 per cent of the vote as opposed to 26.89 per cent for SYRIZA. ND proceeded to form a coalition government together with PASOK and DIMAR, whose share of the votes remained pretty stable. DIMAR left the coalition in June 2013 protesting the abrupt closing down of the national Greek broadcaster

Table 9.2 Abstention rate in Parliamentary elections, 1996–2012

Parliamentary Election Year	Abstention rate, in percentage
1996	**23%**
2000	25%
2004	23%
2009	30%
May 2012	**35%**

Source: Greek Ministry of the Interior. http://ekloges-prev.singularlogic.eu/v2012a/public/index.html#{"cls":"main","params":{}}

ERT. This episode sparked a new wave of protests against the government, seriously destabilizing the coalition. In January 2014 pressure from the Troika to proceed with further restructuring of the public sector, job cuts, tax hikes on private property and salary cuts dealt a decisive blow to the government, as its electoral popularity started collapsing (*Naftemporiki* 2014). The 2012 double elections had been viewed as a de facto referendum by both the coalition government and the opposition. The parties in power wished to optimally receive a clear mandate to continue with reforms, while the opposition was looking for popular support to demand early parliamentary elections. The message from the Greek electorate was largely inconclusive.

Furthermore, in the May 2012 elections we witnessed the concrete establishment of the neo-Nazi party of Golden Dawn as the third power in Greek politics[4] despite the imprisonment of many of its members accused of being part of a criminal network. Ellinas (2013) observes that prior to the 2012 parliamentary elections southern Europe had been largely viewed as being more resistant to the rise of the Far Right parties than elsewhere in Europe, due to their recent experience with authoritarian regimes. As David argues (Chap. 8, this volume), this thesis has to date been proven true for Portugal as well. During the 2012 elections, the electoral success of Golden Dawn came as a surprise to most, with the dominant view being that the voters supporting the neo-Nazi party were punishing the government for the state of the economy. The view that the phenomenon was temporary and that Golden Dawn would soon return to its usual low percentages at election time was widely held but proven wrong. On closer inspection it turns out that the resilience of Golden Dawn is mostly based on the fact that the votes it receives are austerity driven; its widening voter base, which at present includes a range of social groups and a large geographical spread, showcases that it is not just an urban phenomenon created as a reaction to the inflow of immigrants in the Greek metropolitan centres, or a party which attracts voters from the lower-earning social strata of Greek society (Ellinas 2013). Being anti-austerity driven, Golden Dawn will most probably continue to receive popular support as long as the Greek economy does not recover.

The coalition government lasted only until the presidential elections at the end of 2014. New Democracy opted for early elections by pushing for a presidential election before the set date in February 2015. Failure to elect a president by a three-fifth majority in Parliament led to early elections in February 2015 in accordance with the relevant Constitutional stipulation. The Greek electorate now displayed a clear support for anti-austerity parties. Seven parties entered Parliament, out of which four were anti-austerity (SYRIZA, Golden Dawn, KKE and Independent Greeks [ANEL], representing 52.84 per cent of the vote) and three 'pro-bailout' (New Democracy, The River [To Potami] and PASOK representing 38.54 per cent of the vote) (see Fig. 9.5).

Basing its electoral campaign on an anti-austerity but pro-Euro stance, SYRIZA, without reducing New Democracy's electoral base, was able to attract votes from the disintegrating PASOK and Democratic Left (DIMAR), as well as from undecided voters, although it fell short of an absolute majority. This forced the party to form a coalition government with the populist right-wing party ANEL, whose percentage fell by 3 percentage points compared to the 2012 elections, based on a common 'anti-austerity' stance. New Democracy managed to assert its control over the centre-right gaining more or less the same percentage of the vote as in 2012.

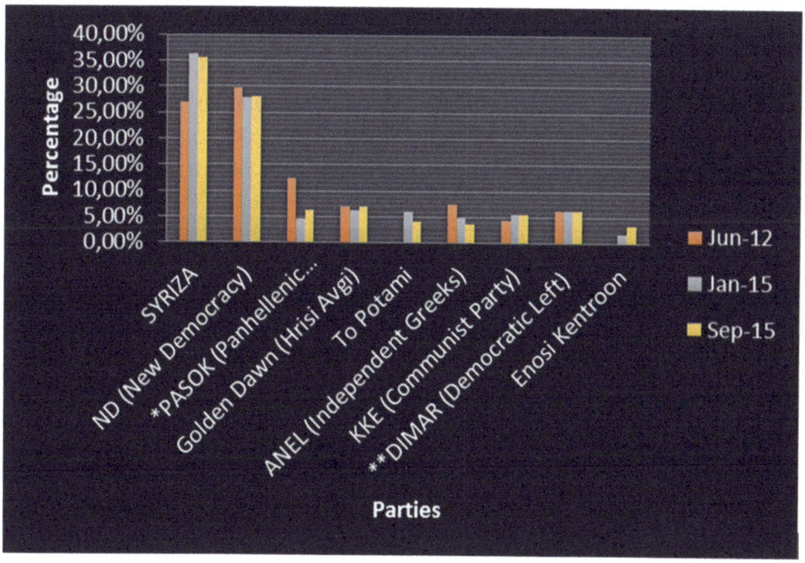

Fig. 9.5 Election results, June 2012–September 2015 (Source: Greek Ministry of the Interior http://www.ypes.gr/en/Elections/; *Electoral results for PASOK as part of Dimokratiki Symparataxi, a coalition between PASOK and DIMAR in the September 2015 national elections; **Electoral results for DIMAR as part of Dimokratiki Symparataxi, a coalition between PASOK and DIMAR in the September 2015 national elections)

The austerity-at-all-costs policy implemented during 2012–2015 was the most critical factor in forming the decisive margin by which SYRIZA won. Despite the imprisonment of most of its members, including its leader, and the lack of a proper political campaign with barely any presence in the media, Golden Dawn managed to retain its percentage of the vote. This showed clearly that anti-austerity-fuelled wrath was as strong as ever among a specific percentage of the Greek population. PASOK and the Democratic Left (DIMAR) were severely punished by the Greek electorate: the former because of its perceived role in the crisis and the latter because of its inability to choose sides between the pro- and anti-austerity coalitions. The River, a party formed in 2014 with a political campaign targeting the pro-bailout moderate middle classes, managed to enter Parliament, as did the Greek Communist Party (KKE), which, despite the unmistakable move of the voters towards supporting anti-austerity parties, failed to gain any significant support.

SYRIZA's victory and the move to form a coalition government with ANEL raised serious questions over the future handling of the debt crisis in Greece and the country's position in the Eurozone. SYRIZA had been accused of populism and had been regarded as one of the Radical Left populist parties on the rise throughout the European South. In the seven months following SYRIZA's ascent to power, the party maintained popular support through its 'anti-Memorandum', pro-welfare rhetoric. The anti-austerity statements found fertile ground among disillusioned voters who felt they had found a party to represent them.

The government decided to hold a referendum on 5 July 2015, asking voters whether they were in favour or against the latest package of austerity measures drafted by the Troika. The result was a clear victory for NO (61 per cent) and showed undeniable popular support for the leader of SYRIZA, Alexis Tsipras, to call off any deal with the Troika. However, the economic turmoil that followed the announcement of the referendum—including the imposition of strict capital controls and the expiration of deadlines for repaying loans to the IMF and the EU—crippled the economy in the middle of the tourist season. In a remarkable U-turn and in apparent contradiction with the referendum result, Prime Minister Tsipras agreed to sign a third MoU, with much harsher conditions. SYRIZA soon split, forcing PM Tsipras to call new elections for September 2015.

The SYRIZA rhetoric during the campaign was based on the claim that the party negotiated hard the terms of the memorandum and although it failed to strike a better agreement, if in power, it would guarantee that corrective measures would be taken to relieve at least the most vulnerable. This was reminiscent of the party's Thessaloniki programme prior to the January 2015 election, when the PM-in-waiting, Tsipras, had promised job creation, restoring the minimum wage to €751, freezing pension cuts and providing new welfare benefits for the poor. The populist rhetoric after the cataclysmic events that followed the July referendum, at a time when unemployment reached 25.8 per cent and the risk of poverty 35.7 per cent, won the populist parties ground. SYRIZA remained more or less at the same level as in January, despite the split in the party. The results remained the same for ND as well, leading the party to reconsider its leadership. The minor changes that occurred involved smaller parties, like the ANEL and To Potami, which barely made the 3 per cent national threshold to enter Parliament, and the addition of the Centre Union (*Enosi Kentroon*), a populist party. What was novel in the last election (to date) was that the political landscape was composed of a large majority of populist and fringe parties (SYRIZA, ANEL, Golden Dawn, the Communist Party and Enosi Kentroon making up 55.13 per cent of the parties in Parliament) and that abstention rose from 36 per cent in January 2015 to 44 per cent in September 2015. This was a manifestation of two tendencies: one towards the populist and extreme/radical parties of both the Left and the Right, and one towards political apathy and abstention. It was a vote that demonstrated the ill health of both the Greek and EU status quo and of representative democracy at large.

Conclusion

Long-lasting structural deficiencies in the functioning of the Greek state continued to hinder the country's efforts in the run-up to the EMU. Further deterioration of public finances in the context of the global financial crisis made Greece the epicentre of the Eurozone crisis. Fear of contagion led to the first Greek bailout, with a mandatory commitment on the Greek side to implement a set of neoliberal reforms. Despite the electoral risks associated with the bailout conditions, consecutive governments attempted to implement the strict programme. The adoption of punitive austerity measures, however, had a profound effect on the socio-political landscape of Greece. Social unrest and political transformation dominated the post-2010 period. The Metapolitefsi system was shaken up causing profound changes in the party system, including the rise of anti-austerity, populist as well as radical/extreme parties.

The particular brand of populist and clientelistic governance that evolved in the post-1974 Metapolitefsi period operated in a dual way in formulating the post-MoU Greek political geography. On the one hand, when the clientelistic relationship between the government and the electorate was disturbed, it caused the dismantling of the indisputably dominant political force during the Greek Metapolitefsi, PASOK, in favour of a more radical party, SYRIZA. On the other hand, Metapolitefsi's populism and clientelism created fertile ground for the rise of other populist parties in power, including the extremist Golden Dawn but also the more moderate *Enosi Kentroon*. Finally, a last tendency is high abstention rates. All these tendencies demonstrate the poor health of the status quo in Greek politics and democracy at the national level but also of democracy and politics at the EU level. In the case of Greece, this was particularly evident during the referendum in July 2015, when voters of different parties and different ideologies voted against a further wave of austerity measures but subsequently saw them imposed.

Following the onset of the crisis, a large proportion of the fragmented centre-ground supported SYRIZA, mostly at the expense of PASOK, and another significant proportion supported New Democracy. As noted in the foregoing, a number of votes also went to emerging small parties, and abstention rates grew significantly. The rise of SYRIZA in particular has echoes of the rise of PASOK in 1981. Like SYRIZA it grew as a radical, non-Communist, alternative to the existing political status quo by drawing support away from centre parties. The hollowing out of PASOK led Labour analyst James Doran to coin the phrase *Pasokification*, referring to the erosion of support for Social Democratic parties throughout the EU and indeed beyond it. Whether SYRIZA can avoid a similar fate in the long-term remained to be seen at the time of writing. If the crisis drags on and more austerity is the only medicine available from a neoliberal-inspired Troika, then it may be difficult to avoid such a fate. The broader consequences of such a direction of travel for democracy and society in Greece—and probably in the EU more generally—are potentially extremely grave.

Notes

1. By the term Metapolitefsi, we refer to the political transition which occurred in Greece after the end of the military junta in 1974 towards representative democracy. The Metapolitefsi period has been characterized by the dominance of PASOK and ND, who alternated in power. The 2012 elections brought about what has been largely regarded as the end of the Metapolitefsi, with PASOK collapsing to single-digit figures and ND severely weakened.
2. During that period, a dual narrative was created and reproduced around the political parties' electoral identity in favour or against passing harsh austerity measures. This pro-Memorandum/anti-Memorandum dichotomy proved to be decisive in the electoral result.
3. It was quite usual during the May 2012 electoral period for 'anti-Memorandum' indecisive voters to paradoxically claim that they were debating voting for either SYRIZA (a left-wing party, quite often referred to as radical Left) or Golden Dawn (a neo-Nazi, right-wing party).
4. Golden Dawn's share of the vote in June 2012 was remarkably stable, registering 6.92 per cent.

References

Algan, Y., and P. Cahuc. 2010. Inherited Trust and Growth. *American Economic Review* 100: 2060–2092.

Couloumbis, T. 1993. PASOK Foreign Policies, 1981–89: Continuity or Change? In *Greece 1981–89: The Populist Decade*, ed. R. Clogg. New York: St Martin's Press.

Ellinas, A. 2013. The Rise of Golden Dawn: The New Face of the Far Right in Greece. *South European Society and Politics* 18 (4): 543–565.

ELSTAT. 2016a. *Unemployment Rates*. http://www.statistics.gr/documents/20181/cf6647b2-0640-49c9-9287-2214de617568.

———. 2016b. *Threat of Poverty*. http://www.statistics.gr/documents/20181/f5f875ea-5cc8-4901-8ce4-6d98b30c6ec0.

Featherstone, K. 2003. Greece and EMU: Between External Empowerment and Domestic Vulnerability. *Journal of Common Market Studies* 41 (5): 923–940.

———. 2005. Introduction: 'Modernization' and the Structural Restraints of Greek Politics. *West European Politics* 28 (2): 223–241.

———. 2008. 'Varieties of Capitalism' and the Greek State: Explaining the Constraints on Domestic Reform? *Hellenic Observatory Papers on Greece and Southeast Europe*, GReeSE Paper no. 11.

———. 2011. The Greek Sovereign Debt Crisis and EMU: A Failing State in a Skewed Regime. *Journal of Common Market Studies* 49 (2): 193–217.

Featherstone, K., G. Kazamias, and D. Papadimitriou. 2000. Greece and the Negotiation Economic and Monetary Union: Preferences, Strategies and Institutions. *Journal of Modern Greek Studies* 18 (2): 393–414.

Gemenis, K. 2008. The 2007 Parliamentary Election in Greece. *Mediterranean Politics* 13 (1): 95–101.

Kalyvas, S. 1997. Polarization in Greek Politics: PASOK's First Four Years: 1981–1985. *Journal of the Hellenic Diaspora* 23 (1): 83–104.

Kalyvas, A. 2010. An Anomaly? Some Reflections on the Greek December 2008. *Constellations* 17 (2): 351–365.

Lyrintzis, C. 1982. The Rise of Pasok: The Greek Election of 1981. *West European Politics* 5 (3): 308–313.

———. 1984. Political Parties in Post-junta Greece: A case of "Bureaucratic Clientelism?". *West European Politics* 7 (2): 99–118.

Mavrogordatos, G. 1997. From Traditional Clientelism to Machine Politics: The Impact of PASOK Populism in Greece. *South European Society & Politics* 2 (3): 1–26.

Moschonas, G. 2001. The Path of Modernization: PASOK and European Integration. *Journal of Southern Europe and the Balkans* 3 (1): 11–24.

Naftemporiki. 2014. *3 Percent Lead for SYRIZA*. http://www.naftemporiki.gr/story/756189/pulse-probadisma-3-gia-ton-syriza.

Pappas, T. 2010. Winning by Default: The Greek Election of 2009. *South European Society and Politics* 15 (2): 273–287.

Philippopoulos, A. 2013. The Eurozone Crisis: Phoenix Miracle or Lost Decade?: Comment. *Journal of Macroeconomics* 39: 309–312.

Rüdig, W., and G. Karyotis. 2014. Who Protests in Greece? Mass Opposition to Austerity. *British Journal of Political Science* 44 (3): 487–513.

Simiti, M. 2014. Rage and Protest: The Case of the Greek Indignant Movement. *Hellenic Observatory Papers on Greece and Southeast Europe*, GReeSE Paper no. 82.

Smaghi, L. 2014. Austerity, A Threat to Democracy? *The International Spectator: Italian Journal of International Affairs* 49 (1): 7–17.

Sotiropoulos, D.A. 1993. A Colossus with Feet of Clay: The State in Post-authoritarian Greece. In *Greece, the New Europe and Changing International Order*, ed. H. Psomiades and S. Thomadakis, 349–365. New York: Pella.

Spanou, C. 1996. Penelope's Suitors: Administrative Modernisation and Party Competition in Greece. *West European Politics* 19 (1): 98–125.

Spourdalakis, M., and C. Tassis. 2006. Party Change in Greece and the Vanguard Role of PASOK. *South European Society and Politics* 11 (3-4): 497–512.

To Vima. 2012. *Survey on the 2012 Legislative Elections*. http://www.tovima.gr/files/1/2012/04/20/E1608%20%CE%A0%CE%91%CE%9D%CE%95%CE%9B%CE%9B%CE%91%CE%94%CE%99%CE%9A%CE%97%20%CE%95%CE%A1%CE%95%CE%A5%CE%9D%CE%91%20%CE%91%CE%A0%CE%A1%20'12.pdf. Accessed 3 Mar 2015.

Trantidis, A. 2014. Reforms and Collective Action in a Clientelist System: Greece During the Mitsotakis Administration (1990–93). *South European Society and Politics* 19 (2): 215–234.

Vasilopoulou, S., and D. Halikiopoulou. 2013. In the Shadow of Grexit: The Greek Election of 17 June 2012. *South European Society and Politics* 18 (4): 523–542.

Venieris, D. 2013. Crisis Social Policy and Social Justice: The Case of Greece. *Hellenic Observatory Papers on Greece and Southeast Europe*, GReeSE Paper no. 69.

CHAPTER 10

Conclusion

Owen Parker and Dimitris Tsarouhas

Abstract The Eurozone crisis had a profound effect on the countries of the periphery—Ireland, Spain, Portugal and Greece—considered in this book as the chapters have articulated. Drawing together the insights from those chapters, this short conclusion suggests that while there were common causes and structural constraints on these countries (see also Introduction), there were also important domestic differences in their political economies, which meant that their trajectories through the crisis were different. It offers a comparative analysis of the cases, pointing to both those differences and important similarities.

Keywords Eurozone crisis • Core–periphery • Asymmetries • Austerity • Neoliberalism

The Eurozone crisis had a profound effect on the countries of the periphery, both in terms of their political stability and economic viability. The

O. Parker
Department of Politics and SPERI, University of Sheffield, Sheffield, UK

D. Tsarouhas (✉)
Department of International Relations, Bilkent University, Ankara, Turkey

O. Parker, D. Tsarouhas (eds.), *Crisis in the Eurozone Periphery*,
Building a Sustainable Political Economy: SPERI Research & Policy,
https://doi.org/10.1007/978-3-319-69721-5_10

country case studies discussed in this book reveal domestic shortcomings in the run-up to the crisis, yet also highlight institutional and, in some cases, structural deficiencies in the set-up of the Eurozone (Parker and Tsarouhas, Chap. 1, this volume). Each of Ireland, Spain, Portugal and Greece encountered a similar external environment and associated constraints. But the impacts of and responses to the crisis were varied because of the different domestic institutions, histories and political cultures that mediated both. Indeed, a first important analytical lesson to emerge from the volume is that global, European and domestic factors—and the linkages and relations between them—each require due consideration if we are to begin to understand the complexities of the crisis that beset the Eurozone and, in particular, its periphery, at the end of the first decade of the 2000s. Only such a comprehensive understanding can permit the formulation of viable ways forward.

A second and related analytical lesson emerging from the volume is that the crisis was irrevocably a crisis of political economy. In other words, the contributions to the book demonstrate the inextricable interconnections between economic and political dynamics in the build-up to and unfolding of the crisis in these so-called periphery states. Politics drove particular economic developmental strategies and associated orientations towards Europeanisation in each of our cases, while such Europeanisation—particularly the socio-economic structures it has imposed—has shaped politics, even as particular domestic historical path dependencies have mediated its effects in particular national and local contexts. As such, while it is heuristically useful to divide the volume into analyses that focus principally on economic and principally on political crises in relation to each of the four countries, each chapter is a work of political economy. Moreover, the two chapters for each country case are best considered as complementary; they are most usefully read together as each helps to explain the other.

Below we seek to add to the analysis offered elsewhere in this volume by briefly engaging in a comparative, cross-country comparison of our case studies. We do so by focusing in turn on the economic and political mechanisms that have led to and sustained the crisis. In so doing we remain cognisant of the aforementioned analytical lessons: the importance of considering vertical and horizontal economic and political linkages and the importance of a political economy analysis that treats both politics and economics as interrelated.

Economics: Bubbles That Burst and Debt-Led Growth

For all the four states considered here, debt was at the heart of their woes (see Parker and Tsarouhas, Chap. 1, this volume). As Neil Dooley argues in his chapter, in many respects Portugal was ahead of the game in terms of its adherence to a model of debt-led growth based on domestic demand. Following an unsuccessful post-authoritarian experimentation with radical Left policies, in the early 1980s the country embarked on a process of Europeanisation that saw a process of radical market liberalisation and the emergence of an economic model increasingly reliant on debt. While leading to significant growth in the late 1980s and 1990s, this model was proving problematic in Portugal well before the onset of the Eurozone crisis, with a severe downturn in the early 2000s rooted in a domestic debt crisis. Its construction sector—which boomed in the 1990s—was faltering in the early 2000s, just as it was taking off elsewhere in the periphery. As Dooley notes, by the time the global financial crisis hit, Portugal's debt-led bubble had long been deflating while the bubbles in the other three cases were, at the same time, still rapidly inflating. In contrast to the other cases—that were perceived to be growing healthily when the crisis struck—in the case of Portugal it was its long-term economic issues that made it vulnerable once the crisis hit Greece.

Spain and Ireland are two such cases, as described in the chapters by Luis Buendía and Sean Ó Riain respectively. Both countries achieved substantial growth rates in the early 2000s and were widely regarded as star students in the Eurozone class. However, like Portugal before them, both countries fuelled development by investing heavily in the real estate and construction sectors—at the expense of productive sectors—which was possible due to easy access to cheap credit facilitated by the single currency (Parker and Tsarouhas, Chap. 1, this volume). Over time this overdependence led to substantial economic asymmetries and left both states exposed the moment their banking sectors started to malfunction following the arrival of the credit crunch and the global financial crisis. The consequences of the crisis for both states have been dramatic, especially in terms of their distributional effects and the rise of inequality that has become a major hindrance to long-term, sustainable economic recovery. Their position in the periphery of the Eurozone is of importance here, given the distribution of labour that the Eurozone has created (Buendía, Chap. 3, this volume), but the role of agency is not to be underestimated: Ireland has been characterised by a type of 'aggressive liberalism' (Ó Riain, Chap. 2, this volume) that deliberately advocated a low tax, low regulation regime, therefore bypassing the need to develop endogenous types of sustainable investment and industry-led development.

A similar story of debt-fuelled growth is true of the main casualty of the crisis, Greece, as Pavlos Gkasis outlines in his analysis. In addition, Greece, suffered from more severe structural public sector weaknesses than any of the other cases, including extremely weak tax revenues in the years of prosperity and boom, which left the country particularly vulnerable when the bad times succeeded the good. This, Gkasis argues, is one of the reasons that the country found itself still under surveillance and in a significantly more difficult position than the other states considered, each of which had managed to exit their bailout programmes at the time of writing. That said, above all the Greek case speaks to the problems inherent in the structures of monetary union and (a revamped) economic governance—rooted in austerity and so-called internal devaluation—that we outline in Chap. 1. At the time of writing, it was the starkest example of the way in which the rescue of the single currency was being implemented at the expense of democracy (Streeck 2014) and of the way in which the current model came close to an 'authoritarian' form of neoliberalism (Tansel 2017). In that context, the political instability that has emerged from the economic crisis is hardly surprising.

Politics: Fragmentation, Breakdown, Reform

The near break-up of the Eurozone had huge political consequences, nowhere more so than in the country cases considered in this volume. The crisis was of course an important trigger for political developments in each of our country cases, but their particular form was also dependent on long-term domestic legacies. Politics has certainly become a lot more fluid and unpredictable in all four cases, with the emergence of public protest, the rise of new political parties, the formation of new coalitions of pre-existing parties and, in some cases at least, the demise of long-standing political entities, whether individuals, political parties or both. As Brazys and Regan (2017: 412) note, 'since 2008, no government in Ireland or Southern Europe has managed to return a governing majority'.

This story of political turbulence is not unique to our case studies; it extends to the core of the Eurozone and, indeed, beyond both the

Eurozone and the EU more generally. A new era in European (and Western) politics has been emerging for some time now. Its principal characteristics have been declining party membership rates (Mair and van Biezen 2001); falling party identification among the electorate; the electoral rise of new 'populist' parties (Zaslove 2008); and the inability of mainstream parties to compete over systemic political change, instead adopting an anodyne managerialism (Blyth and Katz 2005). In short, we have seen ever-greater and intense depoliticisation as the counterpart to a neoliberal economic trajectory, certainly since the 1980s. However, over the past decade or so, and particularly in the context of the recent crisis period, we have seen evidence of a nascent repoliticisation. This has not followed the same trajectory everywhere, and even in our four case studies, the political consequences of the crisis have been far from uniform. It may, however, be indicative of a benign consequence of the crisis, namely the re-emergence of political struggle as an essential aspect of contemporary democracy and a healthy antidote to the passive acceptance of a market-led strategy of political contest.

The crisis initially prompted the emergence of protest movements as the social and individual effects were felt in the periphery. Such protest was first seen in 2010 in Greece. As Alexandra Prodromidou informs us in her contribution, these constituted an angry, and sometimes violent, reaction to the harsh social consequences emerging from the first 'Memorandum of Understanding' signed by Greece and the Troika (consisting of the EU, ECB and IMF). The various movements in different parts of the periphery certainly inspired each other and, indeed, other protestors and activists beyond the periphery (and beyond the EU). In particular, the famous '*indignados*' or '15M' movement that erupted in Spain in 2011, described in this volume by Monica Clua-Losada, is widely thought to have prompted similarly designed movements in Greece ('*oi Aganaktismenoi*'), as well as the various 'Occupy' movements that emerged in response to the broader global financial crisis. As Isabel David explains in her contribution, '15M' was shortly preceded in Portugal by a large wave of demonstrations under the banner 'Generation in Trouble', and the latter was important in inspiring the former. Perhaps the outlier as far as the politics of protest is concerned was Ireland, where social movements were notably absent, or certainly not in evidence on the scale seen in the other three countries, notwithstanding the comparable social hardship that its citizens have had to endure. That said, as Nicholas Kiersey notes in his chapter, even in Ireland this changed from around 2014 as further austerity policies—notably a proposed tax on water—were for many perceived as the final straw and prompted widespread opposition and protest.

In various ways these social movements were institutionalised in local and national politics in our four country cases. In Spain and Greece in particular, this led to the rise of new electoral forces. In Greece, as Prodromidou informs us in her contribution, such forces sprang out of hugely strengthened existing movements (SYRIZA, Golden Dawn), while in Spain, as Clua-Losada explains, new parties emerged in the context of the crisis (Podemos, Ciudadanos). Podemos, in particular, was built upon the success of the 'Indignados' movement and both drew strength from and supported the institutional forms of resistance to the mainstream political formations emerging at a local level. While the party system has been surprisingly unscathed in Portugal throughout the early years of the crisis, in recent years it has also witnessed an important political change. Following elections in 2015 an unprecedented governing coalition between the Portuguese Socialists (PS), the Communist Party (PCP) and the Left Bloc (BE) was formed. David argues that the protest movements during the early years of the crisis brought together the disparate actors on the political left that would make such a unique pact possible. We see a similar story in Ireland, where the—in many ways belated—anti-austerity 'water protests' helped to create the conditions for an electoral upset in 2016. As Kiersey argues, this was a result that dealt a serious blow to the mainstream parties that had looked surprisingly resilient until that point and saw the rise of various leftist parties.

At the time of writing in 2017 the upshot of these political shifts varied between our cases. In Spain and Ireland, the status quo was significantly weakened as a consequence of elections in 2016, but at the same time established, mainstream parties remained resilient and in power. In Spain the *Partido Popular* (PP) and in Ireland *Fianna Gael* (FG) remained the governing parties, though neither had the majority to effectively govern alone and enjoyed only conditional support from other parties. In both cases political parties on the left or centre-left had failed to unite for their respective 2016 elections in ways that might have allowed for a clear anti-status-quo and anti-austerity government to emerge. However, the potential for a more dramatic national political change remained present in both cases. Compounding these issues in national politics, in Spain the politics of separatism was live, with Catalan nationalism in particular on the rise and posing a threat to the territorial integrity of the Spanish state. And in

Ireland, the prospect of Brexit—the withdrawal from the EU of Ireland's key export market, the UK—cast further uncertainty on domestic politics.

In Greece and Portugal, anti-austerity governments of the left were already in place. With respect to Greece, the successes and failures of SYRIZA have been well documented. As Prodromidou informs us, the rise of the party to government was certainly a remarkable achievement that shattered the mainstream and, in particular, was a key factor in the demise of PASOK, the Socialist party that had been a fixture of Greek politics for much of the period since the end of military rule in 1974. However, despite SYRIZA's critique of austerity from opposition and massive popular opposition to it (starkly demonstrated in the context of the 2015 referendum that rejected further EU austerity), in government it has been implementing further welfare and public services cuts given its support for continued Greek membership in the single currency. The 2015 referendum was indeed a chastening experience for the party and for the European left in general, begging the question: can the politics of austerity be effectively resisted within the structures of the EU's neoliberal economic governance? At the time of writing, the case of Portugal offered some hope in that respect as the new Portuguese government succeeded both in cutting its public deficit *and* raising pensions and wages (*Economist* 2017). As recounted by David (Chap. 8), in this volume, notwithstanding the suspicion or outright hostility to this coalition from many in the EU elite, the country offered an interesting, and potentially unique, example of how the crisis can be dealt with from an anti-austerity point of view.

There were broader signs at the time of writing that a politics from below might influence national and, indeed, supranational positions on contemporary Europe's socio-economic governance. While the austerity morality tales—about 'saints and sinners', 'reaping what you sow' and 'taking your medicine'—temporarily lent legitimacy to austerity, at the time of writing, such tales were wearing thin in each of our cases as reflected most clearly in their most recent national elections. The same was true in countries beyond our cases, such as France, Italy and the UK.

In each of our cases the resilience of the neoliberal message had as much to do with the identity of the messenger as it had with the message itself. The EU has been regarded as a positive developmental and democratising force in countries that had lagged economically (all our cases) and had experienced long periods of authoritarian political rule or semidemocratic conditions (Spain, Portugal and Greece). Thus, while the Troika and its governance prompted anger and protest, the EU—and for the most part, the euro—remained popular with the majority. However, it cannot be assumed that this will remain the case in any of our country cases in the face of an economic governance model that continues to impose punitive austerity, and certainly not in a country such as Greece whose government has to a large extent been forced to cede economic control to the Troika, whose approval is a precondition for the exercise of economic policy.

Perhaps the EU institutions were beginning to recognise the truth of such an assessment at the time of writing. The European Commission was not strictly or consistently enforcing its own rules on austerity any longer, using its discretion to interpret data and define terms in ways that eased the pressure on, for instance, France, Italy and Spain (Schmidt 2016: 1044–1045). Moreover, in 2017 the Commission began to talk the talk on a 'Social' Europe, with publications on the importance of a 'social dimension' and its launch of a 'pillar of social rights', (Parker and Pye 2017), even if the Troika and many in the core, particularly Germany, were still very far from walking the walk (see Parker and Tsarouhas, Chap. 1, this volume). Thus, although the neoliberal paradigm remained at the core of the Eurozone's toolbox—having repeatedly proven its resilience to change (Schmidt and Thatcher 2013)—other possibilities were at least starting to be considered by some in the mainstream.

Only if the EU remains legitimate for all its citizens will a hard Euroscepticism, and the disintegration that would follow, be kept at bay. For such an outcome to become feasible and eventually possible, forms of collective organisation premised on political economy principles antithetical to the current neoliberal orthodoxy will need to materialise at regional, national, European and indeed international level. After all, the Keynesian revolution of the 1930s and 1940s as well as the neoliberal turn of the 1970s and 1980s acquired a systemic, lasting character through the interplay of structural and agency-related factors that spread from the local to the global level. For a lasting and meaningful change of the current paradigm, a similar process will need to take place. In short, we need nothing short of a Polanyian countermovement but cannot assume that such a movement is predestined or that it will be easily and painlessly navigated. Politics and the choices made by leaders as well as organised groups matter as much as they ever did.

References

Blyth, M., and R.S. Katz. 2005. From Catch-All Politics to Cartelisation. *West European Politics* 28 (1): 33–60.

Brazys, S., and A. Regan. 2017. The Politics of Capitalist Diversity in Europe: Explaining Ireland's Divergent Recovery from the Euro Crisis. *Perspectives on Politics* 15 (2): 411–427.

Economist. 2017. Growing Out of It: Portugal Cuts Its Fiscal Deficit While Raising Pensions and Wages. April 1.

Mair, P., and I. Van Biezen. 2001. Party Membership in Twenty European Democracies. *Party Politics* 7 (1): 5–21.

Parker, O., and R. Pye. 2017 Mobilising Social Rights in EU Economic governance: A Pragmatic Challenge to Neoliberal Europe. *Comparative European Politics*. Online First: https://doi.org/10.1057/s41295-017-0102-1.

Schmidt, V.A. 2016. Reinterpreting the Rules 'By Stealth' in Times of Crisis: A Discursive Institutionalist Analysis of the European Central Bank and the European Commission. *West European Politics* 39 (5): 1032–1052.

Schmidt, V.A., and M. Thatcher, eds. 2013. *Resilient Liberalism in Europe's Political Economy*. Cambridge: Cambridge University Press.

Streeck, W. 2014. *Buying Time: The Delayed Crisis of Democratic Capitalism*. London: Verso.

Tansel, C.B., ed. 2017. *States of Discipline: Authoritarian Neoliberalism and the Contested Reproduction of Capitalist Order*. London: Rowman and Littlefield.

Zaslove, A. 2008. Here to Stay? Populism as a New Party Type. *European Review* 16 (3): 319–336.

Index[1]

[1] Note: Page numbers followed by "n" refer to notes.

O. Parker, D. Tsarouhas (eds.), *Crisis in the Eurozone Periphery*,
Building a Sustainable Political Economy: SPERI Research & Policy,
https://doi.org/10.1007/978-3-319-69721-5

The manufacturer's authorised representative in the EU is Springer Nature Customer Service Centre GmbH, Europaplatz 3, 69115 Heidelberg, Germany. If you have any concerns regarding our products, please contact ProductSafety@springernature.com

Printed and bound by CPI Group (UK) Ltd, Croydon, CR0 4YY
25/09/2026
02222859-0001